Inquisitorial Inquiries

Inquisitorial Inquiries

Brief Lives of Secret Jews
and Other Heretics

Edited and Translated by
Richard L. Kagan and Abigail Dyer

The Johns Hopkins University Press
Baltimore and London

The Johns Hopkins University Press
2715 North Charles Street
Baltimore, Maryland 21218-4363
www.press.jhu.edu

Library of Congress Cataloging-in-Publication Data
Inquisitorial inquiries : brief lives of secret Jews and other heretics
/ edited and translated by Richard L. Kagan and Abigail Dyer.
    p.   cm. — (Heroes and villains series)
ISBN 0-8018-7923-x (alk. paper)
ISBN 0-8018-7924-8 (pbk. : alk. paper)
1. Marranos—Spain—Biography. 2. Jews—Spain—Biography.
3. Sephardim—Spain—Biography. 4. Inquisition—Spain—Sources.
5. Jews—Persecutions—Spain—Sources. 6. Trial (Heresy)—Spain—Sources.
7. Spain—Ethnic relations—Sources. I. Kagan, Richard L., 1943–
II. Dyer, Abigail. III. Series.
DS135.s8A155 2004
272'.092246—dc22
2003018310

A catalog record for this book is available from the British Library.

Lives of a few lines or a few pages, nameless misfortunes and adventures gathered into a handful of words. Brief lives, encountered by chance in books and documents. *Exempla,* but unlike those collected by the sages in the course of their reading, they are examples that convey not so much lessons to ponder as brief effects whose force fades almost at once.

—MICHEL FOUCAULT, *Lives of Infamous Men*

Contents

Maps

Preface

The Spanish Inquisition is not an institution customarily associated with autobiography, let alone the stories people tell. Rather, the Holy Office, as the Inquisition is also known, evokes the darker side of life—arbitrary justice, racial hatred, and religious persecution, along with images of dreary prisons, torture, and human suffering. Cognizant of these grim realities, we do not pretend to offer a revisionist account of either the aims and methods of the Inquisition or the many individuals, starting with the inquisitor general, who made it tick. Our aim is simply to give this institution something of a human face by offering a close look at some of the unfortunate men and women who found themselves caught in the Inquisition's net. For this purpose we make use of trial transcripts housed in the Inquisition archives and focus in particular on the moment in the trial proceedings when the inquisitors asked the prisoners who had been brought before them to recite the stories of their lives. The resulting autobiographies, coupled with other information these same prisoners provided during the course of their inquisitorial ordeal, are the subject of this book.

By definition, therefore, this is a collaborative effort. It could never have been written without the men and women whose lives we recount here or without the inquisitorial scribes who prepared the transcripts upon which we have relied. We would also like to acknowledge the directors and staff of Madrid's Archivo Histórico Nacional, Cuenca's Archivo Diocesano, and Mexico City's Archivo General de la Nación. Without their assistance and, even more importantly, the microfilms and photocopies produced in their photographic labs, this book could never have been completed. Others who provided assistance and support include James Amelang, Robert Ferry, Kimberly Lynn, Sara Nalle, David Nirenberg, and Jack Owens. Our thanks also go to Manuel Colas, Ana de Leon, and Molly Warsh for their many useful comments and suggestions when, somewhat under duress, they read an earlier draft of this study as part of their assigned readings in a graduate seminar at the Johns

Hopkins University. Finally, we are grateful to Henry Tom, Executive Editor of the Johns Hopkins University Press, his staff, and our excellent copy editor, Lois Crum, for their help in transforming what once seemed a far-fetched idea about inquisitorial autobiographies into a volume that we hope our readers will both profit from and enjoy.

Inquisitorial Inquiries

Introduction

On 23 November 1624, in the city of Toledo, the inquisitorial trial of Francisco de San Antonio was about to begin. San Antonio had been residing in Madrid, capital of the Spanish monarchy, when, on 21 November, he was arrested and brought to Toledo, Spain's de facto ecclesiastical capital, at the order of the Holy Office of the Spanish Inquisition. There, the Inquisition held him in its secret prisons. A bailiff ushered the prisoner into the tribunal's audience chamber and ordered him to sit down. Before him were three judges, or inquisitors, seated behind a long table. San Antonio knew little about these judges, not even their names. However, he was almost certainly aware that their primary task as inquisitors was to root out and then punish Catholics accused of heresy, a category the Holy Office expanded to encompass crimes such as bigamy and blasphemy.

These judges, thanks to testimony previously gathered from several witnesses, including San Antonio's wife, Mariana de los Reyes, already knew a great deal about the prisoner who was seated before them on a bench. They knew he was born and raised as a Jew in the city of Fez, in Morocco, where he

1. *Inquisitorial Tribunals*

went by the name of Abram Rubén. They also knew that he had emigrated to the Netherlands and worked as a rabbi but later converted to Catholicism. In doing so Abram, aka Francisco de San Antonio, became what the inquisitors understood as a New Christian, or *converso*. Yet the inquisitors also had information that San Antonio was a *judaizante*, or crypto-Jew, a convert who secretly practiced his ancestral faith. Several witnesses had indicated that, after leaving the Netherlands for Portugal, he secretly resumed his activities as a rabbi. They had also learned that San Antonio had left Portugal for Madrid, where, accompanied by his wife, he reconverted to Catholicism in 1621 in an elaborate ceremony held in the chapel of the royal palace. Making things worse for San Antonio was evidence that, following his second conversion, he continued to teach Hebrew together with the rudiments of the Judaism to a small group of New Christians residing in Madrid. As proof of these activities, the inquisitors had in their possession several printed Hebrew primers that had been found among San Antonio's possessions at the moment of his arrest. This evidence, none of which had yet been presented to Francisco, had already convinced the inquisitors that this prisoner was a *judaizante dogmatizador—* a dogmatizing Judaizer—and guilty of apostasy, a major heresy. Armed with this knowledge, they began questioning him as follows: Why do you think you have been arrested? What is your name? Your age? Your profession? Where are you from?

These questions were routine. All important inquisitorial trials began in this fashion. Yet San Antonio's answers to these formulaic queries were perfunctory; he told the inquisitors what they asked for and no more. But when asked for what the attending scribe noted in the transcript of his trial as the "discurso de su vida," or "narrative of your life," San Antonio, as if waiting for a cue, became more verbose and launched into a full-blown life story that offered the inquisitors new information about him: details about his boyhood in Fez, his travels as a merchant-cum-itinerant-rabbi in the Ottoman Empire, his decision to become a Catholic and subsequent baptism in Antwerp. He also expounded upon his return to Judaism and his marriage to a young woman, a Catholic, whom he had met in Portugal. He continued by telling the judges about his arrival in Madrid. In answers to other questions posed by the inquisitors, San Antonio provided more details about his wife, as well as his activities in Madrid. He also used his answers as an opportunity to explain that the Hebrew books found in his possession had nothing to do with his adherence to the Roman Catholic faith.

Inquisitorial Autobiography

Embedded in Francisco de San Antonio's *discurso* is an autobiography, albeit an autobiography of a special sort. It is perhaps best defined as an involuntary or inquisitorial autobiography, one crafted under duress and partly in response to the judges' prompts. Francisco de San Antonio's inquisitorial autobiography is one of six that we examine at length in this volume. As autobiography, it is quite different from contemporary understanding of this genre. We generally conceive of autobiography as a wholly voluntary act. It tends also to be equated with truth-telling and the idea that the autobiographer is uniquely positioned to address questions relating to his or her emotions and personal motivations in ways that biographers are not. Yet early modern notions of autobiography, as James Amelang has explained, did not necessarily entail the presumptions of truth and autonomy of narration currently associated with the genre.[1]

In the sixteenth century, when the practice of autobiographical writing in Europe was still relatively new, autobiographers had standards quite different from our own. The first autobiographies were largely confessional endeavors, documents meant to prepare the souls of men and women for the afterlife. These "confessional" autobiographies had their roots in Acts 26, where the Apostle Paul defended his religion before King Agrippa, as well as in the *Confessions* of Augustine of Hippo, the fourth-century prelate who wrote a first-person account of his perilous spiritual journey from sinner to aspiring saint.[2] Over the centuries the *Confessions* inspired other holy men and women to craft spiritual autobiographies of their own. Notable examples include Peter Abelard's *Historia calamitatum,* or *The Story of my misfortunes,* dating from the twelfth century; *The Book of My Life* by Margery Kempe (b. 1373); and to cite one sixteenth-century Spanish example, Teresa de Avila's *Life* (first published in 1588), in which the future saint recounts her transition from youthful sinner to religious visionary and founder of convents.[3] In many cases, however,

---

1. See *The Flight of Icarus: Artisan Autobiography in Early Modern Europe* (Palo Alto, CA: Stanford University Press, 1998), esp. the introduction, which offers a succinct introduction to the difference between early modern and modern (that is, post–eighteenth-century) autobiography.

2. *Confessions,* trans, R. S. Pine-Coffin (Baltimore: Penguin, 1968).

3. Abelard's *Story of My Misfortunes* is included in Peter Abelard, *Heloise and Abelard,* trans. Betty Radice (Harmondsworth, Eng.: Penguin, 1978). For Kempe, see *Book of Margery Kempe,* ed. Barry Windeatt (New York: Longman, 2000); and for Teresa, *The Life of Saint Teresa of Avila by Herself,* trans. J. M. Cohen (London: Penguin, 1987).

confessors and spiritual advisers helped shape the character as well as the content of these autobiographies, generally with an eye toward crafting an exemplary life that could not only serve as an inspiration for others but also smooth out the autobiographer's road to sainthood.

Late medieval and early modern spiritual autobiographies, then, were not necessarily autonomous or even factually correct works, and the same is true of many of the first secular autobiographies written by lay persons, both male and female. That of the famous sixteenth-century Florentine sculptor Benvenuto Cellini, for example, set issues of personal honor and reputation ahead of verisimilitude. Others, among them the *ricordi* (memories or records) composed by the fifteenth-century Florentine merchant Gregorio Dati, emphasized family matters as opposed to personal experiences.[4] The idea of confession as understood by the Church—the sacrament through which repentant Catholics could expect to receive remission of actions or statements the church determined to be sinful—also figured prominently in many early modern autobiographies. As a result, these "lives" are very selective, focusing on particular actions and incidents that the writers deemed relevant to their afterlife. In this respect, few early modern autobiographies, whether spiritual or secular, were what we might consider complete. Nor were they necessarily wholly transparent and truthful works. They were most often collective products of the authors' experiences, the specific context in which they were written, and the nature of the emergent autobiographical genre.

The life stories we examine in this volume have much in common with these autobiographies. They too are collective products, a mixture of the prisoners' own life experiences and the particular context—in this case, a trial chamber—in which they were composed. Confessional ideas also governed their content, inasmuch as everything uttered by prisoners during the course of an inquisitorial trial was considered to be part of their "confession." Yet inquisitorial autobiographies were in other ways quite unique. Most began, somewhat spontaneously, as first-person oral accounts that were copied, although not necessarily verbatim, by inquisitorial scribes. Others, as described in chapter 2, were produced in response to direct, often pointed questioning by the inquisitors themselves. Yet all authors produced their inquisitorial auto-

4. Gregorio Dati's *ricordi* are available in *Two Memoirs of Renaissance Florence: the Diaries of Buonaccorso Pitti and Gregorio Dati,* ed. Gene Brucker, trans. Julia Martines (New York: Harper and Row, 1968). For Cellini, see *The Autobiography of Benvenuto Cellini,* trans. George Bull (New York: Penguin, 1998).

biographies under duress and within the confines of a coercive juridical environment especially designed to provide inquisitors with information they could use against the prisoner before them as well as against other heretics yet to be identified. Most other early modern European judicial systems were similarly coercive. Together with the Inquisition, they considered confession a vital aspect of any criminal trial, the sine qua non for affirming a prisoner's presumed guilt. What set the Inquisition apart from these other tribunals was its insistence on secret trials and its refusal to reveal to the accused the identities of witnesses whose testimonials had contributed to the presumption of guilt. Through these measures, the Inquisition sought literally to scare prisoners into providing them with a "truthful" confession that would reveal aspects of their lives that they might otherwise seek to conceal.[5]

Such conditions, however intimidating, produced varied responses. Inquisitorial autobiographies were surprisingly eclectic, in both substance and style. Some prisoners, having internalized the importance of confession, constructed life stories designed specifically to beg inquisitorial forgiveness and mercy. Consequently, they spoke with an excess of candor. Others saw in the narrative a chance to justify their actions, defending themselves against what they believed would be the inquisitors' charges. Still others, cautious in the extreme, dissembled; they used their life story to displace their guilt and to blame their perceived heresies on the influence of others: neighbors, relatives, or even the Devil himself. It follows that the life stories prisoners told were not always, or even usually, truthful relations of events. Then too, the surviving transcripts of these life stories are the products of the scribes who transcribed them.

The "lives" included in the trial proceedings are not necessarily exact replicas of the "lives" originally relayed—orally—to the inquisitors. Clearly, in the process of transcription, much has been lost: emphasis, tone, gesture, even language as well, as the scribes, acting under inquisitorial direction, refashioned these narratives in ways that rendered them both easily intelligible and

---

5. Inquisitorial autobiographies are briefly discussed in Adrienne Schizzano Mandel, "Le procés inquisitorial comme acte autobiographique: Le cas de Sor María de San Jerónimo," in *L'autobiographie dans le monde hispanique* (Paris: Publications Université de Provenu, 1980), 155–69; Antonio Gómez-Moriana, "Autobiographie et discours rituel: La confession autobiographique au tribunal de l'Inquisition," *Poétique* 56 (1983): 444–60; and Gómez-Moriana's "Autobiografía y discurso ritual: Problemática de la confesión autobiográfica destinada al tribunal inquistorial," *Imprevue* 1 (1983): 107–27. They also appear in Sonja Herpoel, *A la zaga de Santa Teresa: Autobiografías por mandato* (Amsterdam; Atlanta: Rodopi, 1999). Otherwise, scholars of Spanish autobiography have paid scant attention to the life histories collected by the Inquisition.

coherent. Nevertheless, the form of the narratives, together with the incidents they highlight, still reveals much about the men and women who originally crafted them. To be sure, these lives—to paraphrase the French philosopher Michel Foucault—are brief; they are broken, fragmentary, incomplete. Yet they still enable us to examine the interplay between inquisitorial procedures and a collection of individuals whose lives were sufficiently out of the ordinary to attract attention and, eventually, arrest. By definition, therefore, these lives are unusual—they speak of the margins of early modern Spanish society and of the limits of acceptable social and religious behavior. As such, they reveal the diversity of a society customarily, and stereotypically, rendered as one so rigid and conformist that it was unable to tolerate any form of difference, divergence, or dissent. Finally, these lives, apart from their intrinsic interest and ability to provide what is colloquially known as a "good read," restore to the historical record of early modern Spain the quotidian experiences of a series of individuals whose stories, were it not for their brush with the Inquisition, would have been forgotten or even lost.[6]

The lives included in this collection are by no means representative of the men and women who lived in early modern Spain. Nor are they necessarily representative of all the individuals—estimates place this figure at more than forty thousand—who appeared before the Spanish Inquisition during its 350-year history. They are drawn from the sixteenth and seventeenth centuries, the era when the Inquisition, an institution founded in the late fifteenth century for the express purpose of extirpating heresy among Spain's large converso population, was most active, targeting, in addition to conversos, suspected Protestants; former Muslims, known commonly as *moriscos,* accused of secretly practicing Islam; and Catholic deviants charged with minor heresies ranging from bigamy to blasphemy to sorcery and superstition. In parts of Spain, notably the eastern kingdom of Aragon, the Inquisition also claimed jurisdiction over the "crime" of sodomy.[7]

The geographical range of the individuals whose autobiographies we have

6. "Brief lives" is the term Michel Foucault uses to describe the capsule biographies of ordinary men and women found in the judicial records of Old Regime France. See his essay "The Lives of Infamous Men," in *The Essential Works of Michel Foucault,* ed. James D. Faubon, 3 vols. (New York: New Press, 2000), 3:157.

7. Starting with Henry C. Lea, *A History of the Inquisition in Spain,* 4 vols. (New York: Macmillan, 1906–7), there are many books on the history and structure of the Spanish Inquisition. The best recent survey is Henry Kamen, *The Spanish Inquisition: A Historical Revision* (New Haven, CT: Yale University Press, 1998). For inquisitorial persecution of sodomy, see William C. Monter, *Frontiers of Heresy: The Spanish Inquisition from Basque Lands to Sicily* (Cambridge: Cambridge University Press, 1990).

translated is equally circumscribed. In the sixteenth century the Spanish Inquisition comprised a network of local tribunals whose judges were supervised by an inquisitor general and a central council, the Consejo Suprema y General de la Inquisición, more commonly known simply as the Suprema. Sixteen of these tribunals, each headed by two or three judges assisted by a subaltern staff that included a prosecutor *(fiscal)* and several secretaries, as well as bailiffs, prison wardens, and other officials, were located within the Spanish kingdoms of Castile and Aragon. Two more tribunals—one in Naples, the other in Sicily—could be found in those parts of southern Italy then under Spanish rule. Starting in 1569, two other tribunals were established in Spain's American colonies, in Peru and in New Spain (roughly today's Mexico), primarily to prevent conversos and their descendants from acquiring a permanent foothold in the New World.[8] But wherever its location, each of these tribunals maintained copious records, among them complete transcripts of individual trials. The tribunals also maintained regular contact with the Suprema and, in an effort to prove that they were responsibly fulfilling their assigned tasks, provided the council with annual summaries *(relaciones de causas)* of the cases that had been successfully prosecuted. After the Inquisition's dissolution in 1834, the Spanish state preserved the archives of the Suprema (these are now in Madrid's Archivo Histórico Nacional) almost intact, but those of the local tribunals were mostly destroyed along with the individual case files—an irreparable loss. The only ones to survive are certain case files belonging to the tribunals of Cuenca and Toledo, which together had jurisdiction over those parts of central Spain known as New Castile and La Mancha, as well as others from New Spain, which are currently housed in Mexico City's Archivo General de la Nación. As a result, the cases we have selected all come from these regions.

By the late sixteenth century, the Inquisition routinely dispatched hundreds of cases involving blasphemy, "injurious words," and "scandalous propositions." It also arrested numerous individuals who had declared that sex ("simple fornication" in legal terminology) between unmarried individuals was permissible. In doing so, the Inquisition was less interested in prosecuting fornicators—it never closed any brothels or arrested cohabiting couples—than

---

8. In addition to secret Jews, the Mexican and Peruvian tribunals prosecuted Old Christian Spaniards who were suspected of heresy together with New World *mestizos* (those of mixed Spanish, Indian and/or African heritage). Indians were initially exempt from its jurisdiction, although by the seventeenth century they too could be arrested and tried for minor heresies such as superstition and sorcery.

in enforcing recognition of the Catholic doctrine that sexual union outside the bonds of matrimony was, in fact, a sinful act. Yet these cases, however mundane, kept the inquisitorial tribunals busy. They also reminded Spaniards that the Inquisition did not countenance religious deviance of any sort. And they served to create the Protestant image of the Holy Office as an omniscient institution, an "eye that never slumbered" in the memorable words of one nineteenth-century historian, and thus one that peered regularly into every nook and cranny—even the bedchambers—of Spanish life.[9] But because so many of these cases involved only petty infractions, only rarely did the inquisitors bother to inquire deeply into the lives of the accused. It was quite different, however, in cases involving *judaizantes,* Protestant sympathizers, moriscos, and other persons accused of heresies believed to pose a major risk to the orthodoxy and general well-being of Spanish society. In these cases, inquisitors could be expected to look closely at the lives and backgrounds of the accused, partly because they believed that heresy, like eye color, could be inherited (more on this below) and partly in an effort to garner information about possible other heretics with whom the accused had contact.[10]

We also selected those cases containing life stories that, within the confines of the genre under review, are fairly complete. For this reason, the individuals whose lives are recounted here are not altogether typical of the individuals who appeared before the Holy Office. When inquisitors asked the accused to narrate their life stories, biography was not necessarily their major interest or concern. They expected these life stories to lead them to other heretics and thus enable the Holy Office to get on with its work. In this respect, the cases included in this volume are less representative of the kinds of persons brought to inquisitorial trial than of the issues the Inquisition deemed particularly important or compelling.

Nonetheless, these cases offer a fascinating, if somewhat unusual, look into the society and culture of early modern Spain, one that highlights such issues as ethnic and religious discrimination, sexual difference, and the place of religion in everyday life, as well as the extraordinary mobility characteristic of so many early modern lives. These cases also enable us to appreciate the range

9. William H. Prescott used the phrase "an eye that never slumbered" to refer to the Inquisition in his *History of the Reign Philip II,* 3 vols. (Boston, 1855), 2:446.

10. Even then, our portrait of inquisitorial concerns is only partial, as our search in the Inquisition archives for an interesting autobiography of a person charged with Protestant sympathies proved unsuccessful.

of individuals (nonconformists, in modern parlance) that this society tended to regard as deviant, or at least different, and consequently the norms and values that stood at the center of Spanish life. At the same time, the stories—some might call them fictions—that these nonconformists constructed enable us to locate the margins of what Spaniards of this era considered to be acceptable behavior.

In addition to Francisco de San Antonio and his wife (chapter 4), we meet a series of individuals whose lives are comparable to, and possibly even models for, those of the *pícaros,* the sharpsters and tricksters who were stock figures in the famous picaresque novels of Spain's golden age. *Pícaros* such as Lazarillo de Tormes or Francisco de Quevedo's Buscón were generally outsiders, men (and women) living highly mobile, unpredictable, and often dangerous lives.[11] Such was existence of Luis de la Ysla (chapter 1), a Jew expelled from Spain in 1492. He subsequently converted to Christianity and reconverted to Judaism, only to be rejected by the Jewish community in Alexandria as a false convert when he was stricken with blindness. Ysla eventually reconverted to Christianity, returned to Spain, and presented himself—voluntarily—to the Inquisition in 1514 in order to avoid arrest. We also meet Elena/Eleno de Céspedes (chapter 2), who was born female (Elena) but chose to live as a man (Eleno) and marry a woman. She was originally arrested by a royal judge for the crime of sodomy, but in 1587 the Inquisition claimed jurisdiction over the case and tried Elena/o on charges of bigamy and sorcery. Miguel de Piedrola (chapter 3), who was punished in the same *auto de fe* as Elena/o de Céspedes, was a soldier who claimed to have talent as a visionary. When he announced the imminent downfall of the Spanish monarchy and claimed that his prophetic authority superseded the authority of the king and the pope, the Inquisition arrested him (in 1587) for false prophecy and sedition. Diego Díaz (chapter 5) was a descendant of converted Muslims who reentered Spain after being exiled in 1609. He was caught and deported to Algiers but escaped aboard a fishing boat and swam the rest of the way back to Spain, where the Spanish Inquisition arrested him thirteen years later for certain practices it connected with Islam. Blanca Méndez de Rivera (chapter 6) fled the Seville Inquisition with her husband and five daughters in 1621, finding safety in Mexico City. Blanca, soon widowed, and her daughters became the hub of Mexico City's converso

11. The stories of these two famous *pícaros* are available in translation in *Two Spanish Picaresque Novels,* trans. Michael Alpert (Harmondsworth, Eng.: Penguin, 1969).

community. In 1642 they made the tactical error of welcoming into their community an Inquisition spy who was posing as a secret Jew. The Mexican Inquisition arrested Blanca and all her daughters a few months later. Each of these chapters offers, in addition to a transcription and translation of the autobiographies these prisoners related, a brief discussion of their trials and the wider issues they raised.

The Spanish Inquisition

The common denominator linking these diverse lives is, of course, the Spanish Inquisition, otherwise known as the Holy Office of the Inquisition (Santo Oficio de la Inquisición). No matter how unusual the case before it, the Holy Office acted in accordance with a consistent set of internal procedures that applied equally to all of its far-flung tribunals. Integral to these procedures was the requirement that its judges collect detailed information about every individual it prosecuted, a stipulation that harks back to the beginnings of the institution itself.

The Spanish Inquisition belonged to a long line of ecclesiastical tribunals, also called inquisitions, that the papacy created for the purpose of extirpating heresy from within the confines of Christendom. The name *Inquisition* derives from *inquisitio,* a particular form of juridical procedure that evolved out of earlier Roman practices and found its way into the canon law of the medieval church. This procedure, utilized only in exceptional circumstances, empowered the presiding judge or judges to order arrests, gather evidence, interrogate witnesses, and render judgment, that is, to direct the entire court proceeding. The papacy first deployed this legal weapon in the late twelfth century against deviant communities of monks and nuns and then, with greater determination, at the start of the thirteenth century against Cathar heretics gathered in southwestern France. Subsequently, it authorized individual bishops to institute inquisitorial tribunals whenever the need arose. But whereas these medieval inquisitions were essentially papal or at least episcopal institutions,[12] the Spanish Inquisition, authorized by papal bull in 1478, was directly under the auspices of the Spanish Crown. Initially, the papacy, fearing loss of power, was reluctant to sanction this new arrangement, but the reigning Spanish monarchs, King Ferdinand (1479–1516) and Queen Isabella (1479–1503), pre-

---

12. The bibliography concerning the medieval Inquisition is immense. A useful recent introduction is Edward Peters, *Inquisition* (New York: Free Press, 1988).

vailed, having insisted that a new and somewhat extraordinary institution was necessary to suppress heresy among Spain's large and growing population of New Christians or *conversos*, a term that initially applied to converts from Judaism but which later, and for reasons discussed below, also applied to the descendants of converts.

Spain's converso problem dated from 1391. In that year a wave of violent pogroms that swept across the Iberian peninsula prompted large numbers of Spanish Jews to convert, at least nominally, to Christianity. Subsequent pogroms prompted further conversions, as did the royal decree of 31 March 1492 ordering all Jews in Spain to convert or face expulsion. Numbers are vague, but in the course of the fifteenth century, perhaps as many as one-third to one-half of the kingdom's former Jewish population had been baptized. These Jews officially changed their faith, becoming what was popularly known as *cristianos nuevos*, or New Christians, a term that distinguished them from *cristianos viejos*, or Old Christians, individuals whose lineage was supposedly free from either Jewish or Muslim blood. Some of these conversions were sincere, and many others were not, but whatever the circumstances of their private devotions and religious rituals—and there was astonishing array of such practices, many of which had little to do with orthodox Judaism per se—New Christians were widely suspected of "relapsing" into the faith of their ancestors. Canon law classified *relapsi* as guilty of the sin of apostasy, a capital crime. More prosaically, the Spanish Inquisition labeled these heretics as *judaizantes*, or Judaizers. In Portugal they were known as *marranos* (pigs), a term that was occasionally used in Spain as well. The important to thing to remember here is that whatever the terminology employed—conversos, *judaizantes*, or *marranos*—these New Christians were not all alike. Their backgrounds differed, and so did their devotions. But in general the Inquisition erroneously lumped these individuals together into a single, homogeneous group. Modern scholars, using such labels as crypto- (secret) Jew, have done likewise. While these terms also appear in this book, largely for the sake of convenience, we employ them guardedly and with the understanding that they do not do justice to the broad range of religious devotions followed by New Christians, whether in Spain, Portugal, or the New World.

But whatever the precise nature of New Christian belief, central to inquisitorial understanding of this religious group were issues of inheritance and blood. As David Nirenberg has argued, the sudden appearance of ever-increasing numbers of converts in late-fourteenth- and fifteenth-century Spain fundamentally transformed the nature of Spanish society itself.[13] In the Middle Ages Jewish converts to Christianity were by no means unknown—the twelfth-century scholar Petrus Alfonsi is a famous example—but, starting in 1391, conversos emerged as a large, powerful, and in many ways unclassifiable social group that did not mesh neatly with the tripartite division of Spanish society into separate "nations" or ethnoreligious groups: Christian, Jewish, and Muslim. Conversos were regarded as outsiders, individuals whose very existence threatened the cohesion of the existing religious communities. Jews labeled sincere conversos as apostates, or *meshumud*. Old Christians were reluctant to accept them as equals, as repeated fifteenth-century outbreaks of anti-converso violence among Old Christians readily attest. Furthermore, starting in the early fifteenth century, various cathedral chapters, religious orders, and university colleges instituted *estatutos de limpieza de sangre* ("purity of blood" statutes) in an effort to restrict membership to individuals of proven Old Christian blood. In the process, genealogy, formerly something that mainly concerned the high nobility, acquired new importance: ordinary Spaniards sought to demonstrate a lineage free from converso taint. Once an Old Christian, always an Old Christian; and by this same logic New Christians were accorded a separate and seemingly immutable social status, one that not even the sacrament of baptism had the power to erase. As a result, the term *converso* was applied not only to actual converts, but also to their children and grandchildren, even those who were devout Catholics.

It follows that the Holy Office had a particular interest in the family history of conversos arrested on suspicion of heresy. Previous papal inquisitions had been aware that heresy tended to propagate itself in family groups, but in general medieval inquisitors were more interested in belief than in blood and questions of inheritance.[14] In accordance with the trial procedures outlined in Nicolau Eymeric's *Directorium inquisitorum* of 1339 and other inquisitorial manuals of the late Middle Ages, these judges secured information about a prisoner's place of origin and current residence, along with others, "both living and dead" with whom she or he had been in contact. However, inquisitors rarely made a systematic effort to extract detailed biographical information

---

13. "Mass Conversion and Genealogical Mentalities: Jews and Christians in Fifteenth-Century Spain," *Past and Present* (February 2002): 3–41.

14. James B. Given, *Inquisition and Medieval Society: Power, Discipline, and Resistance in Languedoc* (Ithaca, NY: Cornell University Press, 1997), 38, notes the interest of medieval inquisitors in the families of the individuals they interrogated.

from accused heretics.[15] They were more concerned with having these individuals expound upon their particular religious ideas and practices, and
they forced the accused to do so by means of lengthy question and answer
sessions that formed the heart of inquisitorial trials, otherwise known as "trials
of faith."

The Spanish Inquisition was equally concerned with such matters, and its
question and answer sessions were modeled upon those of earlier inquisitions.
In keeping with contemporary notions of purity of blood, moreover, Spanish
inquisitors also subscribed to the notion that heresy could be inherited along
with other family traits, such as eye color, stature, and the like. They consequently set out to learn about the family history of the accused, generally by
asking them questions about their genealogy and family background. Initially,
only conversos had to answer these questions; but by the sixteenth century,
genealogical queries, as noted above, formed part of most important inquisitorial trials. By 1561 the Inquisition's trial procedures, called "instructions,"
included these specific requirements:

> [Inquisitors are to have accused heretics] state their genealogy as expansively as
> possible, beginning with their fathers and grandfathers, together with all the
> collateral lines they can remember. [They are also to] state the professions and
> residences of their ancestors, and the persons to whom they were married,
> whether they are living or dead, and the children descended from these ancestors
> and collateral lines. The accused are also to state whether they are married and
> with whom, the number of times they have been married, and the names and
> ages of their children. And the Notary will write this genealogy into the tran-
> script, putting [the name of] of each person at the start of a line, and listing if any
> of his ancestors or members of his lineage has been arrested or punished by the
> Inquisition.[16]

Later "instructions" included even more detailed questions, and by the 1580s
the accused, as part of what was by this time expressly referred to as "el
discurso de su vida," was required to provide information about where he (or

15. For the procedures of the medieval inquisitions, see Nicolau Eimeric, *Manuel de inquisidores
para uso de las inquisiciones de España y Portugal* (Barcelona: Editorial Fontamara, 1974); and *Les regi-
stres d'inquisition de Jacques Fournier,* trans. Jean Duvernoy, 3 vols. (Paris; La Haye, Mouton, 1977).

16. The inquisitorial "instructions" of 1561 are printed in their entirety in Miguel Jiménez
Montserín, *Introducción a la inquisición española* (Madrid: Editorial Nacional, 1950), 198–240.

she) was raised, the places where he had lived, and the persons with whom he had contact and communicated with, "all extensively and with great detail."[17] Thus, by the end of the sixteenth century, life histories became a regular and distinctive feature of inquisitorial practice, although, as noted above, inquisitors had considerable leeway to prosecute individual cases as they saw fit.

Inquisitorial procedures were also unique in other important ways. One was the secrecy with which Inquisition trials were marked at every stage. The Inquisition initiated its cases by a secret process called *denunciation,* which differed substantially from the secular and ecclesiastical court process of *accusation.* Crimes prosecuted in these latter tribunals had human victims who, assisted by a prosecutor, had the right to enter an accusation of wrongdoing against the perpetrator. Accusers could expect monetary compensation for their suffering in case of a guilty verdict and could themselves be prosecuted in case of false accusation. In contrast, the individuals who reported heretical acts to the Inquisition were, technically speaking, not accusers since they were not victims. They were more like witnesses, persons who had stepped forward to alert the Holy Office to crimes that had been committed against God and his Church. Furthermore, the persons who filed these reports could not expect any compensation if the denunciation resulted in a guilty verdict. Nor, on the other hand, did they have to fear punishment for "false witness," a real possibility in other criminal proceedings where the accused was judged innocent. In inquisitorial trials, "witnesses" were offered the additional guarantee of anonymity, which protected them from reprisal. Keeping the names of witnesses secret helped provide the Inquisition with cases, but it also led to many abuses, among them denunciations that had less to do with actual instances of heresy than with personal enmity and ill will.

Following an anonymous denunciation, inquisitors began an investigation into the accused's alleged heresies. Inquisitors interviewed witnesses to the heresy and known associates of the accused, conducting their depositions with the utmost secrecy. These witnesses swore never to reveal that they had spoken with inquisitors, and inquisitors did not inform prospective defendants that they were under suspicion. If the depositions lent credence to the initial denunciation, the judges put the case before a *calificador,* a theologian or canon lawyer especially appointed to determine the merits of a case. Pending the

17. Ibid., 401.

calificador's approval, inquisitors dispatched their bailiffs to make an arrest and imprison the accused in a secret Inquisition jail to await the start of her or his trial.

Once imprisoned, accused persons could often wait for months, sometimes years, before the inquisitors summoned them for an *audiencia* (audience, or hearing). Even then, inquisitors did not reveal to the accused the reasons for the arrest. Instead, as already seen in the case of Francisco de San Antonio, they began the first interrogation by asking, "What do you think you have done to be arrested?" hoping for a complete and truthful confession. It was also during this initial hearing that inquisitors posed a series of routine questions to defendants, among them the request for a life history. No matter how much or how little information prisoners revealed in the course of their first audience, inquisitors ended the audience by "warning" them to make a "full and complete confession," adding that the Holy Office did not arrest prisoners without good reason. "The Holy Office [of the Spanish Inquisition]," they announced, "is not accustomed to arresting people without having sufficient information that they have said, done, and committed . . . an offense against God and against the Holy Roman Catholic Faith."

Once this initial session was over, bailiffs escorted the accused back to their cells, to await the next audience. In the meantime, the inquisitors warned them to search their consciences and provide the inquisitors with the confession they sought. After three such *audiencias,* the Inquisition's prosecutor (*fiscal*) drew up a list of charges and presented it to the accused. It was only at this point that the accused had an opportunity to examine the witness testimony against him or her (with the witnesses' names omitted) and consult with a lawyer and prepare a written defense. Yet the legal assistance provided was often quite dubious. Paid by the Holy Office, the lawyer's primary task was not to "defend" the accused but rather to persuade the accused to make a full confession. The lawyer had the further obligation to reveal to the judges any additional information he may have garnered about the heresy of the accused. Following these consultations, the accused submitted a response to each of the prosecutor's charges.

It was also after the completion of the three initial audiences that inquisitors had the power to have the accused tortured in order to hasten a full confession. These tortures ranged from forcing the prisoner to swallow huge amounts of water to the use of such instruments as the *potro* or rack (to stretch the prisoner's body) and the *garrucha,* a kind of pulley system in which the prisoner was hung by the wrists; none of these means violated the (narrowly construed) clerical injunction against spilling blood. Make no mistake: inquisitorial justice was harsh justice, although compared to other courts of the era, the Holy Office was actually rather sparing in its use of torture, and by the seventeenth century some of its judges went so far as to discount entirely the veracity of confessions extracted by means of torture. But whether or not the trial involved torture—most did not—after more witness interviews and more responses, the prosecutor drew up a final list of charges and a request for sentencing. The inquisitors then weighed the merits of the case, voted, and handed down a sentence.

Unlike royal and ecclesiastical courts, which understood their sentences as retributive for injuries done to the accuser, the Inquisition framed its punishments as atonement, a penance that had to be done in order to make amends for the defendant's injury to God, the Church, and the sacraments. Penance, as imagined by the Holy Office, usually included large doses of public humiliation. Most minor offenses—blaspheming, for example, or insulting an inquisitorial official—often resulted in little more than a private reprimand from the inquisitorial tribunal. This might be coupled with an order to attend a certain number of Sunday masses and offer a designated number of prayers. The Holy Office punished most heretics, however, in a public ceremony of penance called an "act of faith," or *auto de fe*. An *auto* was a public gathering in which the "penitents," as the Inquisition called them, paraded before a gathered crowd, wearing garments known as sanbenitos (smocks bearing an insignia symbolizing the prisoner's crime) and *corozas* (similar to dunce caps), symbolizing shame. At the *auto,* the crimes of the penitents were read aloud. One by one, those who confessed their guilt stepped forward for sentencing. Individuals accused of minor offenses who had willingly repented of their "sins" and promised to reform were "reconciled" to the Church in a short, formulaic speech pronounced by one of the Inquisition's officials: "Considering that Our Lord does not wish the death of sinners, but that they turn from their ways and live, since said [name of prisoner], with a pure heart, converts to our Holy Catholic faith, we should and do admit him to be reconciled."

The penalties were then announced. Those accused of minor heresies could expect to receive what was called an *abjuración de levi* (literally, abjuring or forswearing minor heresies). These individuals generally could get off with as little as a whipping and a public shaming, although the Inquisition often required these penitents to wear their sanbenitos on Sundays and holidays for a specified period of time. Thereafter, the Holy Office mandated that the penitential garments be hung from the rafters of the penitent's parish church, where they remained on display as permanent reminders of the person's crimes. Those guilty of more serious offenses *(abjuración de vehementi)* could suffer seclusion in a monastery, exile, or (as in the case of San Antonio) several years of galley slavery in the king's Mediterranean fleet. The harshest penalties were reserved for heretics who had not confessed or who were repeat offenders, the infamous *relapsos.* They were "relaxed" (handed over) to the secular justices to be burned at the stake. By not executing prisoners itself, the Inquisition could claim that it was acting in accordance with the canonical injunction prohibiting clergy from engaging in bloodshed. Otherwise, the Inquisition was determined not to allow any heretic to go unpunished. Adhering, moreover, to the concept that heresy could be inherited, the Inquisition regularly subjected the heirs of *relapsos,* as well as those who confessed to serious heresies, to *infamia* (infamy). *Infames* and their descendants for three generations could not hold public office, join clerical orders, wear luxury items, carry arms, or ride horses.

As the late Francisco Tomás y Valiente has observed, the true horrors of the Spanish Inquisition were not the numbers of prisoners burned at the stake nor the excessive use of torture commonly attributed to this institution.[18] The Inquisition was, in fact, less prone to torturing and executing prisoners than were secular courts in Spain and other parts of Europe. Further, as the case records presented in this volume suggest, the Inquisition was something less than the faceless, monolithic machine that it is commonly conceived to have been. The Holy Office maintained a set of uniform procedures, but individual tribunals and individual inquisitors applied them in differing ways and in a manner that often allowed prisoners room for maneuver and even for negotiating their trial's eventual outcome. The same cases further suggest that, contrary to expectation, the Holy Office exercised a considerable degree of leniency in the handling of individual cases. Nonetheless, it remained for most Spaniards a terrifying institution, and as Tomás y Valiente has suggested, perhaps the Inquisition's most sinister aspect was its "mechanism of secrecy"—its practice of holding prisoners incommunicado and in undisclosed locations, its refusal to reveal to its prisoners either the nature of the charges against them or the names of the witnesses who had originally denounced them, and its deter-

---

18. "El proceso penal," *Historia 16, extraordinaria inquisición* (1976): 19–36.

mination to drape a mantle of silence over every aspect of its proceedings. In some cases, this mechanism of secrecy ground to a halt, but generally it served to foster fear of the Holy Office, a fear that the Inquisition ably exploited to its own advantage. This fear also had its creative side, inasmuch as it was directly responsible for the creation of the autobiographies assembled in this book.

Note on Transcriptions

The process of editing these lives has been a balancing act, with a need on one hand to maintain the integrity and flavor of the original trial transcripts and, on the other, to render them in a legible, concise format. The documents used are preserved in Madrid's Archivo Histórico Nacional, which contains the case files of the inquisition of Toledo; Cuenca's diocesan archive, with the case files of the tribunal that was once located in that city; and the Archivo General de la Nación in Mexico City. They are handwritten accounts of the actual trial proceedings as transcribed by an Inquisition scribe. The transcripts have no standardized spelling or punctuation and no regular spacing between words, and they are padded with gratuitous legalese. Transcripts range anywhere from tens to hundreds of pages long. Included in this volume are lengthy excerpts from each case file that shed light on the prisoners' life experiences and defense strategies as well as the Inquisition's institutional framework. On occasion, we include various inquisitorial marginalia—marked marginalia—written in the original documents, as they help pinpoint certain issues or facts that the inquisitors found pertinent to the case. However, we have omitted other information included in the trial transcripts for the sake of streamlining and shaping each narrative.

The task of translating these documents by its nature involved editing as well. Run-on sentences, which often ran on for several pages, had to be corralled and shortened into manageable bits, spelling of proper names standardized, spaces put back between words, abbreviations spelled out, and legalese reduced. Furthermore, the scribe's third-person transcription ("she or he said . . .") of the prisoner's first-person narrative has been transformed into an approximation of the original first-person testimony. It is our hope that through the process of editing and translation we have made it possible for the prisoners' stories, coerced, untruthful, or too truthful for the defendant's own good, to reach a wide audience, one much larger than the panel of inquisitors for whom these brief lives were originally designed.

FURTHER READING

As recommended background reading on the European context of early modern Spain, see Evan Cameron, ed. *Early Modern Europe: An Oxford History* (Oxford: Oxford University Press, 1999). The classic political history of early modern Spain remains John H. Elliott, *Imperial Spain* (London: Arnold, 1963 and later editions). Elliott's collection of essays, *Spain and Its World* (New Haven, CT: Yale University Press, 1989), provides a more complex understanding of major issues in early modern Spanish history. For an introduction to Spanish social history of this same period, see James Casey, *Early Modern Spain: A Social History* (London: Routledge, 1999): and Teofilo F. Ruiz, *Spanish Society, 1400–1600* (Harlow, Eng.: Longman, 2001).

For an excellent discussion of ethnicity, religion, and the interactions of Jewish, Muslim, and Christian cultures in medieval Spain, see David Nirenberg, *Communities of Violence* (Princeton, NJ: Princeton University Press, 1998).

For early modern autobiographies and life stories, see James S. Amelang, *The Flight of Icarus: Artisan Autobiography in Early Modern Europe* (Palo Alto, CA: Stanford University Press, 1998); and three now-classic studies by Natalie Zemon Davis: *The Return of Martin Guerre* (Cambridge, MA: Harvard University Press, 1983); *Fiction in the Archives: Pardon Tales and Their Tellers in Seventeenth-Century France* (Palo Alto, CA: Stanford University Press, 1987); and *Women on the Margins: Three Seventeenth-Century Lives* (Cambridge, MA: Harvard University Press, 1995). For life stories based primarily on inquisitorial sources, see Carlo Ginzberg, *The Cheese and the Worms: The Cosmos of a Sixteenth-Century Miller,* trans. John Tedeschi and Anne Tedeschi (New York: Penguin, 1982); Richard L. Kagan, *Lucrecia's Dreams: Politics and Prophecy in Sixteenth-Century Spain* (Berkeley: University of California Press, 1990); and Sara T. Nalle, *Mad for God: Bartolomé Sánchez: The Secret Messiah of Cardenete* (Charlottesville: University of Virginia Press, 2001).

An excellent overview of both the papal and the Spanish inquisitions may be found in Edward Peters, *Inquisition* (New York: Free Press, 1988). The best starting point for the history of the Spanish Inquisition remains the classic study by Henry C. Lea, *A History of the Inquisition in Spain* (New York: Macmillan, 1906–7; reprint, New York: AMS Press, 1988), although it should be supplemented with Henry Kamen, *The Spanish Inquisition: A Historical Revision* (New Haven, CT: Yale University Press, 1998).

CHAPTER ONE

Renegade Jew

Luis de la Ysla

Abraham Abzaradiel (1484–1514), a native of Illescas, a small Castilian town near Toledo, was among the thousands of Sephardic Jews who were expelled from Spain by the order of the monarchy in 1492. As part of the great Mediterranean diaspora, Abzaradiel, only eight years old at the time of the expulsion, found his way to Italy, where, just shy of his thirteenth birthday, he was baptized, converted to Christianity, and took the name Luis de la Ysla. Under this alias he returned to his former homeland to learn a trade and to meet up with family and friends.

Ysla, however, was a wanderer. He soon left Spain, going first to Italy, then to Turkey and the Middle East, where he found other Spanish Jewish exiles and returned to his ancestral faith. On other occasions, Ysla lived as a Christian, and as he moved from port to port, he regularly altered his religious identity in an effort to survive. Living as a Christian in Alexandria, Egypt, Ysla went blind as a result of some illness and decided, around 1514, to return permanently to Spain.

Back in Toledo, Ysla's friends advised him that in order to avoid arrest by the Inquisition, he should appear voluntarily before its judges to confess his former "sins." Ysla did what he was told, and the story he recounted to the Inquisition offers a fascinating window onto the diaspora of 1492 along with valuable information about the Jewish communities that Ysla encountered in the course of his travels.

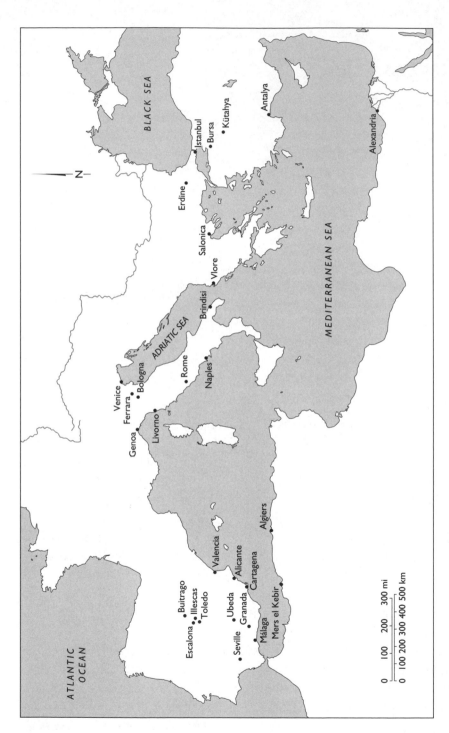

2. *Travels of Luis de la Ysla*

In the very noble city of Toledo, on 15 May 1514, the Reverend Licentiate Pedro Ochoa de Villanueva, Inquisitor of the Holy Office of the Inquisition, ordered Francisco Maldonado, warden of the prison of the Holy Office of the Inquisition, to bring into the audience room a blind man who was a prisoner there. Maldonado appeared with this man before his Reverence, who, presiding, asked the prisoner his name.[1]

"My name is Luis de la Ysla, and I am a New Christian of Jewish origin, age thirty. I was born in Buytrago, but raised in Illescas as a Jew.[2] I was also a native of the kingdom [of Castile] at the time of the expulsion of the Jews from these kingdoms [in July 1492]. I then went abroad, going to the city of Algiers in Barbary [North Africa], where I stayed for two months. From there I went to Venice and remained there, living as a Jew, for three and one-half years. From there I then went to Genova [Genoa] became a Christian, and resided there for just about a month.

"From Genova I traveled to Escalona[3] and lived in the house of the archdeacon of Toledo for four months. From Escalona I went to Úbeda [in Andalucia] and lived there for twenty-two months, learning the trade of spinning silk in the house of Juan de Torres, who is now deceased. From Úbeda I went to Granada, where, for about five or six months, I plied my trade. From there I returned to this city [Toledo]. I lived here for about two months in the house of Juan Francés, a spinner. I next went to Seville, living in the house of García Bondina, a Genovese [native of Genoa], for two months. I then returned to this city and to the house of Juan Francés.

"From Toledo I next went to Valencia, working for four years in the house of Nicolás Carbonero, who is now deceased. I also lived in a house belonging to a member of the Borja family.[4] He was executed because he stabbed a certain Francisco Calderon. From Valencia I went to Alicante and was there about three or four months. I then went to Mers el Kebir[5] and from there returned to Valencia, and then came again to this city, where I lived for two months. I next went to Málaga, and then traveled to other places in these kingdoms.

1. Our translation is based upon the text published in Fidel Fita y Colomé, "El judío errante de Illescas (1484–1514)," *Boletín de la Real Academia de la Historia* 6 (1885): 130–40.

2. Buitrago is a small town, located north of Madrid. In the fifteenth century it was known for its many Jews and conversos. Illescas is located to the south of Madrid, on the road to Toledo.

3. A town east of Toledo, the seat of the powerful Marques of Villena. It is likely that Ysla went to Escalona because of the archdeacon, a churchman with whom his family probably had connections before the expulsion of 1492, inasmuch as Luis's grandfather, Yuçufa Abzaradiel, was a tax farmer who had dealings with the church in villages and towns near Toledo.

4. A prominent Valencian family whose members included Pope Alexander VI (1492–1503).

5. A small coastal town near Oran in modern Algeria.

"In the year of the plague [1506], I went to Cartagena and embarked for the port of Livorno [in Italy], and from there went to Rome. From Rome I went to Bologna, and then to Ferrara. While living in Ferrara and needing money, I heard someone speak about a Jew who was originally from Murcia [in southeastern Spain]. I cannot remember his name, but he was residing in the city. I asked the Jew if they spun silk in Ferrara, and the Jew had one of his servants take me to the house of another Jew, named Çabahon, a native of Guadalajara[6] and a weaver of *tocas*.[7] I went to this house and asked the Jew where they spun the silk for headdresses. The Jew responded by asking me where I was from. I told him that I was a Castilian and a native of Illescas. I also told him that I had been a Jew but was now a Christian. The Jew then invited me to return to his house another day to dine. I went to eat with him on Saturday, and we ate meat that had been cooked on Friday for the Saturday meal, along with some fish pies. On that day, Saturday, before eating, at the hour when Jews customarily pray, I went with this Jew to a synagogue and we arrived during the middle of the prayers. The Jew sat along with the other Jews, while I sat on a small low bench along with some Jewish boys, as there was not room left to sit among the adult Jews. I remained with the Jew in the synagogue until the prayers were over and we left. After eating dinner with the Jew, I went back into the city and did not return to the house of this Jew until another day, a Sunday. I asked him whether he had spoken with the Jew from Murcia, the silk spinner, who I hoped would give me some work and a wheel to spin silk. The Jew said he had spoken with the Murcian Jew, who told him that he could not hire anyone to wind silk as it cost more to wind silk than to spin it.

"From Ferrara I went Venice and boarded ship along with some Portuguese merchants. One of them was called Juan Pentenado, the other Maestro Rodrigo Cirujano, and both were from Lisbon. [Inquisitorial marginalia: "lisbon. Juan pentenado, New christian. master Rodrigo, surgeon, New christian."] These two merchants said that if I was willing to serve them aboard the ship, they would pay for my passage. So I served them, and they fed me. I think the two merchants were going to the kingdom of Naples, but when we were at sea the ship began to break apart. It was then that the merchants told me that they had once been Jews and that they were going to Brindisi [in southeastern Italy]. I told them that I too had been a Jew. [Once in Brindisi,] the merchants

---

6. A city in central Spain, thirty miles east of Madrid.
7. *Toca* is form of female headdress, traditionally worn by nuns and widows. Note that *cabahon* is the Hebrew for *spinner*.

boarded a small ship and headed for Velona [Vlore], which is in Turkey, and I accompanied them.[8] We arrived in Velona at the beginning of Lent, and I spent all of Lent with the two merchants. These merchants lived like Jews, performed all of the Jewish ceremonies, and ate meat throughout Lent. I spent Saturdays with these Jews, eating the same food, which was cooked on Fridays, that they ate. During Lent, the two merchants celebrated the holiday of unleavened bread [*pan cenceño* = Passover] and I did so along with them. Occasionally, on Saturdays, I also went to synagogue with my two masters, but when they arrived at the door of the synagogue, I left them and stayed outside and walked around the corrals and along the marshes along with other servants like myself.

"From Velona I went to Salonica, accompanied by some Jews, Greeks, and Turks, calling myself a Jew and known to the two merchants who I went with as a Jew. There I bumped into [met] a Valenciano [native of Valencia], called Castellar, a spinner of *bivos* [?] whom I had known as a Christian in Valencia. But in Salonica he was a Jew, and I spoke to him and we recognized one another. He persuaded me to become an interpreter for a group traveling to Adrianople [Erdine, in European Turkey]. It was also in Salonica I met someone named Gabriel Roca, a native of Valencia and a veil-maker. He was also there as a Jew and married to a Jewess from Sicily. He invited me to his spinning shop, where we ate some beans and cheese and bread. It was also in Salonica that I met Castellar's father, a velvet weaver. He also had been a Christian and a resident of Valencia, but was now a Jew in Salonica. I don't remember his name except that he was called Castellar. Also in Salonica I met a servant called Galiana, who was from Valencia. He told me he was the nephew of Suhau [?], a merchant, who had silk looms in Valencia. The boy was around eighteen or nineteen years old, and told me that he had a brother in Mallorca, also called Galiana, a cloth merchant. The boy also told me that he was the nephew of Moisés Velarte, a Jew, resident in Salonica, who had previously been a Christian and a resident of Valencia. The boy was named Isaac, and he had been a Christian, and had stayed on in Salonica, determined to be a Jew. It was also in Salonica that I visited the house of a Jewess, bringing her some letters from her son, who was living in Brindisi. I stayed three days in her house. I also saw, in Velona, dressed as a Jew, Baltasar Valeriola, a resident of Valencia. I believe he is called Mosén Valeriola. [Inquisitorial marginalia: Valencia. Castel-

---

8. Velona, or Vlore, an Adriatic port town in what is now Albania, then was part of the Ottoman Empire, and for this reason Ysla located it in Turkey.

lar, weaver of bivos; graviel (sic) Roxa, veil-maker; the father of the aforesaid Castellar, weaver; galiana alias Isaac, a youth.—Valencia. Baltasar valeriola.—Valencia. Valencian conversos turned jews.]

"From Salonica I went to the city of Adrianople [Erdine, in European Turkey], a two-day journey. I stayed there for two weeks, as a Jew and among Jews, and I saw there many Jews, originally from Toledo, Torrejón [de Velasco],[9] Madrid, and Guadalajara, all of whom had gone there after the general expulsion [of 1492]. I spoke with them, told them who I was, and how things were going. One Saturday I dined with a Jew who invited me [to his house], and we ate meat and cherries.

"From Adrianople I went to Constantinople [Istanbul], and I was there two days. I lodged in the Jewish quarter, and there I met several Castilians dressed as Jews but who once were Christians. I recognized some of their faces, as I had seen them in Valencia and elsewhere in these kingdoms, but I did not know their names.

"From Constantinople I went to Bruça [Bursa], which is located in old Turkey [the Asian mainland]. I was there for two days, dressed as a Jew. I saw there several Jews, originally from these kingdoms, and other Jews who had once been Christians, but I did not meet them. I recognized them by their folded hoods, which are different from those worn by Jews; these hoods are signs that they had been Christians. From Bruça I traveled to Cuté [Kütahya], a town in Old Turkey, with a Jew from Maqueda [a village near Toledo] who called himself Hasamel. I went dressed as a Jew, and with a Jewish name. In Cuté, once at midday, I ate apricots and rice with a Jewish peddler. I then wanted to go to Setabías [Antalya], a port town, in order to get to Alexandria, and I arranged with a Turk to get me there. I thus traveled to Setabías. There I was in the house of a Jew named Abenxuxen, who was originally from Guadalajara. I was there for two weeks, working in the company of some Jews.

"From Setabías I embarked for and traveled to Alexandria. In the ship I was accompanied by a natural Jew and ate with him. Once in Alexandria, this Jew took me to a shop to eat, and once we had finished, he invited me to accompany him to Cairo. I said no, as I wanted to stay on and earn some money. So the Jew left, heading for Cairo, while I went to the "factory" *[alhóndiga]* of the Catalans, the exchange hall *[casa de negociación]* for Christians. There, being among them, I publicly declared myself a Christian. Yet being there, I also

9. A village near Toledo.

happened to speak with several Jews, among them one Jacob Çaban, a native of Córdoba, who I was told had been a Christian and about whom I don't know anything more except that he called himself Çaban." [Inquisitorial marginalia: "Córdoba—jacó çaban."] These Jews then asked me where I was from, and I told them from Illescas, and that I had been a Jew. Then this Jacob Çaban asked me why I had become a Christian and why a person from such honorable people as those in Illescas could call himself a Christian. I answered that I had wanted to be a Christian and a Christian I was. With that, Çaban begged me to become a Jew again, and he promised to give me money and other things I needed. I insisted: no, I want to be Christian and remain in the faith. Just about then I also came to speak with a boy from Valencia, son of Guillen Nadal, who lived near the plaza of the calle de Avellano and who I believe was a silk weaver. The boy was named Calceranete Nadal. He had been a Christian, but he was in Alexandria as a Jew and called himself such. He also called himself by the name of Jucé, and in my opinion he was then about eighteen or nineteen years old and could now be about the age of twenty-four, more or less. [Inquisitorial marginalia: "Valencia, calceranete nadal, alias yuçe."] This boy made a point of being a Jew and that he went to synagogue in order to give thanks to the Lord for having saved him from a shipwreck. And when these Jews saw that I did not want to become a Jew, they threatened me, telling me that they would have me burned for not wanting to be Jewish.

"I was in the city of Alexandria for about thirteen months, serving two prostitutes [*mujeres enamoradas*], both Christians, one from Vizcaya, the other from Naples. They paid me one and one-half *sarafos* a month, plus food, which is equal to just less than one and one-half ducats. [At that time] the Jews complained about me to the lieutenant governor, because I did not want to become a Jew; and thus I remained a Christian, as I had been and now am, and I was always regarded as a Christian. In Alexandria, I went blind as a result of several fevers, and I was there as a blind man for nine months, living in the *alhóndiga* of the Christians. Once I went blind, the Jews taunted me and said bad words to me, telling me I was blind on account of my sins and for not having wanted to become a Jew. I confessed all of this to a friar of the Order of Saint Francis and to another friar of the same order who was returning from the Holy Land. I confessed to them everything that had happened, and they absolved me.

"From Alexandria I went to Naples. There I confessed with the confessor of the Catalan consul, and he too absolved me from everything I have just recounted. From Naples I came to Valencia, and from Valencia to this city of Toledo. About five years had passed from the time I embarked with the Portuguese merchants [in Brindisi], and it has now been about two years since I returned to this city.

"This past Lent [March–April 1514], when I was one day in the [church of] San Pedro Martyr, listening to a sermon, I heard the preacher say that the sinner was obliged to suffer for his sins, each and every time he remembered them. I then remembered to confess again for what I had done, and I went to confess with a priest in the cathedral. As I began to tell him my story, this churchman told me that I should go to the [Franciscan] church of San Juan de los Reyes and make my confession there to one of its friars as they had a very pious bull [of indulgence] that could absolve me from what I told you before. Shortly thereafter, on Easter Day [16 April 1514], I went to San Juan de los Reyes, but I could not find a confessor; I also quarreled with the porter, because he did not go to find me one. So I left. Going away, I bumped into a certain Alfonso de Illescas. He asked me where I was coming from, and I told him that I was angry with the porter of San Juan because he did not want to find me a confessor. This Alfonso de Illescas then told me to go with him and he would take me to one who was in [the parish church of] San Román, a very good man and learned. Once I got there, this Alfonso de Illescas left me with a clergyman, who called himself the *bachiller* [university graduate] of San Pablo.[10] . . . I told him, outside of confession, everything that had happened to me. Then the *bachiller* told me that all this was important business and something that fell under the jurisdiction of the Inquisition. He then told me that, with my permission, he would report it to the Inquisitors and that he would do so honestly. All this bothered me, inasmuch as I had already confessed and been absolved of everything. I also said that I had not wanted to say anything to anyone, so that it would not come to the attention of their Reverences [the inquisitors], so as not to suffer any insult. Despite all this, the *bachiller* told me that he'd do what he wanted. And then the *bachiller* told me that he would speak to the Inquisitors, and that he would do so honestly; and he tried very hard [to convince me]. I then gave him half a real [some money] to sing a mass to the Holy Spirit on my behalf.

"A few days later the *bachiller* told me that he had already spoken with

10. Ysla is probably referring to the Dominican College of San Pablo in Valladolid, an institution affiliated with the university located in this important Old Castilian city.

Inquisitor Villanueva, and that Inquisitor had told him that I should tell my story to a lawyer, who would then give it to the Inquisition. This bothered me, because I had already told everything to Juan Zapata, the silk weaver. I went next to the San Juan de los Reyes with a document from the vicar's assistant indicating that the [friars] there should hear my confession, inasmuch as I had not confessed during Lent. And I did indeed tell everything to a friar, noting that I had previously confessed and had been absolved. The friar told me that since I had confessed and was absolved, it was not necessary to do so again and suggested that I confess other sins. He also advised me that if the Inquisitors should call me in and ask me about what I had already said, they were persons who would listen mercifully to what I had to say. So I went ahead and confessed my other sins to the friar, and he absolved me, and suggested that I should go to the Inquisitors and confess. I came away somewhat perplexed, since that very same morning the *guardian* [head friar] of San Juan de los Reyes, when we were seated together on some beams, asked me whether everything I said about what happened to me was indeed true and also whether I had already confessed. I told him that I was telling the truth, and also that I had confessed first in Alexandria and then in Naples. The *guardian* then told me that he had already spoken to the judge and that 'those who you fear are those you have to accuse; don't bother to speak with them or try to understand them. But if you are going to call on the Inquisitors, tell them in any case the whole truth, as they are pious men who will treat you with mercy.' I did not speak again with this *guardian*, but as I was afraid of being insulted, I did not dare to come before your Reverences. And, by the way, the friar who confessed me is Fray Juan Sebastián."

[The inquisitors now asked Ysla for the different names he used during his travels.] "While I was in Velonia, I was called Abraham, but while I was traveling toward Alexandria I did not use any name. Once I was in Alexandria, I called myself Luis. . . ."

[signed] Juan Lopes, notary public

On 31 March 1492 the Spanish monarchs, Ferdinand and Isabella, issued a royal decree ordering all Jews in their kingdoms either to convert to Christianity within the space of three months or to go into exile. The order was controversial but by no means unprecedented. Other European rulers had previously ordered Jews into exile.

But the Spanish order of expulsion marked the beginning of what is often referred to as the great Sephardic diaspora, the dispersion of Spanish Jews throughout many parts of the Western world.

How many Jews left Spain at this time is in dispute, but somewhere between fifty thousand and one hundred thousand chose exile over conversion.[11] Some of these emigrated to neighboring Portugal and later to the Netherlands. Others fanned out across the Mediterranean, some heading for North Africa and others for Italy, Venice in particular, as this city was known for its tolerance of Jews. Still other exiles ventured farther east, toward the Ottoman Empire, where the Turkish sultans, in traditional Muslim fashion, welcomed Jews as *dhimmi,* a special status that allowed them to freely practice their religion in exchange for the payment of a tax.

Luis de la Ysla, as his "autobiography" makes clear, was part of this Mediterranean diaspora. Born Abraham Abzaradiel in 1484 into a fairly prosperous Jewish family—his grandfather Yuçaf was a tax farmer—Luis (he adopted the name Luis de la Ysla following his conversion to Christianity) moved as a child with his family to Illescas, a small Castilian town located on the road between Toledo and Madrid.[12] Ysla was only eight at the time of the Expulsion Order. In the company of his family, he left Spain, heading first for North Africa and then Italy, where he took up residence in Genoa. At this point, Ysla, age twelve, was baptized, converted to Christianity, and, under this pretext, returned to his native land in 1496, possibly accompanied by his father. The circumstances surrounding his "conversion" remain unclear, but in November 1492 the Spanish monarchs granted a right of return to those Jews who had left their kingdoms providing they converted to Catholicism. The decision to make Luis into a Catholic—on the eve of his Bar Mitzvah!—was therefore likely part of a family strategy designed to repatriate Ysla and reestablish the family's connections with their native Castile.

Back in Spain, the young Ysla learned to spin silk and eventually found his way back to Toledo, where he met up with friends and presumably family as well. He subsequently worked as an itinerant silk spinner for about ten years, but in 1506, at the age of about twenty-two, he decided to go into exile once again. Ysla does not explain what prompted him to leave Spain on this occasion, but—reading between

11. The most comprehensive study of the expulsion is Haim Beinart, *The Expulsion of the Jews from Spain,* trans. Jeffrey M. Green (Oxford; Portland, OR: Littman Library of Jewish Civilization, 2002). However, as Beinart admits, the number of Jews who actually left the peninsula remains in dispute (284–90).

12. Other than the material provided in the autobiography, what little is known about Luis de la Ysla is summarized in César Martín, "Abraham Abzaradiel: El judío ciego de Illescas (Toledo)," *Raíces* 54, no. 17 (2003): 48–60. We are grateful to David Nirenberg for bringing this article to our attention.

the lines of the testimony he presented to the Inquisition of Toledo in 1514—he apparently did so because he was a crypto-Jew, a convert who was secretly practicing Jewish rites. The Holy Office had been especially created to prosecute these "Judaizers," and Ysla, perhaps sensing danger, emigrated for a second time.

On this Mediterranean journey, Ysla returned to Italy in search of work and the company of the other Spanish Jews, although, interestingly, he makes no mention of ever having contacted his family. Living for a time in Ferrara, he soon headed eastward, into the Ottoman Empire, stopping successively at Vlore, Salonica, Erdine (in European Turkey), Istanbul, various cities in Asia Minor, and finally Alexandria, where, owing to some sort of illness, he went blind. He subsequently found his back to Italy, stopping at Naples, and then Spain, where he returned to Toledo, a city he knew and where he still had friends.

During the course of his travels, the chameleon-like Ysla seemingly altered his religious identity—along with his name—whenever it suited his purposes, living sometimes as a Christian named Luis, sometimes as a Jew called Abraham. Unstable religious identities of this sort were by no means unusual in the sixteenth century: they can also be found on the frontiers between Catholicism and Protestantism in western Europe as well as those separating Christianity and indigenous beliefs in the New World. The Mediterranean, with its complex amalgam of Christianity, Judaism, and Islam, had its own share of overlapping religious identities, especially among the many Jews who were "stateless" as a result of the Spanish Expulsion Order of 1492.[13] Ysla was but one of these stateless persons, a wanderer for whom religion was less an immutable system of beliefs and practices than a malleable instrument to be played in different ways for purposes of daily survival. Instrumentalized religiosity of this kind was more a necessity than a matter a choice, but whatever its origins, it certainly figured in Ysla's first "conversion" to Christianity and subsequent return to Spain in 1496. It further helps to explain why he was prepared to "live as a Jew" in both Ferrara and Salonica, apparently with an eye toward establishing relationships with fellow Spanish Jews who were prepared to offer him hospitality and provide him with work. At other times, as in Alexandria, Ysla professed Christianity, much to the dismay of other Spanish Jews who knew that he was born Jewish. As Ysla later reported, these Jews taunted and teased him, even claiming that he went blind only because of his refusal to live as a Jew.

How much of this story is true? Without corroborating sources—unfortunately,

---

13. A recent study of one such Jew is Mercedes García-Arenal and Gerard Wiegers, *A Man of Three Worlds: Samuel Pallache, a Moroccan Jew in Catholic and Protestant Europe,* trans. Martin Beagles (Baltimore: Johns Hopkins University Press, 2003).

few have been discovered[14]—the overall veracity of Ysla's narrative is difficult to determine. Yet the essential facts—exile, return, exile, and a final return—are entirely credible. So, too, is Ysla's report of finding fellow Spanish Jews—and Spanish conversos—wherever he went. Equally importantly, his life underscores the complexity of the diaspora itself. More than a single event, Ysla's experiences suggest that it more closely resembled a process of gradual disengagement involving closely entwined yet competing notions of religion and nationality. Both Spaniard and Jew, Ysla continually felt the backward pull of his native Castile, so much so that he was ultimately willing to discard his ancestral faith and live as a Christian. In doing so, Ysla was by no means alone. Countless other Jewish exiles, having converted to Christianity, trickled back into Spain, their beloved Sepharad, well into the seventeenth century.[15]

Ysla's narrative reveals other interesting aspects of the Mediterranean diaspora as well. As the exiles fanned out across Italy and then the broad expanse of the Ottoman Empire, they tended to stick together, regrouping to form small but distinctive communities, identifiable by language and dress, as well as by certain religious practices that separated these newcomers—known as *megorashim* in Hebrew—from the autochthonous Jews, or *toshavim*.[16] Ysla's story offers a small window into these diasporic communities and reveals that they were by no means homogeneous despite common origins in Spain. His testimony before the Inquisition reveals a complex amalgam of "natural" Jews (Jews who had never converted), conversos whose attachments to these communities were seemingly predicated less upon religion than on the shared experiences of exile and loss, and cross-over types such as himself. Ysla further offers a glimpse into how members of these communities assisted one another with jobs and other favors. On one hand, Ysla was thus able to put his Jewishness to work, using it to find both hospitality and employment wherever he went. On the other hand, some of these diasporic communities were less fond of conversos than others, and in this respect Ysla's experiences in the port of Alexandria is revealing. He reports that in this city he decided to live as a Christian, primarily, it seems, to establish contacts with the *alhóndiga,* or trading "factory" organized by some Catalan merchants. The Alexandrine Jews, a mixture of long-established, Greek-speaking *toshavim* and *megorashim* recently arrived from Spain, apparently resented Ysla's decision to live as a Christian. Notwithstanding his Se-

---

14. See note 12 above.
15. On seventeenth-century returnees, see García-Arenal and Wiegers, *A Man of Three Worlds.*
16. For these terms, see Bernard Lewis, *The Jews of Yslam* (Princeton, NJ: Princeton University Press, 1984), 127.

phardic roots, they treated him as an alien, a renegade, a *meshumad* in Hebrew. Ysla, in contrast, almost expressed surprise at being treated in this way. Regarding himself as much as a Spaniard—or, more specifically, a Castilian—as either a Christian or a Jew, Ysla had apparently played the national card to worm his way into the other Sephardic communities he had encountered during his travels. Alexandria was different, and it was apparently the refusal of that city's Jewish community to accept him that led to his decision to repatriate in 1513.

Yet for all of the historical insights that Ysla's testimony offers, we must also recognize that he was a dissembler; the incidents he recounts are represented in ways expressly designed to arouse inquisitorial sympathies. Ysla's narrative differs from the those of the others examined in this volume in that he denounced himself to the Inquisition without ever having been formally arrested. He was, however, incarcerated in the inquisitorial prisons to await the start of proceedings against him. Once in the audience chamber, he spontaneously recounted his story with little in the way of inquisitorial prompting. In this respect, his "life" is also a confession, the sacrament required of all practicing Catholics, which, if sincere, led to remission of sin. Forgiveness, in fact, was precisely what Ysla was after when he stepped forward to tell the inquisitors about his Judaizing and other experiences living on the borderline between Christianity and Judaism. It is also worth emphasizing that this testimonial was not the only time Ysla had told clergymen about his sins. He first did so in Alexandria, where, on two separate occasions, he confessed to two Franciscan friars. As he tells it, "in Alexandria I confessed to them [the friars] everything that had happened, and they absolved me." Ysla also claimed to have received absolution from a priest in Naples and from a friar in Toledo, another Franciscan, who heard his story and granted him absolution while also recommending that he tell it again to the inquisitors: "pious men who will treat you with mercy." And mercy was clearly what Ysla had in the forefront of his mind when, on 15 May 1514, he appeared before the Inquisition in Toledo.

Toward this end Ysla crafted a narrative designed to reduce whatever doubts the inquisitors, clergymen trained to be on the lookout for Judaizers, may have harbored about the sincerity of his faith. Ysla did this first by announcing, at the very start of his testimony, his status as a converso, a tactic clearly meant to disarm his judges and to underscore the centrality of Christianity in his life. "My name," he stated boldly, "is Luis de la Ysla, and I am a New Christian of Jewish origin, aged thirty." He also admitted to having associated with Jews and even having "lived as Jew." However, he wanted to impress the inquisitors with his indifference to Jewish rites, emphasizing at one point that when his [Jewish] masters went to synagogue on

Saturdays, he "stayed outside and walked around the corrals and along the marshes along with other [and presumably non-Jewish] servants like . . . [himself]." In making these statements, Ysla, manipulating one of the stock themes of Christian martyrology, represented himself as a Christian whose faith, despite his recent conversion, was of sufficient strength to resist this and other temptations. Notions of martyrdom also underscored Ysla's description of how the Jews in Alexandria taunted and mocked him for his Christianity after he went blind. Such stories were clearly designed to win over the inquisitors, as was Ysla's willingness to provide the judges with the names of Spanish Jews and conversos with whom he had associated in the course of his travels. To gain additional sympathy, Ysla represented himself as a repentant sinner, one who had recognized the inherent wrongfulness of his previous relationships with Jews and one who had already received absolution for these "sins" from three different confessors. Ysla's expectation, no doubt, was that the Inquisitors would react the same way.

Fact or fiction? It is difficult to tell. What matters is that, for Ysla at least, the autobiography he crafted enabled him to escape a full-blown inquisitorial trial and the very real possibility that he would be punished for Judaizing. Perhaps the inquisitors felt sympathy for the blind and repentant converso who stood before them, begging forgiveness. Perhaps they believed his story and accepted him for what he claimed to be: a sincere Christian who, in their eyes at least, had the misfortune of having been born a Jew. Furthermore, they were judges who regarded themselves as the ultimate bastions and guardians of Christian faith, and Ysla's apparently sincere and successful conversion may well have constituted proof positive of the superiority of Christianity itself.

Whatever their ultimate reasoning, the inquisitors who heard Ysla's confession took no immediate action on his case. Rather, they proceeded cautiously, seeking to acquire as much additional information about Ysla as possible while keeping him locked up in the Inquisition's prison. The judges consequently instructed Juan Lopes, the tribunal's notary, to prepare three copies of Ysla's testimony. One of these was forwarded to the bishop of Tortosa, inquisitor general of Aragon. He in turn sent the transcript to the Inquisition in Valencia, a city where Ysla had admitted to having some converso friends, for further review. In Valencia, however, someone, probably the tribunal's secretary, marked the document with the Latin word *nihil* (there is nothing here). The document was then returned to Toledo, at which point someone—we do not know who—added the following notation to the transcript: *Et nihil prodest ad praesens* (nothing further to report). This annotation, dated 7 August 1514, marks the end of the inquisitorial proceedings against Ysla, inasmuch he is reported to have died—we do not from what—in the inquisitorial prisons in Toledo later that year.

The text of Ysla's narrative was first published in 1885 as a short article, "El Judío errante de Illescas (1484–1514)," by the Spanish scholar Fidel Fita y Colomé.[17] In the notes, Fita, a distinguished member of Spain's Royal Academy of History, claims to have obtained the document, once part of the archives of the Inquisition of Valencia, from Manuel Danvila, another member of the Royal Academy. However, the document is not in the archives of the Royal Academy, and its current location is unknown.

FURTHER READING

On medieval and diaspora Sephardim, see Jane S. Gerber, *The Jews of Spain: A History of the Sephardic Experience* (New York: Free Press, 1992); Haim Beinart, *The Expulsion of the Jews from Spain,* trans. Jeffrey M. Greene (Oxford; Portland, OR: Littman Library of Jewish Civilization, 2002); and Jonathan I. Israel, "The *Marrani* in Italy, the Greek Lands, and the Ottoman Near East," in his *Diasporas within a Diaspora: Jews, Crypto-Jews, and the World Maritime Empires (1540–1740)* (Leiden: Brill, 2002), 41–65. Norman Roth, *Conversos, Inquisition, and the Expulsion of the Jews from Spain* (Madison: University of Wisconsin Press, 2002), is also useful, if not always reliable. Gretchen Starr-Lebeau, *In the Shadow of the Virgin: Inquisitors, Friars, and Conversos in Guadalupe, Spain* (Princeton, NJ: Princeton University Press, 2003), offers interesting insights on the fate of conversos in the postexpulsion era. For a thought-provoking discussion of blood purity statutes as an origin of modern, Western racism, see George Fredrickson, *Racism: A Short History* (Princeton, NJ: Princeton University Press, 2002).

17. See note 1 above. Fita's article is cited in J. N. Hillgarth, *The Mirror of Spain, 1500–1700* (Ann Arbor: University of Michigan Press, 2000), 166–67. The text of Ysla's testimony is translated here into English for the first time.

CHAPTER TWO

Sexuality and the Marriage Sacrament

Elena/Eleno de Céspedes

Elena de Céspedes was born a slave in Valencia. Her mother was Moorish and her father Christian, and she was raised as a Christian. Elena's master freed her from slavery when she was a child. At age sixteen, Elena married Cristóbal Lombardo. A few months later, while Elena was pregnant with their child, Cristóbal abandoned her because, Elena said, "she did not get along with him." Leaving her baby with friends, Elena moved from town to town throughout southern and central Spain. In the process, she changed careers several times, from tailor to hosier to soldier and finally to licensed surgeon. She also changed from female to male dress, had affairs with women, and began to call herself by the masculine version of her name, Eleno.

In 1586, at age forty, Elena, living as Eleno, married twenty-four-year-old María del Caño. They lived together as man and wife in a small town outside of Toledo for one year. Then in June of 1587, acting on a neighbor's accusation, the local royal official (*corregidor*) arrested Elena and her wife for committing "the nefarious crime of sodomy," a capital offense, in this case broadly defined as the crime of engaging in homosexual acts. Elena claimed she was innocent of these charges because she was, in fact, male. Shortly after the *corregidor* arrested Elena, the Spanish Inquisition's Tribunal of Toledo claimed jurisdiction over the case and charged Elena with sorcery and "disrespect for the marriage sacrament." Elena argued before the tribunal that she was innocent of their charges because, in reality, she was a hermaphrodite whose two sets of sexual organs made both of her marriages licit and because as a hermaphrodite she could live alternately as a man and a woman without invoking the Devil's aid, as the sorcery charge implied.

Holy Office of the Inquisition, Tribunal of Toledo, Trial of Elena/o de Céspedes:

In the morning audience of the Tribunal of Toledo on 17 July 1587, Inquisitor don Lope de Mendoza presiding.[1] By his command a woman in men's garb was taken from her jail cell and brought before him. She swore an oath in the proper form, in which she promised to tell the truth in this audience as in all other audiences in which she may appear until her case may be resolved, and to keep secret [the contents of these proceedings].

She said, "My name is Elena de Céspedes. I was born in Alhama and I'm forty-one or two years old."[2] When asked for her genealogy, she made the following statement:

Father: "Pedro Hernández, born in Alhama. He's a farmer and owns a mill. My mother, Francisca de Medina, is deceased, but I believe my father is still alive. Francisca de Medina, my mother, was a Berber slave and was dark [*morena*]."

Paternal Grandparents: "I never met my grandparents, paternal or maternal, and don't know any of their names."

Aunts and Uncles on Her Father's Side: "My father didn't have siblings that I know of."[3]

Aunts and Uncles on Her Mother's Side: "My mother didn't have any siblings, that I know of."

Brothers and Sisters of His:[4] "Juan de Medina, who was my mother's son and also, I think, my father's. He lives in Granada and has lived in Vélez-Málaga and in Alhama."

---

1. Our transcription and translation are based upon the materials included in Archivo Histórico Nacional, Madrid, Sección de Inquisición, Tribunal de Toledo, leg. 234, exp. 24.

2. A town near Granada, in southern Spain.

3. The scribe has rendered this in the masculine, "that he knows of," possibly out of confusion caused by Elena's masculine appearance. The scribe writes the rest of Elena's genealogy mixing the masculine and feminine but shifts back definitively to the feminine when he arrives at the question of Elena's marital status.

4. I.e., Elena's.

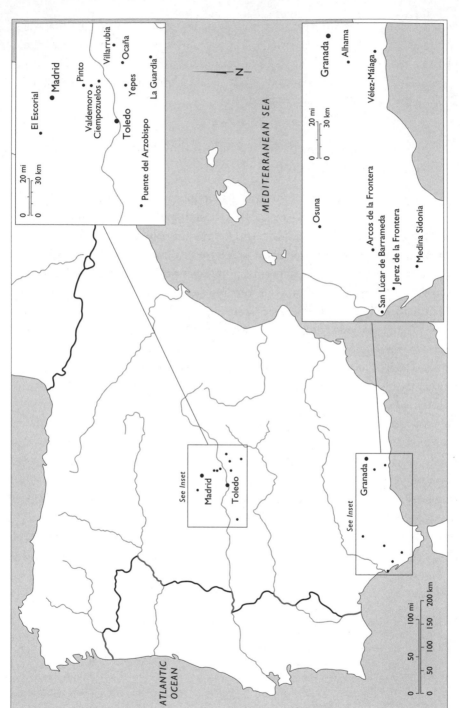

3. *Travels of Elena/Eleno de Céspedes*

Asked if she was married or single and if she had children, she said, "When I was sixteen years old my parents married me in Alhama to Cristóbal Lombardo, a mason, who was a native of Jaén [marginalia: she married as a woman, which she was]. We married and celebrated our veiling in Alhama.[5] We lived together as man and wife for about three months. I had a son with him, who's also named Cristóbal [inquisitorial marginalia: she bore a son]. I don't know if he's alive, since I left him in Seville at Mario Antonio's house. Mario Antonio is a foreigner who lives in La Laguna. He's well known in Seville and leases an oven. I think my son [was raised by?] Catalina, a maid on Losal Street. I haven't had any other children. I think Cristóbal Lombardo died in Baza a short time after he married me.

"About fifteen months ago I got married again, this time to María del Caño, daughter of Francisco del Caño from Ciempozuelos. We married and celebrated our veiling in Ciempozuelos. The priest there married us and the assistant priest of Yepes celebrated the veiling. My godparents were Augustín del Castillo and his wife María de Paz, both from Yepes. There were several upstanding people in attendance, whose names I didn't know."

When asked if she was an Old Christian, she said, "My parents and I, I believe, are Old Christians, although my mother was a slave and was black, and was probably a Gentile.[6] None of us has ever been a prisoner of, or disciplined by, the Holy Office."

Asked if she had been baptized, she said, "I am a baptized and confirmed Christian. I was baptized in Alhama and confirmed there by the Archbishop of Granada, who [lived near?] in my master's house. I confess and attend Mass as the holy mother Church commands. This past Easter I confessed in Villarrubia de Ocaña with Agustín Gómez, that town's assistant priest."[7] She crossed herself and said the Our Father, the Hail Mary, the Credo, and the Salve Regina in Spanish, and said them well.[8]

Asked if she knew how to read and write, she said, "I know how to read and

5. Veiling is a ceremony required by the Council of Trent (1546–63) as a necessary component of a legitimate and valid marriage. The ceremony consists of a nuptial mass following the wedding ceremony, during which the priest covers the newlyweds with a veil.

6. Elena's mother was either a Muslim or a Muslim convert to Christianity, a fact that contradicts Elena's claim of being an Old Christian.

7. The Council of Trent required Catholics to take confession at least once a year, as a minimum. Elena refers here to Villarrubia de Santiago, a village to the east of Ocaña.

8. The Inquisition tested prisoners' knowledge of Catholic dogma by asking them to recite the basic prayers.

write. I haven't studied, but I own books on surgery and medicine in Spanish and Latin, which I bought all at once from a lawyer."

Asked for the story of her life, she said, "I was born in the city of Alhama, in the house of Benito de Medina, my mother's master. I was born a slave [inquisitorial marginalia: she was born a slave], but my master freed me. I was raised with my master until I was eight or ten, at which point Ana Daça, one of my master's daughters, got married in Vélez-Málaga, so I went to live with her. I served Ana for about two years and then returned to Alhama to see my master. Then I went to serve my master's wife, whose name was Elena de Céspedes. I was named in her honor. But when I got [to the house] to serve my master's wife, she had already died. So I went instead to live with my mother in the house in Alhama. In my mother's house I learned to weave.

"I lived with my mother until I was fifteen or sixteen years old, at which time I married Cristóbal Lombardo, as I've said. But because I got along badly with him, he left, leaving me alone and pregnant. I stayed in Alhama, in Gaspar de Belmar's house, for about two years, more or less, at which time my mother died. From there I went to Granada and settled in the house of [illeg.] San Miguel. He later became the treasurer of the Royal Chapel of Granada. I was with him for about four or five months. While I was there I learned the trade of making hose and became a hosier. From there, I began to work as a weaver in Alonso Martínez's house on Gumeles Street. But after six months, I couldn't find anything to weave, so I began to work as a tailor and a hosier.

"I made my living this way in Granada for a year, more or less. From there I went to San Lúcar de Barrameda, and in San Lúcar I practiced the trades of tailor and hosier publicly.[9] I found that I was earning a good living and I stayed in San Lúcar for about a year, more or less. From there, I went to Jerez de la Frontera, where I practiced the same trades of hosier and tailor. But there I got into a fight with a pimp[10] called Heredia. I stabbed him and they arrested me. When I got out of jail, because of the threat this Heredia and his other pimp friends made against me, I decided to disguise myself in men's garb, so I left off wearing women's garb, which until then I'd always worn.

"In men's garb I went to Arcos [de la Frontera], where I found a job as a

9. Although at this point the scribe is consistently referring to Elena with feminine pronouns, he has suddenly switched to identifying Elena's trades by their masculine forms (hosier, *calcetero* instead of *calcetera*; tailor, *sastre* instead of *sastra*).

10. *Rufián.* This term in the late sixteenth century had the primary meaning of pimp and the secondary meaning of scoundrel. It is unclear which definition Elena/o employs here.

farmhand for Antón Marino, since he had lots of work. I called myself Céspedes, without saying Pedro, Eleno, or Juan. I worked for him for a month. He paid me thirty-six reales and bread, and nothing else. So I left his employ and went to work for Francisco the Gabber *[portaboca],* who was called that because he ran on at the mouth. For him, I worked as a shepherd for about fifteen days. But, suspecting I was a woman, the *corregidor* arrested me.

"By chance, Doctor Benesar, who's from Alhama, happened to be passing through. Because I sent word to him that I was from Alhama, he came to see me in jail. He recognized me and told the *corregidor* who I was. The *corregidor* released me and placed me in the house of Juan Núñez, a priest and a native of Arcos, who was the pastor of Santa María.[11] But because the *corregidor* knew I was a woman, he ordered me to put on women's garb. So I put on a skirt, like a woman [marginalia: returned to women's garb].

"I served the priest for about six or seven months, more or less. After that I left his employ because of a grievance I had with him.[12] Because at that time the uprising of the moriscos of Granada had begun, I decided to go to war.[13] So I once again took off women's clothing and put on men's garb. Calling myself only Céspedes, I became a soldier in don Luis Ponce de León's company until the uprising was over. Then I went back to Arcos with his company.

"When the company disbanded, I began to practice the trade of tailor publicly, still in men's garb. I passed the [guild] exam for tailors in Jerez de la Frontera, but they made me put 'seamstress' on the sign [in front of my shop] since they knew I was a woman.[14]

"After that, a military recruiter came to Arcos. One of the town residents who had been drafted paid me well to go to the war in Granada in his place. So I went to war a second time [marginalia: soldier again]. I was with the Duke of Arcos's company until the war was over. All that must have lasted about three years, the same amount of time as the war. When it ended I went back to Arcos and to my trade as a tailor. I stayed there for just over a year. From there I went

11. It was common for secular (as opposed to inquisitorial or ecclesiastical) judges such as the *corregidor* to place female criminals in the homes of "respectable people," usually the town mayor or a priest. There the women would work as domiciled servants and, presumably, learn to imitate the moral behavior of their masters.

12. In all probability it was the priest who had a grievance with Elena since, as Elena (then in women's garb) later testifies, she had been having an affair with the sister of a priest, Francisco Núñez, and another woman, Catalina Núñez, also a resident of the town of Arcos.

13. Elena (who went to war dressed as man) refers here to the War of the Alpujarras (1568–70), in which Miguel de Piedrola (see chapter 3) also fought.

14. *Sastra* instead of *sastre.*

to Vélez-Málaga, where I stayed for just over a year working as a tailor. Then I got into a fight with a *regidor* called fulano Barra,[15] so I left and went to Alhama. There I opened another tailor shop. I stayed there for a year and from there went to Medina Sidonia and Osuna, where I stayed for another year, working in my tailor shop, as I had in other towns.

"From there I went to the Court [Madrid] for about two years and set up shop as a tailor.[16] At Court I became friends with a surgeon[17] from Valencia who took me into his home for a while and began to teach me to cure [marginalia: surgeon]. Because I learned so quickly and in so little time to cure as well as he did, and since the trade proved advantageous to me, I left off the tailor's trade and took up that of surgeon.

"I practiced as a surgeon in the Hospital de la Corte for about three years, at the end of which I went to El Escorial[18] to cure Obregón, who was one of His Majesty's servants. I began to cure publicly and traveled throughout the towns of the Serranía curing for more than two years. But then they accused me of curing without having been examined first, so I went to Court to take my exam and got two licenses, one for bleeding and purging, and the other for surgery. I stayed at Court for a long time, until they took me to [illeg.], where I cured for nine months. From there I went to La Guardia, where I set up shop and cured as a surgeon for about six years, frequently coming and going all this time to and from the Court.

"Due to a sorrow I suffered in La Guardia[19] I went with a company [of soldiers] that was passing through there, curing those who were wounded in the company of don Antonio Pazos. With them, I went to Pinto, and from there to Valdemoro, where I stayed for about two years, though sometimes I traveled to Ciempozuelos, where I went to cure. By chance, I fell ill [while in Ciempozuelos] and was taken in as a guest in the home of Francisco del Caño,

15. Elena apparently cannot recall the *regidor*'s first name. She thus refers to him as *fulano,* the Spanish equivalent of "Mr. so-and-so."

16. King Philip II established Madrid as the seat of the Spanish royal court in 1561.

17. Surgeons *(cirujanos)* and physicians *(médicos)* had separate, thoughcomplementary, functions. Physicians were trained at university in the medical arts. Surgeons, in contrast, learned their trade by apprenticeship and were of lower status. Surgeons performed more rudimentary procedures such as bleeding, purging (through the administering of emetics), and tooth extraction.

18. The Hospital de la Corte was a charity hospital founded by Ferdinand and Isabella at the end of the fifteenth century. The Escorial Monastery, constructed (1563–84) for King Philip II in the mountains north of Madrid, was also a royal residence.

19. Elena never explains what happened in La Guardia, although she may be alluding to the end of an affair she had with a widow named Isabel Ortiz, who would later claim to the vicar of Madrid that Elena had promised to marry her.

my [future] father-in-law. There, they were generous to me, and I became fond of María del Caño, daughter of Francisco del Caño, and María became fond of me, so I asked for her hand in marriage. María's parents said that if it was God's will, we could marry."

Because it was late, given the hour, the audience was ended and the prisoner commanded to return to jail.

Before me,
[signed] Iñigo Ordóñez

The afternoon audience of the Tribunal of Toledo, on the aforementioned day, month, and year, the aforementioned Lord Inquisitor don Lope de Mendoza presiding. By his command the aforementioned Elena de Céspedes was brought from jail and, as is customary, was asked if she remembered anything she could say in order to unburden her conscience. She was still under the oath she had taken in the morning audience, in which she promised to tell the truth in all matters. She said, "When I asked for María del Caño's hand in marriage, and it was given to me, I went to Madrid to ask the vicar for a license to marry and post banns.[20] The vicar, who saw that I was beardless and hairless, asked me if I was a capon. I told him I wasn't, and that he should look at me to see that I wasn't. To this end, they took me to a nearby house, where three or four men looked at me from the front, though I didn't let them look at me from the back, so they wouldn't be able to see my woman's parts.[21] The men testified that they'd seen me and that I wasn't a capon. So the vicar gave me a license to post banns, and I took the license with me. The priest of Ciempozuelos published them, but upon their publication a widow named Isabel Ortiz, who lived in Madrid next to [the convent of] San Francisco and who has children [illeg.], came forward and claimed me as her husband, saying I'd promised to marry

20. Designed to publicize the forthcoming marriage and give those who wished a chance to raise canonical impediments to the union an opportunity to do so, the "posting of banns" consisted of announcements of the coming marriage made in the parish churches of the betrothed during one or more Sunday masses in the weeks preceding the wedding. Posting of banns was a necessary component of a legitimate and valid marriage.

21. This is the first mention of Elena's disappearing penis, which, as she claims at various points in her testimony, to possess or to have lost only recently. Her penis, readers should note, tends to disappear only before she is to be examined by secular or inquisitorial court-appointed physicians. While the editors recognize the possibility of medical hermaphroditism, we suspect that in Elena's case the "male member" was a fiction, endorsed by members of the Madrid and Toledo medical communities whom Elena had befriended or bribed, or both.

her.[22] After talking to the widow, I went before the vicar of Madrid and separated from her.

"Later they set another impediment against me, saying that it was public knowledge and widely rumored that I was both male and female, so I went back to Madrid to see the vicar a second time. The vicar commanded that I be examined by Court doctors, who, in order to determine what was just, and in order to comply with the vicar's command, wanted to examine me. But because I was so well known in Madrid, I came here to Toledo and before the vicar they examined me here. My lawyer was Morales. They examined me in front of [Francisco Pantoja, the Secretary of the Inquisition], and, I think, the physician was Doctor Toro. Although they made many requests toward this end and made many other examinations, they sent me back again to Madrid. During that time I went to [illeg.] to Yepes to cure a man named Jiménez and some other people, for about two and a half months at the most. During this time I prepared certain remedies with wine and alcohol, and many other remedies and potions to see if I could close my woman's part.[23] Even though I couldn't close it completely, I could squeeze it shut to make it look closed.

"With all the remedies I prepared, my woman's part wrinkled up and got so narrow that nothing could be put inside it. When I was ready to be seen, I entered a petition and Juan Gutiérrez, a magistrate from Yepes, ordered the *alcalde*[24] to have surgeons and doctors and other people of good repute look at me to see if my form was a woman's or a man's. The *alcalde* ordered that surgeons and doctors and others from that town, ten men in all, examine me. They came to examine me in my home, during the day and by candle light as well. They felt me and looked at me from the front, though from behind they only felt me. With the artifices I'd devised, I was so tight that none of them could even put a finger inside me or see that I had a woman's part. Though it

22. Although verbal marriage promises were no longer binding after the Council of Trent, a promise of marriage previously given by a betrothed person to a third party would have posed a canonical impediment to the marriage between the affianced coupled. The "separation" Elena received from the vicar dissolved the earlier marriage promise and released her from the limbo of being pledged to one woman and therefore unable to marry the other.

23. Several folk remedies were available to early modern Spanish women who wished to "close their women's parts," though commonly these remedies were used to convince husbands and lovers of the woman's virginity, not to convince a group of doctors of the woman's masculinity. The most extreme remedy, mentioned in Fernando de Rojas's play *La Celestina* and the Cervantes short story "La tía fingida," consisted of sewing the vaginal opening shut with a needle and thread.

24. The mayor of a town or village and head of the town council, who also discharged judicial functions. Unlike *corregidores* and *regidores*, who were appointed by the king, *alcaldes* were appointed by the municipalities in which they served. A municipality could have more than one *alcalde*.

was true that they felt a hard wrinkled spot which was the result of my remedies. When they asked me what it was, I told them it was a hemorrhoid I'd gotten, which I'd cauterized and which had left behind this hard knot. By this ruse, all ten men, including the physicians and the others who'd seen me, declared, said, and affirmed to the *alcalde* that I didn't have a woman's part and that I did have a male member. The *alcalde* made out his report accordingly and I presented it to the vicar, who demanded that I be examined again, according to his instructions.

"Once again I prepared and used all the remedies I'd used in Yepes, plus some other, stronger ones, in order to close myself. I wrinkled myself up to such a point that Doctor Mantilla and Doctor Francisco Díaz, physician and surgeon at Court, when they tried to put a probe inside me, and their fingers, could not do it. When they asked me what I had there, I replied as I had to the other doctors [that it was a hemorrhoid]. With that, they reported that I didn't have a woman's part. With this report, and the recognition [by the witnesses] that I was the same person the doctors had seen and examined, the vicar gave me license to marry.

"With this license I went to Ciempozuelos and got engaged to María del Caño. From there we went to Yepes, where we married and celebrated our veiling *in face ecclesia* in the parish of San Benito. The assistant priest performed our veiling. As I said, we stayed in Yepes for more than a year, living together as man and wife until around Christmas, when, since there was no surgeon in Ocaña, I went to live there. Then the *alcalde mayor*,[25] named Ortega, sent a letter to the governor [to inform him?] that when he was the *auditor del campo*[26] in the War of Granada, he'd known me and that it had been said by some that I was a woman and by others that I was male and female. Because of this letter the governor [*corregidor*], Abraumel, arrested me. From there I was brought as a prisoner to this Holy Office."

[When the *corregidor* of Ocaña arrested Elena, it was for the capital crime of sodomy. In the early modern lexicon, the term *sodomy* denoted a broad range of nonprocreative sexual activities, though it sometimes was used more specifically to signify same-sex relations, as was the case here. The governor also arrested Elena for the lesser crime of having deceived María del Caño and María's father. Elena responded to these charged by claiming that she was, in

25. The chief *alcalde* in a municipality.
26. A legal advocate, serving in a military encampment.

fact, a man, and that, as such, she had not deceived anyone nor had she committed sodomy. In the secular court interrogation, the governor questioned Elena about the charges against her: "Had she, being a woman, about eleven months ago, more or less, deceived María del Caño, daughter of Francisco del Caño, resident of Ciempozuelos, and led father and daughter to believe she was a man? And had she, with little fear of God, out of disrespect for the marriage sacrament and with disdain for the natural order, married and celebrated her veiling and [had carnal relations?] with the aforementioned María del Caño? The defendant responded that she was not a woman but a man. . . . When asked if aside from the aforementioned María del Caño, this defendant had committed the aforementioned unnatural crime of sodomy with other women while pretending to be a man, she replied that she had had relations with other women naturally, as a man, not unnaturally."]

Asked how she, being a woman, could make physicians and witnesses think she was a man, even if she made herself wrinkled and narrow with the remedies and potions she prepared, she said, "In reality I am and was a hermaphrodite. I have and had two natures, one of a man and the other of a woman. What happened is that when I gave birth, I did so with such force in my [woman's] part, that a piece of skin broke out above my urethra and a head emerged about half the size of a thumb, like so, which resembled the swollen head of a male member, which, when I had natural passion and desire, came out, as I said. When I felt desire it got bigger. I gathered the member up and put it back in the place where it had come from so that the skin wouldn't break."[27]

[Elena described her supposed hermaphroditic anatomy in greater detail in a letter to the Inquisition, which she submitted in her own defense shortly after this interrogation took place. The letter included the following text: "I have never pretended to be a man in order to marry a woman as some have impugned.[28] What has happened is that in this world we have often heard of people who are androgynous, or who, by another name, are also called hermaphrodites, who have two sexes (inquisitorial marginalia: Cicero, Pliny, and Augustine).[29] I am and have been a hermaphrodite, and at the time I married

---

27. Tales of sudden sex change and hermaphroditism were common in the popular and medical literature of the day. See, for example, Antonio de Torquemada's *Jardín de flores curiosas* (Lérida, 1573); and Juan Huarte de San Juan's *Examen de ingenios para las ciencias* (Madrid, 1569).

28. This letter is in the first person in the original Spanish.

29. The marginalia, added in a different hand, was probably referring to Pliny's *Naturalis Historia*, in which he describes "beings who possess both sexes, who were once called androgynes and were considered monsters but who are now considered instruments of pleasure." Pliny, *The Natural His-*

[María del Caño] the masculine sex prevailed in me. I was naturally a man and had all the necessary parts of a man in order to marry, as had been proven through examinations by doctors and surgeons licensed in their arts, who saw and touched me and swore legal oaths that I could marry as a man. . . . I have naturally been a man and a woman, and though this may be a prodigious and rare thing that is not often seen, hermaphrodites, as I am and have been, are not unnatural. . . . I married first as a woman to a man, then as a man to a woman, because when I married a man, the feminine sex heated up and prevailed in me. Then, when my husband died, the masculine sex heated up and I could marry a woman."]

"When I was in San Lúcar working as a tailor, which is what I was doing at the time, I worked in the house of a linen merchant named Hernando de Toledo. One day I found myself alone with his wife, who was named Ana de Albánchez and who was very kind and pretty, and I felt the urge to kiss her. Without saying a word, I kissed her, but this frightened her. Then I told her I could have relations with her as if I were a man, which I said [with my face?] half hidden from shame, since I was afraid to tell this woman I had two natures. Ana de Albánchez took me to bed but, even though I was aroused and my head had emerged, as I've described, and I put myself on top of Ana, I couldn't do anything. Aside from this demonstration, I once tried to show myself to Ana de Albánchez, but then Ana's husband walked in, so I couldn't show myself to her at that time.

"Then I went to doctor Tapia, a surgeon in that city. He examined me in secret and told me I was a hermaphrodite. With a probe he put inside me, he made a cut above the piece of skin which had begun to come out. With this cut there emerged a male member, which was as large as a [illeg.] and as long as this line:

It came out bent in an arch, so the surgeon cut it a little bit. With that the member straightened out. He told me it was badly constructed and weak at the root, and he cured me of this. In fifteen days he made me well. I kept this ability to have relations with women and went back to Ana de Albánchez and had

---

tory, trans. H. Rackham (Cambridge, MA: Harvard University Press, 1989), vol. 2, bk. VII, iii.33–34. Pliny also refers to females who change into males (iv.36). Elena (or Elena's defense lawyer) cited this reference from Pliny in the defense statement that Elena sent to the tribunal, making it clear that this model was useful for Elena and her contemporaries as a way to imagine her sexuality. For Augustine, see his *City of God,* trans. Henry Bettenson (London: Penguin, 1984), bk. XVI, chap. 8, p. 663.

relations and dealings with her as a man many times. I was in Ana's house without Ana's husband's knowledge for about four or five months. But at the end of that time, because the *corregidor* of that city was also fond of Ana de Albánchez, and since I'd slept with her, the *corregidor* became jealous and forced me out of the city. So I went to Jerez, as I said."

Asked if she had had relations with any other women as if she were a man, she said, "I've had carnal relations with many other women, especially with a sister of the priest I served in Arcos, whose name was Francisca Núñez, and with another married woman from the same place whose name was Catalina Núñez, and with lots of other women from throughout the places I've traveled. But, aside from Ana de Albánchez, none of the women I've known was aware that I had female organs, since I was always careful to cover them up.[30] At Court, I took as my friend Isabel Ortíz and had relations with her as a man. Isabel never knew I had a woman's nature. My wife María del Caño never knew I had a woman's nature. Even though it's true that many times María desired to put her hand on my shameful parts, I never let her do it, even though she wanted to very much, since she'd been told I had the natures of a man and a woman."

Asked if, as a woman, she had ever had relations with men, and with which men, she said, "I've never had relations with any man other than Cristóbal Lombardo, my husband."

Asked if, being principally a woman and having given birth, she married another woman, like herself, because she thought it was licit for two women to marry, or she thought that two women could marry each other, she said, "Since I found I had a man's member and could have relations with women as a man, and since I'd gone around with so many women, I wanted to leave off sin and marry, and not have relations with anyone but my wife. It was because of this that I married. I didn't think I'd erred, but rather that I'd married in God's service."

Asked if she got her monthlies as other women do, she said, "When I was

---

30. Elena's testimony is inconsistent. She testifies that the *corregidor* of Arcos discovered her to be a woman and ordered her to don women's garb and serve as a maid in the priest's house. When Elena returned to Arcos after having served in the army, she returned in men's garb but "everyone knew" she was a woman. Town authorities allow her to dress as a man but made her hang a sign in front of her tailor shop saying "seamstress." If, as Elena also testifies, she had affairs with the priest's sister and another woman in Arcos, these women must have known Elena was female. By claiming no one but Ana de Albánchez knew about her women's part, Elena may have been trying to protect these women, and her wife, from secular court charges of sodomy.

young I got them a few times and they were very light. They sometimes come now, but not regularly, every month. They come through my woman's nature, as with other women."

Asked if the male member that she said came out served her for anything other than this pleasure she said she had with women, she said, "I urinate through it as other men do, since it's my urethra."

Asked if at present she had the aforesaid male member and the woman's nature, she said, "At present I have only my woman's nature. The male member that emerged from me has just recently come off in jail, while I was a prisoner in Ocaña. It only now finished falling off, after more than fifteen days. What happened is that before last Christmas I suffered a flow of blood through my woman's parts and through my rear end, which caused me great pain in my kidneys. I'd hurt myself while riding horseback and the root of my member became weak. The member became spongy and I went cutting it bit by bit, so that I've come to be without it. It just finished falling off about fifteen days ago, or a little more, as I've said."

Asked if she retained the signs and scars from where she cut said member, she said, "Yes, I still have the wounds."

Asked what kinds of testicles she had, since the witnesses and physicians who examined her said that she had a male member and testicles like a man, she responded, "I have them in a particular form." She described them with her hands but was not able to be understood. She said that if she were to describe the form to a physician, he would understand her, and would see in what form and way she has them.[31]

Asked if the aforementioned María del Caño, when she married the defendant, knew she was marrying a woman, as this defendant is, she said, "María never found out nor did she suspect a thing, since before we got married I took María's virginity and had relations with her several times, so María del Caño could not have known she was marrying a woman, only that she was marrying a man, since this defendant had relations with her as one.[32]

31. It is possible that the unintelligible explanation Elena gave of her testicles was that they were "internal." Early modern medical texts described female sexual anatomy as an inverted ("outside-in") version of male sexual anatomy. Thus the uterus was the female equivalent of the penis, and the ovaries were equivalent to testicles.

32. When doctors hired by the Inquisition examined Elena, they found no trace of a penis. When inquisitors asked how, then, Elena had managed sexual relations with other women, the doctors replied that she must have used a dildo *(baldrés)*. In this context it is interesting to note that in their testimony to the Inquisition, neither Isabel Ortiz, one of Elena's former lovers, nor María del Caño, her

Asked if, when she had relations as a man with said María del Caño and with other women with whom she had confessed [to having had relations], she had from her arousal the pollution[33] that her husband had when he had relations with her, she said, "Yes, I had pollution and completed the act with them as my husband had completed the act with me. There was abundant pollution."

Asked how long it had been since last she had relations as a man with said María del Caño her wife, she said, "I haven't had relations with María del Caño since before Christmas when I fell ill and injured my testicles. To hide my injury during this past Easter, I told María that because it was Lent I couldn't have relations with her.[34] After Easter, for about two months, María del Caño came to Ciempozuelos from Ocaña. During this time María wanted me to have relations with her, so I did, but it caused me a great deal of pain. Since then I haven't touched María del Caño again. It was at this time that I began to cut [my member] bit by bit, as I've said."

She was told that what she said here regarding the male member was fiction and trickery, since she had never been anything but a woman, which was how she was born and was at present, and that what she would have to do in order for this tribunal to show her mercy was to tell the whole truth and tell how the trickery was accomplished, and the ways in which she fooled the witnesses who testified in her favor. She should tell if she gave or promised them anything, and how, being a woman, she married another woman, and whether said María del Caño knew this defendant was a woman when she married her. She replied, "What I've said here is the truth, in that which pertains to my member as in that which pertains to María del Caño and the reasons I married her. I didn't solicit false testimony or say anything against the truth."

Because it was late, given the hour, the audience was ended. Warned that she

---

"wife," ever admitted to having actually seen Elena's "member." Isabel testified that "shame" prevented her from either looking at or touching Elena's penis, although she admitted to having once felt it through her shirt and said that "it felt like flesh." María's "shame" also prevented her from either looking at or touching Elena's penis, although she admitted that it felt "smooth" whenever they copulated. Asked specifically by the inquisitors whether her husband had ever used a dildo or his hand during intercourse, she answered that he had occasionally touched her "nature" with his hand just after they finished "de juntar" (coupling).

33. Pollution (ejaculation) would have been proof of the procreative, therefore licit, nature of the sexual relations between Eleno and his wife.

34. Catholic doctrine prohibits sexual relations during Lent, the season on the liturgical calendar that precedes Easter.

should think about unburdening her conscience, the defendant was commanded to return to her cell.

This passed before me.

[signed] Iñigo Ordóñez

In the morning audience of the Inquisition of Toledo, 18 July 1587, Lord Inquisitor don Lope de Mendoza presiding. By his command, the aforementioned Elena de Céspedes was brought from jail. When she was present, she was asked what her conscience had remembered, and what she could say to unburden her conscience, according to the oath she had taken. She said, "I don't have anything to say, and I don't know anything more than what I've already said and confessed."

Asked, when she was ill and cutting her member bit by bit, who cured her, she said, "I cured myself with powders and ointments made from alum and spices and [illeg.], and an ointment made of lead and pink oil and other things."

Asked when she got well, she said, "I'm still unwell, and at present am ill in my woman's parts. I ask that a physician be allowed to examine me."

Asked if her purpose in putting these things and the strong powders on her woman's parts was to make scars so that she could pull off the trick that it was understood she employed here to make it thought that she had a male member, and if she intended to prove its existence by the scars from the wounds that she artificially inflicted upon herself with said powders, she said, "May God forgive me if I've done so, but I haven't at all."

Asked if she knew or suspected the reason why she was arrested by this Holy Office, she said, "As I've said and confessed here, it is for having married another woman, being a woman myself, as some said I was when I married. But even though I was a woman I was also a man. Since I had the nature of a man, I was fit to marry."

Asked how she knew that the aforementioned Cristóbal Lombardo, her husband, was dead, and what efforts she had made [to verify his death] before getting married a second time, this time to María del Caño, she said, "More than twenty years ago they brought some letters to me in Alhama saying that Cristóbal Lombardo had died in the hospital in Lara. I lost the two letters I had that stated this, since I didn't think they were valuable."

Asked if she testified [to the priest who performed the second marriage] that she was single, and who her witnesses were, and if she promised or gave the witnesses anything so that they would say that she was single,[35] she said, "I neither gave nor promised anything to any witnesses so they'd testify to this. The witnesses present before the Vicar of Madrid, when I wanted to marry María del Caño, had known me for more than two years and believed me to be single, and a man."

She was told that out of reverence for God she should tell the whole truth, with a zeal that would be necessary for the unburdening of her conscience and so she could receive the mercy that this Holy Tribunal customarily showed to those who plainly confess their guilt, especially in the matters about which she has been questioned regarding the spirit and intention with which she married, being a woman. Asked whether she thought or believed that a woman could licitly marry another woman, or that marriage is not a sacrament, since, in opprobrium and derision [of the marriage sacrament], she married a woman and consummated the marriage *in face ecclesia*, making a mockery of said sacrament, she said, "I married because I understood that I was a man, not a woman, and that I could, being a man, licitly marry a woman. I know well that two women can't marry, and I didn't do it out of derision or mockery of the sacrament. Rather, I did it to be in God's service."

[inquisitorial marginalia: first warning] She was told that this Holy Office was not accustomed to arresting people without having sufficient evidence that they had said, done, and committed, or seen others say, do, or commit, something that was or appeared to be against our holy mother Roman Catholic Church or against the right and free exercise of the Holy Office. Thus, she should believe that she has been imprisoned because of said evidence. Out of reverence for our Lord God and His glorious and blessed Mother, the prisoner is warned and charged to go back through her memory and say and confess the whole truth of that for which she feels guilty or that of which she knows others to be guilty, without shielding anyone or anything, or giving false testimony, but that she should do it for the unburdening of her conscience as a Catholic Christian, and to save her soul, and so that her trial might be carried out with all possible brevity and mercy. She said, "I've told the truth and I don't feel there's anything else I can say [illeg.]." She swore this to be the truth by the oath she has taken.

35. In an effort to prevent bigamous marriages, the Council of Trent required parish priests to make inquiries into the marital status of betrothed couples and required witnesses to ratify the couple's answers, before the priest could agree to perform the marriage.

She was asked if the governor and justices of the town of Ocaña took a confession from her, and if she said in that confession what she has said in the audiences before this Holy Office. She said, "Twice they took a confession from me in Ocaña. In some things I told the truth as I've done here, but in all that differed from the confession I've made here, I wasn't telling the truth, but I have told the truth here. I didn't tell the truth before because I feared that the secular justices would not treat me justly, and because I was ashamed."

Because it was late, the audience was ended. The [transcripts of the] audiences the aforementioned Elena de Céspedes had had in this Holy Office were read back to her. Having heard them and understood what was said, she said that these were her confessions and that she had spoken them as they were written. She affirmed this to be the truth and she signed and ratified and confirmed with her name. Warned, she was commanded to return to jail. Signed before me,

[signed] Iñigo Ordónez

[signed] Elen—de Céspedes[36]

[The inquisitors convicted Elena on charges of sorcery and disrespect for the marriage sacrament. They sentenced her to two hundred lashes, public shaming, appearance at an *auto de fe,* and to serve the poor as a surgeon in a charity hospital for ten years, without pay, and with the stipulation that she do so in women's garb.]

When the inquisitors pulled Elena's case from royal jurisdiction, they changed not only the venue but also the nature of the charges against her. Although the royal magistrates and the inquisitors generally agreed on which sexual acts were illicit, they often disagreed as to the reasons why. In Elena's case, the *corregidor* was especially concerned with whether she had committed sodomy, an "unnatural" (nonprocreative, same-sex) sexual act and one which, according to royal law, represented an insult to God. The *corregidor* sought to resolve this issue by means of a simple medical examination. If Elena proved to be a man, she would be innocent, for she would only have engaged in the natural sexual intercourse between a husband and his wife. If, however, Elena turned out to be a woman, she could be convicted of

---

36. There is an ink blot over where the *a* (or the *o*) should have been.

sodomy, a capital crime. In this case, the Inquisition stepped in and assumed jurisdiction over Elena shortly after the medical examination was completed. As it turned out, Elena was lucky. Had she remained in the grip of royal justice, she may well have wound up on the scaffold.

Although inquisitors in Aragon had the power to punish sodomites, their counterparts in Castile did not. Their particular interest in this case sprang from the possibility that Elena had knowingly violated the sacrament of marriage by selecting a woman as her mate. Bigamy was also at issue. At the time of her marriage to María, had Elena ascertained that her first spouse, Cristóbal, was dead? Sorcery was yet another concern. Had Elena employed black magic or invoked demons, possibly even the Devil, in order to trick people into believing that she was a man? None of these charges were major heresies, so even if found guilty of one of them, it was unlikely that Elena would be sentenced to death unless she stubbornly refused to confess.

Elena began her encounter with the Holy Office on the morning of 17 July 1587. Initially, she answered cautiously, disclosing as little information as possible. She also reversed the strategy she had used with the *corregidor,* which was to insist on her maleness despite the absence of a penis. When the inquisitors requested her life story, Elena identified herself as female and omitted any mention of sexual desire for other women. Elena explained that she had dressed as a man only in order to disguise herself and escape the revenge of a pimp with whom she had picked a fight. Elena did not explain why, years after the immediate danger had passed, she remained in men's garb. Nor did she try to explain how she had entered into what inquisitors saw clearly as a same-sex marriage. But Elena was a quick study. By the afternoon audience on that same day, she had figured out where the inquisitors' questions were leading and made a radical change to her defense strategy. Correctly guessing the Inquisition's charges against her, Elena developed a complex life story that justified cross-dressing, bigamy, same-sex marriage, and male identity. She narrated the story in the inquisitorial idiom of adherence to Catholic doctrine.

When the Tribunal of Toledo reconvened in the afternoon, after inquisitors had returned from lunch and, perhaps, a siesta, Elena launched into her new autobiography. Over the course of the afternoon's testimony, the physical body Elena described in her testimony mutated with dizzying speed: she "closed" her vagina, gained a penis and became a man, then regained her vagina and became a woman; next she was a hermaphrodite, with both male and female genitalia; and finally she lost her penis but argued that her nature was still hermaphroditic. And she defended her bigamous, same-sex marriage as being a legitimate use of the holy sacrament.

Elena was more than literate; she was learned and owned a small working library of about two dozen books, mostly on subjects related to her trade as a surgeon. They included copies of treatises, some in Latin, by Aristotle, Galen, Vesalius, and Ambroise Paré, a French sixteenth-century surgeon who wrote, among other things, about hermaphrodites.[37] She was thus able to formulate the argument that hermaphrodites, by virtue of their two sets of sexual organs, could marry both a man and a woman. Apart from the fact that this argument meshed perfectly with the charges against her, given the existing conceptual bank of sexual orientations (on which, more below), Elena was also able to use her reading to express a version of her sexuality that she may have believed to be true. Yet Elena's elaborate justifications fell apart when inquisitors asked if she still possessed the penis she claimed to have had. For the inquisitors, maleness required a penis and testicles, facial hair, and so forth, all of which Elena lacked. Such attributes constituted proofs of sexual identity, inasmuch as postmodern notions of gender identity did not exist. Elena was forced to admit that at the moment she did not have a penis, although, she protested, she had only recently lost it.

Not surprisingly, the inquisitors did not find Elena's story altogether credible, but it at least served to convince them that she was not guilty of any major heresy. In the end they found her guilty of a series of lesser charges—allegations of bigamy (since she could not prove her husband Cristóbal was dead), fakery, perjury, and mockery of the sacrament of marriage. For these crimes she received the inquisitorial equivalent of a slap on the wrist: appearance in the *auto de fe* held on 18 December 1588, two hundred (probably lightly delivered) lashes, and the requirement that she serve for ten years in a public hospital. Following her appearance at the *auto*, Elena—dressed as a woman—began working as a surgeon attached to Toledo's Hospital del Rey, but within a matter of months she was the cause of such commotion that the hospital's director asked that she be transferred to another institution (see below). Elena was subsequently transferred to another, smaller hospital in Toledo and then, one month later, to one in Puente del Arzobispo—a small, somewhat isolated town located about eighty miles west of Toledo itself. There Elena de Céspedes disappeared from the historical record.

Elena's story is remarkable for more than its sexual anomalies, whether those were biological or discursive constructions. In addition to making the transitions from female to male and male to hermaphrodite, over the course of her lifetime Elena shifted from slave to free, New to Old Christian, and weaver to tailor, soldier to

37. Ambroise Paré's *De Monstres* was first published in 1570. It is available in English as Ambroise Paré, *On Monsters and Marvels*, trans. Janis L. Pallister (Chicago: University of Chicago Press, 1982). Hermaphrodites and androgynes are addressed in chapter 6 (pp. 26–31 in the English edition).

surgeon. These transitions reflect the mobility of so much of early modern artisanal and mercantile life, thus contradicting stereotypes about the sedentary nature of premodern society. Elena's constant state of artisanal and geographical transition may have been fueled by her original status as an outsider, a mulatta and a former slave. An itinerant lifestyle may also have helped lower Elena's risk of being discovered as a woman. Itinerancy therefore may have been a necessity, a way of life, much as it was for Luis de la Ysla (see chapter 1). Elena's itinerant sexuality was more unusual than her other states of transition but not so anomalous as to be incomprehensible to her culture, although there was no universal agreement about how to define it.

What do Elena's stories reveal about the ways sexuality and the body were imagined in early modern Spain? Elena's stories, and the reactions of others to them, help us to locate the limits of tacitly permitted sexual transgression and reveal the elasticity possible in early modern imaginings of the body and its sexes. Elena's trial took place in an era when norms for sexual behavior were strictly prescribed in royal law, inquisitorial law, and canon law and by social custom. Each of these legal and social codes of conduct had a different set of rules for proper comportment varied, and the result was an inhibiting profusion of sexual do's and don't's. Some types of sexual peccadilloes, including Elena's affairs with women other than María del Caño, largely escaped judicial notice. Others, such as Elena's cross-dressing and marriage to a woman, went on for months or years before anyone reported them to authorities.

When, for example, Elena moved to the town of Arcos de la Frontera, the *corregidor* promptly arrested her for cross-dressing. But he released Elena almost immediately into the care of the town priest. Elena then had affairs with two women in Arcos, including the priest's sister, for which she suffered no legal consequences. A year or so later, when Elena, once again dressed as a man, returned to Arcos, the town council permitted her to continue wearing men's garb, though they had her hang a "seamstress" sign outside her tailor shop door. Some months after that, when military recruiters arrived in Arcos, a wealthy resident paid Elena to go to war in his place. If everyone in Arcos knew Elena was a woman, did the soldiers in the regiment Elena joined know as well? This seems likely, for Lorencio Gómez, the man who denounced Elena to the secular justices after her marriage, did so because "he had known her as a soldier in the Wars of Granada, where it was said by some that she was a woman and by others that she was a man and a woman." Lorencio did not find Elena's cross-dressing on the battlefield criminal enough to report to military authorities, but he did feel compelled to report her to secular justice once a same-sex marriage entered the picture. The early modern willingness to wink at sexual transgression, it seems, reached its limit at overt instances of homosexual activity.

A willingness to wink at mild to moderate sexual transgression, though, does not explain the enthusiastic reception Elena received after her inquisitorial conviction. According to a letter written by the administrator of the charity hospital where Elena was serving her sentence, a great many Spaniards who were not bound by legal definitions of Elena's sexual acts perceived her as a kind of miracle worker and flocked to the hospital in droves to be cured by her. The arrival of these crowds annoyed the hospital's administrator, who registered the following complaint in a letter directed to Toledo's inquisitors:

> I, Hernando de Aguilar, majordomo of the Hospital del Rey in this city, write that Your Mercies sent me a woman named Elena de Céspedes . . . so that she might come to this hospital to serve the poor. . . . This hospital has suffered in its ministry because it has been forced to attend to the many people who have been causing a great disturbance and tumult since the arrival of the aforementioned Elena de Céspedes. So many people have come to see her and be cured by her that this has caused our hospital great inconvenience. . . . I ask and I beg Your Mercies to please . . . take her out of this hospital and transfer her to another so that this hospital can once again function and serve with the tranquility it used to have.

It was Elena's ability to manipulate her own allegedly anomalous body that, rather than damning her in the eyes of her compatriots, had elevated her to celebrity status and added to her reputation as a surgeon.

The early modern period, in addition to being host to a profusion of sexual limitations, was also an era in which models of sex and gender were not strictly binary. Medical, popular, and juridical literature about sudden sex changes and the wonders of hermaphrodites sat side-by-side on bookshelves with conduct manuals dictating proper behavior for men and women and moralist tracts documenting the dangers of vanity and lust. Medical texts told early modern Spaniards that women and men possessed identical but inverted sexual organs, making it possible for women suddenly to turn into men, and vice versa.[38] Also possible, according to the medical texts of the day, was the existence of hermaphrodites. These were people with "two natures" (the same phrase Elena used) whose bodily humors contained male and female elements.[39] Hermaphrodites and instances of sudden sex change also made appearances in early modern popular literature on monsters and curi-

---

38. See, for example, Juan Huarte de San Juan, *Examen de ingenios para las ciencias,* ed. Guillermo Serés (Madrid: Catédra, 1989), 608.

39. The definition of a hermaphrodite as someone who possesses both sets of sexual organs (as opposed to neither or half and half) is the same one given in Pliny (see note 29).

osities of nature. One popular text on curiosities of nature recounted the tale of a mistreated wife who ran away from home in men's clothing but was so virtuous that she was transformed into a man.[40] This book went on, however, to describe the darker side of sexual anomalies. Two hermaphrodites, the author wrote, each endowed with two sets of sexual organs, were forced to choose to live as one sex or the other. Several years after having chosen to live as women, both hermaphrodites were burned at the stake for "behaving secretly as a man."[41] In this case flexible notions of the physical body had run up against rigid notions of sexual propriety and had decisively been defeated.

Canon lawyers of the period also addressed issues related to hermaphrodites, debating such questions as whether they could marry, how many spouses the hermaphrodite was allowed to have, and whether, if two hermaphrodites married each other, they could alternate taking the male and female roles in sexual intercourse without falling into sin.[42] Majority opinion was that hermaphrodites should choose to live as a member of one sex or the other, forswear all future use of their genitalia that did not match the sex they had chosen, and then marry a member of the opposite sex. The seventeenth-century German jurist Jakob Müller argued that God does not approve of overindulgence of sexual appetites in anyone, including hermaphrodites and (echoing the Tribunal of Toledo) that if a hermaphrodite were to take a husband and a wife, this arrangement would leave all three spouses in an unholy state of polygamy.[43] In a dissenting opinion, the Valencian jurist Lorenzo Matheu y Sanz (1618–80) argued (as Elena had) that hermaphrodites should be allowed to take both a husband and a wife and that if God himself had equipped them to do so, it could not be sinful.[44]

Certainly these texts, popular, medical, and juridical, discussed hermaphroditism and sudden sex change as rare, prodigious, even monstrous. Nevertheless, such concepts were part of a common imagining of the possibilities of the body and part of a common sexual vocabulary. Elena's case brings out tensions between the

40. Antonio de Torquemada, *Jardín de flores curiosas* (1573; ed. Giovanni Allegra, Madrid: Ediciones Castalia, 1982), 112.

41. Ibid., 116, 187–88.

42. For a summary of the early modern debates in canon law regarding hermaphrodites and marriage, see Valerio Marchetti, "La discussione settecentesca sui diritti dei bisessuali," in *Studi politici in onore di Luigi Firpo*, vol. 2, ed. Silvia Rota Ghibaudi and Franco Barcia (Milan: Franco Angeli, 1990), 363–74.

43. J. Möllerus, *Discursus duo philologico-iuridici, prior de cornutis posterior de hermaphroditiseorumque iure* (1692), cited in ibid., 469.

44. Lorenzo Matthaeus et Sanz, *Tractatus de re criminali* (1676), in Marchetti, "La discussione," 465.

flexible notions of the sexed body and tacitly permissible sexual behavior, on one hand, and the many legal limitations on sexual behavior that coexisted in early modern Spain, on the other. Elena's case also exposes a tremendous personal creativity and ingenuity. Just as remarkable as Elena's self-transformations from slave, wife, and mother to soldier, surgeon, and man were her discursive transformations from man to woman to man to hermaphrodite. With each successive defense strategy, Elena adjusted her autobiography to fit the charges against her and to justify her sexual acts and intentions in the eyes of the law that had deemed them criminal.

FURTHER READING

For more on transvestites in Spain, see the autobiographical account of Catalina de Erauso in *Lieutenant Nun: A Memoir of a Basque Transvestite in the New World: Catalina de Erauso,* trans. Michel Stepto and Gabriel Stepto (Boston: Beacon Press, 1996); and Sherry M. Velasco, *The Lieutenant Nun: Transgenderism, Lesbian Desire, and Catalina de Erauso* (Austin: University of Texas Press, 2000). A history of "queer culture" in medieval and early modern Spain can be found in Josiah Blackmore and Gregory Hutcheson, eds., *Queer Iberia: Sexualities, Cultures, and Crossings from the Middle Ages to the Renaissance* (Durham, NC: Duke University Press, 1999). Inquisitorial prosecution of the "crime" of sodomy is examined in William Monter, *Frontiers of Heresy: The Spanish Inquisition from the Basque Lands to Sicily* (Cambridge: Cambridge University Press, 1990).

For female transvestism in early modern Europe, see Rudolf Dekker and Lotte Van de Pol, *The Tradition of Female Transvestism in Early Modern Europe* (Basingstoke, Eng.: Macmillan, 1997). The early modern notions of female sexual organs are central to Thomas Laqueur, *Making Sex: Body and Gender from the Greeks to Freud* (Cambridge, MA: Harvard University Press, 1990).

For comprehensive discussions of female homosexual acts and the law in early modern Europe, see Louis Crompton, "The Myth of Lesbian Impunity: Capital Laws from 1270–1791," *Journal of Homosexuality* 6 (1980–81): 11–25; and Lillian Fadderman, *Surpassing the Love of Men: Romantic Friendship and Love between Women from the Renaissance to the Present* (New York: William Morrow, 1981).

As for Elena herself, she figures prominently in several recent essays by Israel Barshatin. They include "Written on the Body: Slave or Hermaphrodite in Sixteenth-Century Spain," in Blackmore and Hutcheson, *Queer Iberia,* 420–56; "Interrogating Hermaphroditism in Sixteenth-Century Spain," in *Hispanisms and Homosexualities,* ed. Sylvia Molloy and Robert Mckee Irwin (Durham, NC: Duke University Press, 1998), 3–18; and "Elena alias Eleno: Genders, Sexualities, and 'Race' in the Mirror of Natural History in Sixteen-Century Spain," in *Gender Reversals and Gender Cultures: Anthropological and Historical Perspectives,* ed. Sabrina Petra Ramet (London: Routledge, 1996), 105–22.

CHAPTER THREE

Miguel de Piedrola

The "Soldier-Prophet"

A native of the village of Marañón in northern Spain, Miguel de Piedrola was alternately a tinker, a soldier, a prophet, and, following his arrest in 1587, one of the Inquisition's most celebrated prisoners. The exact date of his birth, which probably occurred sometime around 1540, remains unknown; by his own admission Piedrola, orphaned at the age of five or six, was raised by a priest who taught him to read. After fleeing his native village "because of some mischief" he had made, Piedrola "took to wandering," working "in various places for assorted masters." He eventually found his way to Sicily, where he entered the Spanish army as a foot soldier, serving successively in Granada, Flanders, North Africa, Naples, Florence, and Rome. He even seems to have gone to Istanbul, where he claimed to have been held prisoner on no fewer than four different occasions after being taken captive by the Ottoman Turks.

None of these claims can be independently documented, but it was apparently during his first captivity in Istanbul that Piedrola discovered his "supernatural gift of prophecy." He then used this "gift" to escape the Turkish prison and to advise the Spanish viceroy in Sicily and the commander of the Spanish navy on military matters. From the outset, moreover, Piedrola's prophetic gift proved consistent. His prophecies, laden with biblical symbolism and peppered with quotations from Old Testament prophets, were directed exclusively at the wealthy and powerful of the early modern Mediterranean.

While Piedrola's visions won him a large following in both Italy and Spain, his prophetic messages were also politically and religiously unsettling. Piedrola insisted that by virtue of his prophetic gift, he was above the authority of kings and clergy and warned that all those who did not abide by his message, regardless of rank, would suffer the wrath of God. Thus in September 1587, even as Castile's representative assembly, the Cortes, entertained the possibility of appointing Piedrola as the kingdom's first "royal prophet," the Inquisition's Tribunal of Toledo arrested him on charges of false prophecy.

Following his imprisonment, Piedrola initially defended himself by asserting that he was a true prophet and his arrest was unjust. But he soon launched into a full-scale counterattack that culminated in his claiming that the Inquisition had no jurisdiction over prophets. He predicted that if the inquisitors proceeded against him, they too would confront divine punishment.

Miguel de Piedrola de Beamonte, called the Prophet[1]

We, the Apostolic Inquisitors who fight heresy, depravity, and apostasy in the city and kingdom of Toledo, together with the ecclesiastical magistrates, have heard the testimony in the criminal case that was and is pending before us, between the party of the first part, Licenciado Sotocameño,[2] Prosecutor for this Holy Office, and the party of the second part, the accused defendant Miguel de Piedrola of Beamonte, born in Marañón in Valle de Campes [Campezo], near Logroño, who currently resides in Madrid. Because of the information against him, the defendant has been brought before this Inquisition. Asked to give the story of his life, he said:

"From the time I was five or six years old, I was cared for by a priest who

1. Piedrola's Inquisition case file has not been preserved, but his inquisitorial autobiography is recorded in an abbreviated copy of his trial record that was sent to Philip II. Our transcription and translation are based upon this document in Archivo General de Simancas: Estado, leg. 165, fol. 340. An eighteenth-century copy, "Vida y sucesos estranissimos del profeta, ni falso ni santo Miguel Piedrola en tiempo de Phelipe segundo," may be found in the Biblioteca Nacional, Madrid, ms. 10,470, fols. 1–117.

2. Pedro de Sotocameño was appointed *fiscal* (prosecuting attorney) of the Toledan tribunal of the Inquisition in 1565. He served in this office until his death in 1607. The inquisitors who presided over this case were Dr. don Rodrigo de Mendoza, Dr. don Lope de Mendoza, and Lic. Andrés Fernández. The recording secretary was Joseph Pantoja.

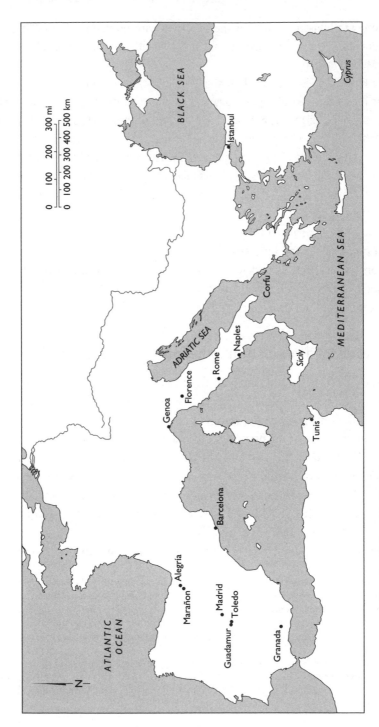

4. *Travels of Miguel de Piedrola*

taught me to read. Because of some mischief I had made, I was afraid [to remain in Marañon] so I went to Alegría, where I stayed with a potter *(ollero)*. The potter's trade didn't appeal to me, so I decided to go to a village near Logroño where the priest, to help me, gave me the vessel *(acetre)* of holy water, which is the way they help poor boys pay for their studies. On Sundays I carried the holy water and a knapsack from house to house, begging for alms.[3] With money I got, I paid for grammar lessons. I studied for about three months, but, seeing that I was stupid and couldn't learn anything, I decided to stop studying. I started singing and took to wandering, working as a servant in various places for assorted masters. Then I went to Sicily and became a soldier. There, during the Gelves [Djerba] campaign, I was captured [by the Turks] and sent to Constantinople.[4] I had been previously taken captive three different times. I was in Constantinople for six or seven months when I heard the voice that used to speak to me. The voice told me to escape and bring certain words of warning to Naples, which I brought to the general and he in turn to His Majesty.[5] I believed what the voice had said, since it told me the way to escape and the escape route, and I escaped. I made it to Corfu and was once again captured and taken to Constantinople [Istanbul], where this time I was imprisoned for about seven or eight months. There, the same voice told me to escape and bring with me the same words of warning as last time. Believing what the voice said, as I did, I got safely to Naples. After I'd wandered around Italy and Spain for a while, I rejoined my regiment and was captured a third time. I was in Constantinople working as a boatman for more than a year. As I traveled from Constantinople to Galata and other points along the Black Sea in a ship, the same voice as before came to me and told me to escape and take with me nine other captives and a guide. I escaped with them and took my words of warning to the Viceroy of Sicily and the Commander of the Navy. Serving as a soldier in various places, I ended up badly wounded after one skirmish and was again taken prisoner. The voice told me that I should escape and that on the road I would find someone to guide me. Thus, having served with distinction

3. Piedrola is describing work as an altar boy.
4. Piedrola refers here to the defeat of the Spanish forces gathered at Djerba, in North Africa, by a Turkish fleet in July 1560. The victorious Turks captured and enslaved hundreds of Spanish soldiers. Some of these, Piedrola apparently among them, were transported to Istanbul. Note that Piedrola refers to Istanbul, capital of the Ottoman Turks since 1453, by its former Christian name of Constantinople.
5. In the sixteenth century the Spanish Habsburg monarch was also king of Naples and of Sicily and was represented in both by a viceroy.

in the war and having given many important words of warning, I returned to Spain. There, His Majesty showed his thanks to me with a certain annuity from [lands in] the Kingdom of Navarre. I then went to serve him in the rebellion of the Kingdom of Granada.[6]

"When I came back to Madrid, I learned that I was a fourth degree descendent of the valiant nobleman de Piedrola. Because of my lineage and my pretensions to the title, I won a sentence [of nobility] in my favor."[7] [In a shining example of Piedrola's lack of concern for linear narrative, he next tells of his return from Flanders without having mentioned his departure, which appears to have been sometime around 1566.]

"When I came back from Flanders, I gave His Majesty certain advice and letters signed with my name, which dealt with how he could best preserve his kingdoms and estates. All these letters were written in a natural discourse, in which I reflected on such matters as a man naturally does. However, other information I knew supernaturally, such as the news that the Frisians and the Malines[8] in Flanders would be the first to rebel [against the king] and that if the situation were not dealt with as I advised, a certain prince would not succeed his father in the monarchy. And really, this is the way it was. The Frisians and the Malines rebelled about six or seven years after that, and the royal person I referred to died within the same period of time I had specified.[9] His Majesty sent a secretary to inform me that I was to leave the Court and never again to take up a pen to write. I told the secretary that I trusted in heavenly justice. I also told him that if he did not do penance for bringing me this news, as I had [noble] lineage and the title of Prophet, and in light of the information and ability these gave me, [I warned him that] his son would marry in a foreign

6. Piedrola refers to an uprising of the moriscos living in the southern city of Granada and its surrounding mountains, known as the "Second Revolt of Alpujarras," 1568–70 (the first revolt took place in 1499). Following the second revolt, Philip II forcibly resettled the granadine moriscos in small groups throughout Castile. These moriscos were later expelled from Spain in 1609–14. See chapter 5.

7. Petitions for nobility were relatively common in early modern Spain. In this case, Piedrola was claiming to be the descendant of a certain Luis de Beamonte, a nobleman from the town of Piedrola and the leader of a faction that had successfully defended the kingdom of Navarre against the territorial pretensions of the fifteenth-century Aragonese monarch Juan II.

8. These are references to people living in Friesland, a region in the Netherlands, and the Flemish city of Malines, both of which then were part of the Spanish Netherlands. The so-called Dutch revolt against Spanish rule began in 1566 and marked the beginning of a protracted conflict that culminated in the independence of the Dutch Republic—today's Netherlands—in 1648.

9. Piedrola's chronology is confusing. The Revolt of the Netherlands began in 1566. Here he is probably referring to the death of Philip II's eldest son, don Carlos, in 1568.

land and he would burn in a fire of pitch, which later came to pass. The secretary asked me why this should be his fault, since he was only obeying orders. I told him that he should ask Elijah why the captains who had burned in the fire were at fault, since they, too, could make the excuse that they were only obeying orders.[10]

"After the secretary made inquiries as to why I hadn't left the Court as I'd been ordered, I received notice that the king had, after consulting with an important adviser, ordered a fort built near [the city of] Tunis.[11] I said that it wasn't a good idea to build [the new fort] before taking down the one that was already there. Instead, the king should route people, munitions, and artillery through La Goletta.[12] If he didn't, within a year all would be lost. This last bit of information came from my supernatural gift for prophecy, while the idea of dismantling the fort, reusing its artillery, and the rest was human discourse and the result of my experience as a soldier with that particular site and fort and as a man of war.

"I told the secretary that I was going to serve in a certain battle. I went to Naples, where, as in other places, I repeated my warning about La Goletta. The same day the news arrived that this fort had been lost.[13] I had been dictating to a friend a letter to His Holiness [the pope], their Majesties the Emperor and the King of France, and the confessor [of Philip II of Spain?], in which I cited the prophet Malachi where he warns the kings and princes about a certain thing and tells them that, among other curses that the prophet would bring upon them, he would curse them with poverty and with constant persecution.[14] My friend asked me how I knew what the prophet Malachi had said if I

10. Here Piedrola refers to the Old Testament prophet Elijah, who chastises messengers sent to consult a pagan oracle on the king of Israel's behalf (see 2 Kings 1). The king orders three of his captains, each with fifty soldiers, to summon Elijah. Two of these captains and their regiments are burned to death by heavenly fire, but the third captain recognizes Elijah as a man of God and pleads with him for his life. This captain and his men are spared the fate the others suffered.

11. This fortress Piedrola refers to is probably that of Bizerta, constructed in 1573 as part of the Spanish war effort against the Ottoman Turks.

12. La Goletta was a Spanish fortress near Tunis.

13. La Goletta was captured by the Turks in August 1573.

14. There is no reference in Malachi to the prophet's rebuking kings and princes, though he does take issue with priests. Piedrola here may be referring to Malachi 2, where the prophet brings Hebrew priests this message from God, "If ye will not hearken, and if ye will not lay it to heart, to give glory unto My name, saith the Lord of hosts, then I will send the curse upon you . . . ye have corrupted the covenant of Levi, Saith the Lord of hosts, therefore have I made you contemptible and base before all people" (Mal. 2:2, 9). (All quotations from the Old Testament are from *Tanakh: A New Translation of the Holy Scriptures according to the Traditional Hebrew Text* [New York: Jewish Publication Society, 1985].) The confessor Piedrola refers to here is probably Fray Diego de Chaves, whom he met in 1578.

had never read a book or studied. I told him he could go look it up, but this was what the prophet had said. I got so mad at him over this that I tore up the letters. Later, when I saw my friend again, I told him that I hadn't really been angry, but that I'd felt a spirit inside me that made me do that and the rest of the things I had done since I was a child.[15] My friend and I got back together and rewrote the letters.

"While I was walking [with my friend] around Naples, near the Spanish barracks, at dusk, a very little child, about fourteen months old, came out of a house. He was holding a dried palm leaf, about half a foot long, in his right hand. It sounded to me like he was saying, 'Ah, Ah, Ah.' When the child came near me, I moved aside so as not to step on him, and I let him pass. The child gave me his hand (his left hand came up to the tops of my stockings, or hose) and he stayed that way until I took the palm, which he held out to me in his right hand, showing me that he wanted to give it to me. I refused to take the palm, saying, 'Innocent, this palm is not for me but for others responsible for having brought me out of my country so that I could do my duty.' But my friend told me to take it, because it was a divine mystery. I told my friend that at the entry to Jerusalem it was said that Christ had received the children saying 'ex ore Ynfantium perficisti laudem.'[16]

"On our way back to the house, I suggested that my friend and I take a closer look at the text of Malachi that we'd discussed before, in which it says 'revertimini ad me, et revertar ad vos Dio.'[17] I decided to buy a Bible from the booksellers, and having bought it, I brought it to my house and placed it on a table on its spine. The book fell open to the aforementioned prophecy of Malachi, and there was an illustration of Malachi with a palm in his hand.[18] I was astonished to see the engraving of the prophet Malachi holding a palm and also to see that the book had turned to that page without anyone's having opened it. Since the child had given me a palm the previous afternoon, when I saw Malachi painted holding a palm, it seemed to me to be a mystery that the

15. Note that Piedrola makes several references to the "mischief" or misdeeds he has committed since childhood but that these references are always oblique.

16. Matthew 21:16: "Out of the mouth of babes and sucklings thou hast perfected praise." As the inquisitorial scribe noted in the margin of the transcript, the correct quote reads, "ex ore infantium et lactantium perficisti laudem." When Jesus enters the temple in Jerusalem, the children in the temple cry out, "Hosanna to the Son of David" (Matt. 21:15). It is this "perfect praise" to which Jesus refers. This and all further quotations from the New Testament are from the King James Version.

17. Piedrola here refers to Malachi 3:7, "Return unto Me, and I will return unto you, saith the Lord of hosts." The correct Latin quote reads, "revertimini ad me et revertar ad vos dicit Dominus exercituum et dixistis in quo."

18. Note that no reference to palm leaves occurs in Malachi's text.

child had given me a palm and then that Malachi had one. The Bible had opened to the part God had wanted it to, the part where Malachi warns the princes. I decided, on my own [initiative], to go through the Bible page by page to see if any other prophet had a palm. None did. But in one of God's mysteries, when I went back to the Bible and turned the same pages backward, I found another prophet with a palm. I told myself that I should not believe that it was another prophet, since this engraving was simply a duplicate of the first.

"Some very important people heard about this, and together with them I went to find the child who had given me the palm the day before. We found him in his mother's arms. In response to our questions, she said that the child was fourteen or fifteen months old, and that he could only toddle a little, holding on to things, like all children his age. She didn't know who had given him the palm. The child's name was Marco Antonio. One of the people present swore by the habit of Santiago[19] that Saint Matthew and Saint Mark are mentioned the margin of the text of Malachi and that he thought Saint Anthony had written on the subject. He told me to take his words down as testimony, but I didn't consent, explaining that God's works would be discovered in their own time. With that, I ended the conversation and we all left, each to his own home and me to mine, where I returned to writing the letters I sent the princes.

"After that, I gained courage and pride and began to say what I felt, which is that I was in God's service. A short while later I had various meetings with the Lord Don Juan of Austria[20] and the Viceroy of Naples, during which I tried to get them to make peace. In particular, I spoke with Lord Don Juan and told him that I would have to write to his servants that which is written in Ecclesiastes, 'vidi servos in equis,' which means, 'I have seen servants upon horses.'[21] [I told him that] unless he followed the orders I was about to give him, when he left for Flanders things would begin to go badly for him.[22] If he followed my instructions, he would rule over all his enemies in the states of Flanders. But if

19. The habit of Santiago is the cloak emblazoned with the insignia of the Spanish military order of Saint James, or Santiago.

20. Don Juan of Austria, King Philip II's half brother, commanded Spain's Mediterranean fleet in the early 1570s. He had previously commanded troops in the Alpujarras War, which may have been how Piedrola was acquainted with him.

21. "Vidi servos in equis," from Ecclesiastes 10:7, "I have seen servants upon horses and princes walking as servants upon the earth." In early modern Europe, riding horseback was a sign of nobility. Ecclesiastes 10:7 is preceded by this quote, also germane to Piedrola's warning to Don Juan: "There is an evil which I have seen under the sun, like an error which proceedeth from a ruler: Folly is set on great heights and the rich sit in low place" (Eccles. 10:5–6).

22. If this conversation actually occurred, it probably can be dated to 1576–77, as Don Juan was sent to Flanders to 1577 in order to quell the Dutch revolt against Spanish rule. Don Juan had little time to accomplish this goal, because he died the following year.

he didn't do as I said, he would lose and end up bad off. His servants would become lords and he a servant. This is what I wrote in a memo I sent him. . . .

"At this time, various noblemen [passed through Naples] on their way to Turkey, where they planned to do very difficult things. Consulting with the Viceroy of Naples, I told him that for various reasons, which I gave him, the noblemen's task was an impossible one and that they should not go forward with it. The Viceroy responded that they had to try. I then set in writing, with my signature, [my prediction] that the noblemen would come to no good, and that they should not go forward. If they did, it would cause great loss and offense and the noblemen would end up on the gallows or suffer some similar punishment. I said all of this speaking as a prophet and as prophecy, and this is what came to pass, as is well known. One was garroted, one was hanged, and the third went blind and deaf.

"At this same time the Commander of the galley fleet in Naples had been run over by a carriage. Believing that he was about to die, the Commander wanted to pass his property on to his son, but I stopped him, saying that he was not going to die. I went to the Commander's house and told him that he wasn't going to die, since his heart, which at other times could be troubled when he was suffering adversities, was healthy and calm. In short, he wasn't going to die. That very afternoon, the Commander recovered. The next day he was fit and soon he was cured. I attributed [my knowledge of] this to supernatural and divine inspiration, which God reserves for His divine mysteries.

"I also counseled the Viceroy of Naples about the governance of his kingdom and his household. Much, or most, of what I told him I said as a human man. But along with that, as later events would show, part of what I said came from my supernatural gift. Seeing that Naples was not well governed, as it should have been, and that in some ways this was my fault, in His Majesty's service I left Naples and returned to Spain. While I was traveling through Rome, His Holiness sent word that I should come and see him at a certain time, which he indicated. I replied that I wished to be excused from the audience, since my first thought was with His Majesty and no other living person. If it pleased His Holiness, however, he could command that I be brought to him forcibly, since I was in his court and jurisdiction. With that, he told me to go on my way. I promised to pay him a longer visit on the way back.

"A few days after I left Rome, I arrived in Florence, where the Duke [of Florence] begged me to go and see him. I told him that if I had business with him, I would go and see him. But if he had business with me, he should send me his questions. If, after that, he still had to see me, he would have to bring me to him by force of law, as the Holy Office has done, since I didn't have the authority to come to him any other way. I said, 'tollierre me et mitite me in mare' (take me up and cast me forth into the sea), as Jonah had said.[23] Even though my life is not equal to that of Jonah, as far as prophecies were concerned, like Jonah, I had said things about the future as a prophet. Thus spoke the Lord through the Prophet Ezekiel, chapter 33, where it says, 'That which is predicted will come to pass, because I have placed here, as I have already done, prophets among you and they will know.'[24] If the duke still wanted to see me, well, I was on his lands and in his city and he could have taken me by force to his palace to see him, which he didn't do. Rather, he let me go without seeing me.

"From Florence I went to Genoa, where, after I had seen its most important buildings, the [Spanish?] Ambassador who happened to be there asked me how I liked the city. I told him, resolutely, that my spirit had moved me for various reasons to say that there would soon be plague and discord in the Republic. He asked me when this would come to pass. I told him that the plague would come in less than five months. And so it happened, because it [the plague] arrived after only four months. I said all of this as a prophet, since this is how I understood it in my spirit. In short, as I have said, it happened in this way.

"From there I went to Barcelona, where I saw a certain important person and tried to persuade her to make peace [with certain people]. She did not do this or other things I asked her to do. As it says in the Holy Scripture, [I predicted that] she would forget the death of her husband with the death of her son, though I didn't say when her son's death would happen. This frightened her. I told her, moreover, that for other reasons, she would be punished by seeing no male of her line survive to inherit. Her son would die within a very short time. I said all of this with the utmost assurance, knowing infallibly that this person's son would die, as I have said."

[We, the Inquisitors] asked whether or not he had said this as a prophet or not. He answered that proof of the gift of prophecy required the [involvement

---

23. When a storm hits the ship on which Jonah is traveling, the passengers draw lots to see which of them has provoked the wrath of God. Jonah draws the short straw and is asked to name his own punishment: "Then said they unto him, 'What shall we do unto thee, that the sea may be calm unto us?' " Jonah replies, "Take me up and cast me forth into the sea; so shall the sea be calm unto you" (Jon. 1:11, 12).

24. There is no reference in Ezekiel that matches Piedrola's misquote. Ezekiel 3:3 reads, "And He said unto me: 'Son of man, cause thy belly to eat, and fill thy bowels with this roll that I give thee.'" The reference to Ezekiel 33 as opposed to 3:3 may have been a mistake of the scribe who prepared this transcription, although it may also have been Piedrola's error.

of] the Pope [*summo sacerdote*], and that he did not know how the Inquisitors, without a special letter from His Holiness, could have jurisdiction over him and his affairs. [Piedrola continued as follows:]

"As you know, I am a prophet. As such, I have spoken to pontiffs, kings, and magnates and to the guardians of these kingdoms. Many of my prophecies have come true. I state this clearly because I don't want harm to come to you, as has come to all others who have dared to persecute me without my having committed a crime deserving [of punishment]. I won't tell you any more than I've told everyone else."

Continuing with his story, he said:

"When I arrived in Madrid, some advisers told me that His Majesty wanted me to tell him about things I spoke of earlier, that had happened while I was in service in Naples. I replied that I would have to meet either with his royal person or in his presence, with a small group of priests and other ministers of state, so that I could speak more effectively. What I proposed was approved, in accordance with the reasons given by His Majesty. A few days later, His Majesty sent certain important ministers of his to meet with me. When we met, they told me that His Majesty wanted me to tell them whatever it was I had to say. I replied that on matters concerning his office it was the king's duty to hear people so that he could act on what was said. It was better not to go through third parties because kings have the virtue of being able to understand advice better when they receive it [personally] than when they receive it through other means. If His Majesty wanted to hear me, I was ready to speak with him. If not, I had carried out my duty in predicting what it was my duty to predict. If His Majesty didn't want to hear me, I would return to Rome, as I had promised His Holiness.

"The ministers told me that the king's hand would not be forced. They told me I would do well to say what I had to say to those who were here. I replied that kings must hear prophets in person, and that when Nebuchadnezzar asked of Daniel that which was now being asked of me, the prophet responded that the reason such a cruel sentence had been imposed was because he was not in the King's presence and that they should take him to Nebuchadnezzar.[25] I myself didn't want to follow any path except that which the Prophet Daniel had

25. Once again, Piedrola has managed to mangle Scripture. In Daniel 2, King Nebuchadnezzar orders the wise men of Babylon, Daniel included, to be imprisoned and then executed on account of their failure to recount and interpret his dream correctly. He also believes that their prophecies have been false. When Daniel is told the reason for the order, he asks the king's guard to bring him before Nebuchadnezzar. He then provides the king a true interpretation of his dream, upon which "the King Nebuchadnezzar fell upon his face and worshiped Daniel" (Dan. 2:46).

taken. Even though I wasn't as saintly as the Prophet Daniel, as far as predictions were concerned, I had my supernatural gift of prophecy and I was a prophet nonetheless. The Catholic Church does not prohibit this, but if it did, I would serve the hand [of the Church].

"Just before dawn, while I was sleeping, about two days before the ministers and I had this chat, I dreamed that I saw the figure of a kind and well-proportioned priest with gray hair and a beard and a biretta pulled down until just above his eyes. He came over to my bed and stood over me, straddling my legs. Lacing his fingers together but with his palms open, he bent over three times, striking my chest and saying each time, 'Dominus Piedrola, Dominus Aaron' (The house of Piedrola is the House of Aaron).[26] The second time he said this, he raised his voice and hit me harder. The third time he struck me so hard that it seemed that the blow had crushed my chest into my ribs, and his voice was so strong that it rang in my ears as if someone had shot off a cannon next to them. With the last blow and at the sound of his voice, I awoke, awed and frightened of the vision.

"I began to wonder what it could mean. Then I remembered the text of Saint Paul, where it says that none but he who is called by God as Aaron was will be given honor.[27] It seemed to me that the three times I was called represented the same thing as when God called to Samuel three times while he was sleeping.[28] Or, perhaps, if this vision wasn't meant to call me to prophecy, perhaps it was meant to call me to the priesthood. But considering that in the past I had predicted so many things, I was persuaded that it was meant more to call me to prophecy and predictions rather than to the priesthood.

"Two or three days later, after the meeting [with the king's ministers] I mentioned, I heard a voice in my sleep which called to me three times, saying 'Piedrola, Piedrola, Piedrola.' When I opened my eyes and looked around, I was on a high mountain. At its top was a large nest of eagles, brown, white, and black.[29] On their heads they wore imperial and ducal crowns, heavily adorned with different stones. As I was looking up from the base of the mountain, I saw a black raven in the sky, coming [from the west] as if from Portugal. In his beak the raven held a round sphere like the ones astrologers draw, except this sphere

26. See Psalm 115:12: "The Lord remembers us and will bless us: He will bless the house of Israel, he will bless the house of Aaron."

27. Hebrews 5:4: "And no man taketh this honour unto himself, but he that is called of God, as was Aaron."

28. 1 Sam. 3:3–18.

29. In Ezekiel 17 a similar dream is narrated, in which eagles represent the king of Babylon who displeased the Lord by breaking his covenant with him.

was dripping and was the color of recently spilled blood. A few drops of blood from this ball fell to the ground. The raven arrived and landed on the western part of the nest, from whence he had come flying. The eagles in the nest fled toward the east, where I was, turning their beaks and faces toward the raven, who flew out of the nest. The raven flew toward me in pursuit of the eagles and landed on my left arm with the ball, dripping blood, still in his beak.

"When the eagles saw the raven leave the nest, they went back to the other side of it, across from where the raven had been, but they kept their heads and faces turned to the spot where the raven was. It should be noted that the eagles, even though they had fled from the raven, never left their nest unprotected. Instead, they were on the other side of it, across from where the raven was, with their faces and beaks turned [toward him]. The raven on my arm called to me three times, saying 'Piedrola, Piedrola, Piedrola, feed the eagles this, which I have brought.' I, frightened to see that I had approached the eagles' nest and they had fled from me, told the raven, 'Since you are naturally so contrary, you must dare to feed the eagles.' The raven laughed and told me, in Spanish, that since he was supernatural he was not afraid of eagles.

"In reply, I said, 'Well, now, there's no reason you should ask me [to feed the eagles]. I know perfectly well that supernatural things can't be judged as natural things can. Try again.' Then the raven flew up to the nest on the eastern side to where the eagles had gone when the raven flew in from the west. Perched on the nest, the raven opened his wings and flapped them three times, like swans do when they call their children. I saw that the eagles had gone toward the raven and had begun to eat the ball he carried in his beak, which showed that they approached him with fear and awe. Then, frightened by seeing the eagles eat what the raven had carried, I awoke and remembered my dream with the certitude that it was a prophetic vision, as I will explain shortly.

"I had doubts as to whether I should tell anyone of my prophetic vision or whether I should keep quiet for fear that talking about the vision could put me in danger. Suffering thus, I decided to look at the Bible which I called [Scripture?] which was the name of the one I had in my hand, the one I had bought in Naples. I took it off the table and opened it. The first thing I came upon was Jeremiah, the part where the Prophet says, 'He who has a dream, tell it now. He who has a word, tell the word.'[30] I wasn't satisfied with this, so I went back and

---

30. Piedrola may be referring to this passage in Jeremiah 23:28: "Let a prophet who has a dream tell the dream; and let him who has received My word report My word faithfully."

opened the Bible a second time. By chance, I opened it to the part where it says, 'If there is among you any prophet of the Lord, I will appear to him in a vision or a dream and I will speak to him now.'[31] With that, it seemed to me that duty obligated me to tell of this vision.

"I gathered the members of my household together, men and women, and I told them the same things I just mentioned, reminding them of some previous predictions that they knew had come to pass. [The Raven,] I said, . . . was the messenger of death for a generation of the House of Austria.[32] The ball was the grave state of the Christian republic, especially of the priesthood. The rings that encircled the ball were the scheming and violent treachery that hindered any attempt at good government. The blood that fell to Earth was the injustice of those who suffered unjustly with no remedy for their pain save their cries to the heavens. The blood that fell to Earth was also a cry to God against the oppressors, like the cry of the just Abel's blood against his brother, the homicidal Cain. The mountain was Christianity, while the nest was the generation and the house of Austria, the guardians of Christianity. The different colors the eagles had were the generations of the House of Austria. That is to say, the black eagles were the kings and emperors, male and female, who are currently reigning. The brown ones were those who are to succeed to the throne. The white eagles were those from the House who were not to succeed or govern. The different crowns represented the different states. The different stones which adorned the crown were the virtues that all princes have and also the obligation they have to be virtuous so that they may bring glory to their kingdoms. I told everyone of this vision and interpretation since that was the will of God and was from God, and so that I would not incur the punishment of the prophet Ezekiel, where Ezekiel says that if a watchman sees the knife coming and doesn't sound the horn and the sword comes and kills, the guard should be arrested for his evil act.[33]

31. Numbers contains this passage in which the Lord addresses Miriam, Aaron, and Moses: "And He said: 'Hear now My words: if there be a prophet among you, I the LORD do make Myself known unto him in a vision, I do speak with him in a dream' " (Num. 12:6).

32. The House of Austria refers to the Habsburg monarchy, which came to power in Spain starting with Charles I (aka Charles V) in 1516 and ended with the death of Charles II in 1700.

33. Ezekiel 33:1–7: "The word of the Lord came to me: "O mortal, speak to your fellow countrymen and say to them: When I bring the sword against a country, the citizens of that country take one of their number and appoint him their watchman. Suppose he sees the sword advancing against the country, and he blows the horn and warns the people. If anybody hears the sound of the horn but ignores the warning, and the sword comes down and dispatches him, his blood shall be on his own head. Since he heard the sound of the horn but ignored the warning, his bloodguilt shall be upon

"When a certain person told me that His Majesty wished to know what complaint I had with him, I asked only why His Majesty had not met with me, as I mentioned above. I had not stopped wanting to see him. Even though I had made up my mind because of this to go back to Italy, some people immediately detained me. I sent His Majesty a letter explaining what I needed him to do to right the wrong and redress my complaints. Later, these people brought me a letter from His Majesty. In it, he commanded me to go on a certain day to the [royal] palace, where he would grant me an audience and where we would discuss our business. In response, I asked why His Majesty had written this if he didn't have to. He didn't have to see me, except that, in some way, what happened with the Prophet Micah and the king Ahab might happen to him.[34]

"Even if I were to go to the king and talk to him, he didn't have to make use of what I told him, since he didn't have to do anything. My response frightened the person and he told me I was crazy. I replied that I had always been this way. Those who denounce things in God's name have always been taken as crazy. Look at Job and his friends. So that the truth may be known, I told this person I would go to the palace whenever His Majesty wished, though His Majesty would not see me for some time to come. To date I have not yet spoken with him.

"I had decided to go back to Italy when by order of His Majesty I was detained and ordered to tell a gentleman about the dream of the raven and other predictions regarding Flanders, which I mentioned earlier, which threatened, among other things, the death of a certain prince. I looked up at a crucifix and said to it, "Well, you know, Lord, that this must be true. I beg you to let it be known." Within four days' time there came letters with the news of the deaths of some important personages. As it seemed to me that the heavenly punishment had begun, I left Madrid, shaking the dust from my boots and

---

himself; had he taken the warning, he would have saved his life. But if the watchman sees the sword advancing and does not blow the horn, so that the people are not warned, and the sword comes and destroys one of them, that person was destroyed for his own sins; however, I will demand a reckoning for his blood from the watchman. Now, O mortal, I have appointed you a watchman for the House of Israel; and whenever you hear a message from My mouth, you must transmit My warning to them."

34. Piedrola has incorrectly attributed the prophecies of Jeremiah to Micah, who does not mention King Ahab at all. It is likely that Piedrola was referring to Jeremiah 29:21, "This is what the LORD Almighty, the God of Israel, says about Ahab son of Kolaiah and Zedekiah son of Maaseiah, who are prophesying lies to you in my name: "I will hand them over to Nebuchadnezzar king of Babylon, and he will put them to death before your very eyes.""

garments at the outset, as testimony that I had done my duty by telling of the vision. I was now on my way to do my duty to His Holiness.

"A certain person asked me how I had seen and then denied the aforementioned prophecy of the raven. I told him not to tire himself out and to go with God. The duty of the Prophet is not to be subjected to those sorts of questions, and I was under no obligation to answer them. Even Jeremiah, a Prophet from the time when he was in his mother's womb, had never dared to ask questions of Baruch, the prophet whose secretary and servant Jeremiah had been.[35] As my interlocutor was a certain doctor, he could not touch me. Although he may have worn a great crown, in return for his impudence it would not be covered with a miter. The same thing happened to another doctor who bothered me, while nothing happened to me. Since I was a child it has been my experience that those who persecuted me have come to bad ends. . . ."

[In the next passage Piedrola went to Barcelona, where the viceroy, without the king's knowledge, ordered Piedrola to participate in an ecclesiastical debate with various learned clerics. Piedrola, according to his own version of events, made an excellent showing. The clerics were amazed and wondered if Piedrola's knowledge was diabolical. Piedrola then traveled to Rome, where he had an audience with the pope. No visions came to him during his audience, so Piedrola asked the pope for indulgences and left. He then went to Sicily where he met with the viceroy, talked about Spanish misgovernment of the island, and predicted that the viceroy's son would die if he left Sicily to join the Spanish army about to invade Portugal, a reference that suggests that this conversation occurred in 1580 as Philip II's forces invaded Portugal in the spring of that year. In passing, Piedrola repeated the claim that the inquisitors had no right to arrest him or to keep him in prison without special permission from the papacy, since only the pope had jurisdiction over prophets. In making this argument, in which he invoked Joseph and other Old Testament prophets, Piedrola asserted, "I am a prophet, neither holy nor false."]

We [the Inquisitors] asked Piedrola what kind of voice he heard and if he saw a body along with the voice or if he only heard a voice. He answered:

"Sometimes the figure of a man or a woman appears to me in dreams. Other times I only hear a voice and can't see the body it's coming from. In

---

35. In Jeremiah 36:4, Jeremiah mentions Baruch as an inferior (a scribe commanded to take down Jeremiah's own words). No mention is made of Baruch as Jeremiah's master or teacher.

some dreams I see people wearing all manner of dress. Some are priests, others monks, farmers, or courtiers. Some are naked or dressed in various types of women's clothes. When I'm alone, these spirits talk to me and, only when I'm asleep, they talk to me about things that are in the Lord's service. . . .

"I wish, if it please God, that I didn't have the gift [of prophecy] or that the Church and its ministers would order me not to have this ministry so that it would no longer torment me. The figure of Christ himself has spoken to me, but sometimes I don't know who it is who's speaking to me. I do know that it's a good spirit, because of what it says. It always tells me things about the glory of God and His Catholic Church. Anything else that might be against this, I reject as a diabolical illusion."[36]

We [the Inquisitors] asked Piedrola various questions, to which he responded:

"That which I know as a prophet may be corrected by another, greater prophet, as when Jeremiah corrected Baruch. But, on the subject of who is allowed to correct me, I'm not sure if the Pope alone has the authority to distinguish between true and false prophets. I do know, however, that prophets are obligated to appear before their superiors and the judges who call them. If I have said anything wrong, such as the prediction that the Inquisition has no jurisdiction over me because of what I thought the Lateran Council had said (which is that priestly authority is secondary to the gift of prophecy), I have only said it out of zeal and with the best of intentions.[37] If I've committed a crime, any judge can arrest me. The Holy Office is the greatest tribunal in the world. I give myself over to it as the Catholic Church demands I do. If you have found me lacking in anything, then bear my good intentions in mind and pardon me."

In another audience we [the Inquisitors] had with him, which we had at his own request, Piedrola said:

"I've remembered that when I was arrested I may have said some disrespectful words in anger. This weighs on me because I didn't behave humbly, which would have been the right thing to do. It also weighs on me that in this tribunal I have said some disrespectful things. For this, I beg you to pardon me and have mercy on me, an illiterate idiot who has studied the Bible only a little bit. I only

36. Diabolical illusion was itself an inquisitorial crime *(iluso, ilusente)*. Piedrola here may have been trying to avoid adding more charges to the list the Inquisition had already compiled against him.
37. The Fifth Lateran Council (1512–17), at the start of its 11th Session, decreed that the papacy was the ultimate arbiter in matters of prophecy and prophetic discourse.

did what was necessary with the dreams as with the prophecies written in my letters. If I've said anything the Holy Catholic Church doesn't agree with, pardon me and have mercy on me. I am an idiot. Correct me. If I've said or written anything against the Holy Catholic Church, I'll retract it since I, from the first, have retracted it in my mind. . . . I've never had a pact with the Devil nor been deceived by him. I never meant to seek honors for being a prophet. The truth is that much of what I've said I've said as a human being, based on the vast experience I've had in the business of war. Because these things, and a couple of things I've said in relation to them, turned out to be true, and because I couldn't have known them through human knowledge as I could with some other things, it seemed to me that, somehow, they were prophecies, as I've said and as my papers show.

"I think I've erred most in believing that certain things have happened and in believing that the things I dreamed were prophecies and in giving these dreams more credit than they were due. . . . Many times I've written papers that told of when I heard the voice, but the truth is that the voice didn't tell me anything. I didn't even hear it. Instead, all of what I've said I've said according to human knowledge and then embellished with some sayings from the writings of the Prophets, from the flower of the Bible and the Holy Doctors and other similar authors, and the Catechism written by the Pontiff and other prelates and people, so that I could use their words. . . .

"The truth is that I'm not a prophet, God forgive His Holiness, the Cardinals, the Inquisitors General, His Majesty, and the rest of His Majesty's servants, ministers, and counselors, both clerical and lay, whom I asked twenty years ago to disabuse me of the notion that I am a prophet. Since others told me that I was, you should pardon me since I acted in good faith, modeling my actions on those of the prophet Baruch. . . .[38] Have mercy on me and consider my noble blood, my life, past and present, and my intention, which was to glorify God and ensure the good governance of the state, since the poor were oppressed and the clerics did not always pay attention to that which Saint Paul said, 'curio en anathema en pro fraccuibus meis,'[39] and that which Moses said,

38. Baruch, son of Neriah, is mentioned only briefly in Jeremiah (Jer. 36:4–32). Baruch faithfully transcribes the prophecies of Jeremiah. When Jeremiah is unable to go to the temple to deliver the prophecies himself, Baruch goes in his place.

39. It is likely that Piedrola refers here to the following biblical quote, which he has uttered in mangled form. Romans 9:2–4: "optabam enim ipse ego anathema esse a Christo pro fratribus meis qui sunt cognati mei secundum." For I could wish that myself were accursed from Christ for my brethren, my kinsmen according to the flesh (KJV).

'Give me the Book of Life.'[40] I have erred out of a Christian desire to do good and from not having anyone to disabuse me [of the belief that I am a prophet] until now. I beg God, if He hears me, to make me my own judge as He did with Jonah when they asked Jonah what sentence he wanted to give himself when the fates turned against him. He said, 'Take me and throw me into the sea.' I say to you, take me and put me in an insane asylum for however long you think is necessary."

[Piedrola again called himself an "illiterate idiot" and pleaded for mercy on the grounds that he was noble. He then repeated his request to be put in an insane asylum. The prosecutor Sotocameño formally accused Piedrola of "being a prophet who was neither good nor approved by the Church," who "preached to frighten people" and who "pretended to be a prophet" when in fact he was not. Piedrola defended himself by claiming that he was "soft in the head" and unable to understand the Bible that he had purchased in Naples.]

"I have only sinned in that I was dishonorable and passed myself off as a prophet. . . . From my childhood I've naturally been inclined toward piety and, seeing that there was no other way to become [closer to God], I thought it a good idea to fake these things to frighten and entertain people, though not to harm them. I know that each one of us fulfills his obligation as best he can. Nobody forced me to do this, but since I didn't take up any other sort of craziness, I took up this one. . . . I have lived the most exemplary and virtuous life I could, and I hope you, in your mercy, will take this into account. Because I am crazy, I ask that you please put me in an insane asylum. . . . I lost my wits after I purchased the Bible in Naples, and people in my hometown, where I committed a certain offense, have always thought I was crazy. . . . Pardon me for having offended the Holy Book and for having wanted to count myself among the number of the prophets.

"Most of the fault lies with all those who put it into my head that the visions I had were prophecies. It is not surprising that a crazy man like myself should believe these people. Because of them, others were fooled. I didn't understand the harm I had done until I came before the Holy Tribunal of the Inquisition, where I thank God for having brought me, which made me see that I had chosen a path to evil."

[Prosecutor Sotocameño closed the case for the Inquisition by stating that

---

40. Piedrola may be misquoting from this passage, in which Moses says to God, "But now, please forgive their sin—but if not, then blot me out of the book [of life] you have written. The Lord replied to Moses, "Whoever has sinned against me I will blot out of my book [of life]" (Ex. 32:32–33).

Piedrola was a "heretic, apostate, disturber of the peace in the republic, usurper of divine and celestial authority, arrogant, seditious, scandalous, a trickster, and a con man who had a pact with the Devil and who declared and signed himself to be a true prophet of God, neither false nor meritorious . . . and who claimed to be subject neither to His Holiness nor to His Majesty in Earthly things. As far as divine things were concerned, they were subject to him, but not he to them." Sotocameño added that he also suspected Piedrola of necromancy and Protestant (or, in Inquisition parlance, "Lutheran") heresies. Piedrola admitted to having "spoken like a mad man, like an unbridled horse" but maintained that his intentions were good and that he deserved inquisitorial mercy because he was "an idiot."

In the end, because of his "good confession, repentance and tears," the inquisitors granted Piedrola mercy, according to their definition. They sentenced him to appear in an *auto de fe,* abjure *de levi* and forbade him to ever again read the Bible or other Holy Scriptures, own paper, write letters, or speak of religious matters. They also sentenced Piedrola to a five-year prison sentence, which in inquisitorial vocabulary was called "perpetual jail."]

Born a commoner in a remote village in Navarre, in northern Spain, Miguel de Piedrola was orphaned at an early age. Raised by a priest, he became a tinker, a maker of pots, and like most artisans in early modern Europe, he was likely to have remained a tradesman for the rest of his life. But Piedrola was ambitious. If the life story he provided the Inquisition contains within it a grain of truth, the pot-maker embarked on the road to advancement first by learning to read Latin and then by adopting the wandering life of a troubadour and a servant. The army came next, and soon Piedrola was a soldier in the service of Philip II. Yet Piedrola wanted more: recognition from the monarchy for his military valor and a grant of noble status as well. Indeed, his appetite for advancement went beyond legal provisions and monarchical prerogatives. By laying claim to a "supernatural gift," Piedrola also sought to transform himself into a prophet and thus, in biblical fashion, into an adviser of kings.

Piedrola's penchant for prophecy was by no means unique. The belief that God had the power to communicate important messages through selected individuals stood at the very core of the Judeo-Christian tradition. Over the centuries, this same belief had inspired countless individuals, men and women alike, to step forward and speak with what they claimed was a divine voice. For the Church, the problem was to separate true prophets—that is, individuals who were truly divinely inspired—from false prophets sent by the Devil in order to sow division and dissent among the faithful.[41] Starting in the fifteenth century, a series of church councils established certain criteria as well as the procedures through which this decision might be made, but in general it remained difficult, if not impossible, for the clergy to determine whether the ultimate source of a prophet's message was diabolical or divine. For this reason, church authorities tended to take a dim view of prophets, especially those who went public with their messages without seeking clerical approval. To be sure, the majority of these prophets were either ignored or simply dismissed as mad. Those whose prophetic messages touched upon matters of church doctrine or challenged the policies of a particular prince were subject to closer scrutiny and, in especially serious cases, arrest. Such was Miguel de Piedrola's fate.

In essence the inquisitorial charges against Piedrola were of "sedition" and "usurpation of divine and celestial authority." "Usurpation of divine and celestial authority" referred to Piedrola's refusal to submit to the jurisdiction of the Church and the Inquisition. "Sedition" addressed his refusal to respect the authority of the king. Sixteenth-century Castilian law defined a seditious person as "anyone who speaks badly of the king and his family."[42] The minimum penalty for sedition was the forfeiture to the Crown of half of one's goods. However, if the accused had "advised or counseled anyone to rebel against or refuse to obey the king's law," the penalty for sedition was death. The royal courts had jurisdiction over sedition, whereas, in theory, the Inquisition could prosecute only heresy. The Holy Office, however, was the only legal system in Spain that could guarantee secrecy and thus prevent Piedrola from using his trial as a political platform. In addition, it possessed the power to deflate Piedrola's self-proclaimed religious authority and, along with it, the basis of his political influence. The Inquisition, in short, was ideally suited to prosecute Piedrola, and in this instance at least, the monarchy did not hesitate to use it against a potential enemy.

Piedrola's inquisitorial autobiography was a direct refutation of the charges against him. He claimed not to have "usurped" divine power; rather, he said it had been bestowed upon him from above. Moreover, Piedrola argued, because he was a

---

41. For a discussion of Piedrola and prophecy in sixteenth-century Spain, see Richard L. Kagan, *Lucrecia's Dreams: Politics and Prophecy in Sixteenth-Century Spain* (Berkeley: University of California Press, 1990), esp. 86–113.

42. See the *Nueva recopilación de todas las leyes . . .* (Alcalá de Henares, 1569), libro 8, título 18, ley 1; título 26, ley 11. Cited in Kagan, *Lucrecia's Dreams*, chap. 3, note 11, p. 194.

prophet of God, neither the king, nor the pope, nor the inquisitors had any authority over him. If they dared to move against him, God would surely punish them.

Piedrola's life story emerged in response to the inquisitors' formulaic request for the *discurso de la vida,* but it differed from the others examined in this volume in that it did not constitute a straightforward narrative, nor did it proceed in strict chronological fashion. In fact, the chronology is so confused that it is easy to believe that much of Piedrola's "wanderings" were the product of a rather fertile imagination. Piedrola centered his story on the various predictions and "warnings" he had provided to various Spanish officials in an effort to offer evidence supporting the divine nature of his calling as well as the veracity of his prophetic visions.

It follows that much of Piedrola's life story can be related to the experiences of the Old Testament prophets he cited (often wrongly).[43] Indeed, by focusing on his supposedly divinely inspired dreams and visions, Piedrola transformed his own narrative into that of a biblical prophet. In so doing, he turned his autobiography into a bid for political and religious legitimacy and, ultimately, a rationale for his release from inquisitorial arrest. The logic of these arguments was in direct competition with the logic of the Holy Office. What he saw as proof positive of his innocence, the inquisitors regarded as heresy, but these competing understandings are central to both the form and the content of Piedrola's autobiography.

After an abbreviated story of his childhood, Piedrola fast-forwarded to his military career and the time he supposedly spent as a captive Christian in the Ottoman capital of Istanbul. It is difficult to ascertain whether this part of Piedrola's story is true. Throughout the sixteenth century, Ottoman and North African corsairs in the Mediterranean made a practice of seizing and then enslaving Christians. The majority of these captives were held in the notorious bagnios located in the North African port cities of Tunis and Algiers, but some found their way to Istanbul, where they fetched a high price. The point is that Piedrola, by identifying himself with the well-publicized sufferings of Christians in Muslim hands, sought to gain the sympathy of his judges. He further explained that it was during this captivity, something the inquisitors would have understood as a kind of protomartyrdom, that he first heard "the voice," that is, the medium through which his prophetic visions supposedly came to him. The voice, in addition to giving Piedrola the information he needed to escape, ordered him to bring "words of warning" to the king. Confirmation of

43. On the information usually included in biblical prophet biographies, see John Sawyer, *Prophecy and the Biblical Prophets* (New York: Oxford University Press, 1993), 34.

Piedrola's prophetic gifts came in the form of a series of small-scale miracles, notably the "miracle of the palm," in which Piedrola compared himself to Jesus, and the miracle of Piedrola's magical Bible. In his view, this Bible transformed him into a latter-day version of the biblical prophet Malachi, the last of the Old Testament prophets and one who warned the Israelites to repent of their sins or risk destruction: "For, behold, the day cometh, that shall burn as an oven, and all the proud, yea, and all that do wickedly, shall be stubble: and the day that cometh shall burn them up . . . that it shall leave them neither root nor branch" (Mal. 4:1). Piedrola's warnings were similarly dire, and the fact that some of them, as he claimed, came true, confirmed his status as a prophet who deserved respect.

Ultimately, Piedrola's prophetic powers and his claim to authority rested with the efficacy of his visions. But visions, however powerful their imagery, were elusive. Were they fabrications? Or real? Illusions sent by the Devil? Or true prophecies inspired by God? Piedrola's judges, following canon law procedure, sought answers to these questions, whereas Piedrola, as he constructed his autobiography, sought to provide the proofs that would convince his inquisitors that his prophecies had been not only accurate but attributable to a divine source. Even then, his answers were somewhat ambiguous. Although eager to prove that the prophecies he uttered were eventually fulfilled, he was somewhat reticent to attribute them to God, preferring instead to call them, somewhat vaguely, "my warnings" and "my supernatural knowledge." Biblical prophets made it clear that they were mouthpieces of God, speaking directly for him when commanded (for example, Ezekiel 33:1–2: "And the word of the Lord came unto me, saying, 'O mortal, speak to your fellow countrymen and say to them . . .'"). Piedrola, cognizant, perhaps, of the punishments that awaited prophets who proved to be false, was more oblique, steadfastly refusing to represent himself as the chosen agent of God. However, the consequences he warned of—a world turned upside down—were comparable to those Malachi had predicted. He was therefore eager to inform the inquisitors that he had once provided don Juan of Austria, governor-general of the Netherlands, the "orders" he needed to achieve victory in the struggle against those who had rebelled against the Crown. Failure to accept these orders would, as he forewarned, necessarily lead to humiliation and defeat, with don Juan, the master, becoming a servant, and his servants, the inhabitants of the Low Countries, masters. As it turned out, the otherwise energetic don Juan was not in the Low Countries long enough to quell the revolt. Following his arrival there in 1576, don Juan contracted an illness that some identified as typhus and died precipitously, and rather prematurely, at the age of thirty-three.

By recounting this and similar incidents, Piedrola tried to convince the inquisitors that his predictions were valid, and his prophetic authority as well. Yet he was cautious, pointedly avoiding any direct reference to himself as the voice of God. Was this a discursive strategy purposely designed to please the inquisitors? Or was Piedrola oblivious to the finer points of prophesying? Whatever the precise answer, the inquisitors dismissed Piedrola's prophetic claims and instead interpreted his many predictions as evidence of little more than unbridled hubris. "Woe unto the vile prophets," Ezekiel warned, "that follow their own spirit and things they have not seen" (Ezek. 13:3). The inquisitors would have agreed.

Before his arrest in September 1587, Piedrola had enjoyed remarkable success as a prophet. His prophecies came to the attention of Philip II as early as 1577, when one of the king's secretaries presented the king with a copy of one of Piedrola's "letters" and described him as a "soldier who is said to be a good man ["hombre de bien"] and someone whom "Your Majesty already knows." To this Philip scribbled a brief reply: "I know him and I don't think he is very stable [asentado], although he is probably well-intentioned."[44] A year later, Philip's confessor, Fray Diego de Chaves, after having discussed some of Piedrola's prophecies with the king, expressed an interest in meeting with the prophet. Upon learning of the confessor's interest, Piedrola, impatient for recognition, did not wait for a formal invitation but showed up unexpectedly at the door of Chaves's lodgings in Madrid.[45]

Piedrola was soon asked to leave Madrid and headed for Italy, but he was back again in 1584. By this time Madrid had more than its share of prophets, several of whom roamed the streets ranting about the sins and proximate destruction of the ruling House of Austria. In comparison, Piedrola was somewhat more discreet. He avoided the streets, preferring instead to cultivate a following among important personages at the royal court. The times were bad: economic crisis at home and political difficulties abroad. Skepticism about the wisdom of Philip II's policies was growing, especially in the wake of Francis Drake's successful raid of the southern Spanish port of Cádiz in April 1587 and with resident foreign ambassadors beginning to report that Madrid was consumed by rumors of the kingdom's "defenselessness." In such a charged atmosphere, Piedrola's dire prophecies concerning Spain's future rang true. His following grew, and by the summer of 1587, on the eve of Philip II's decision to launch the "Invincible Armada" against England, several members of

44. British Library, London, Egerton ms. 1506, fols. 59–60, letter of 1 June 1577. The original reads, "Yo le conozco y no le tengo por muy asentado aunque de necesidad [?] hombre de bien."
45. Ibid., fol. 94, letter of 19 November 1578.

the Castilian Cortes, meeting in Madrid, recommended that Philip create the office of Royal Prophet and make Piedrola its first incumbent. Piedrola was at the peak of his popularity, but whatever his successes, his continuing prophecies about the imminent collapse of the House of Habsburg and the destruction of Spain created enemies as well. In late July the king ordered an inquiry into the activities of the "soldier-prophet," and a special committee was assembled to advise on the nature of his prophecies. Among those consulted was the famous theologian Fray Luis de León and the noted Jesuit scholar Pedro de Ribadeneira, both of whom expressed certain doubts about both the man and his message. On 1 August the committee made up its mind and, in a meeting held in the lodgings of Chaves, the royal confessor, recommended to the king that "the Holy Office ought to handle this business," because some of Piedrola's propositions were intolerable to "Our Holy Catholic faith."[46] A month later, with the king's acquiescence, the Inquisition stepped in, ordered Piedrola's arrest, and remanded him to its secret prisons in Toledo to await trial.

Once he arrived in Toledo, Piedrola's prophesying came to a halt, but the soldier-prophet continued to demonstrate remarkable mental agility. His first tactic, as noted above, was to justify his actions through a lengthy, somewhat rambling, and ultimately unconvincing autobiography. Angered by his arrest and possibly annoyed at the inquisitors' repeated questions about whether he was a prophet speaking with the voice of God, he openly declared that he was "a prophet, neither holy or false," and challenged the inquisitors' authority to judge him by referring both to the Old Testament and to the Fifth Lateran Council, which had remitted cases entailing both prophets and prophecies to the pope or his chosen representative.[47]

But then, somewhat unexpectedly, Piedrola switched gears. Perhaps acting on the advice of one of the Inquisition's attorneys, Piedrola, anxious to avoid serious punishment, devised a new story. This retreat and capitulation took several forms: apologies for inadvertent commission of heresy, obsequious praise of the Holy Office, and claims of insanity, an admissible defense. Piedrola now assured the inquisitors that the only voices to which he gave credence were those of good spirits speaking "about the glory of God and His Catholic church," while he rejected

46. For this inquiry, see Instituto de Valencia Don Juan (Madrid), Envio 89, fol. 186.

47. On this issue, see the comments of Pedro de Ribadeneira on the validity of Piedrola and his prophecies, as published in Patris Petri de Ribadeneira, "De Michaele de Piedrola et Veamonte Pseudopropheta . . .," *Monumenta historica societatis Iesu,* vol. 60 (Madrid: Editorial Ibérica, 1923), 415–23.

"anything else that might be against this . . . as a diabolical illusion." In the same breath, Piedrola renounced his prophetic gifts as an unwelcome burden. "I wish, if it please God, that I didn't have the gift [of prophecy] or that the Church and its ministers would order me not to have this ministry so that it would no longer torment me." Following this renunciation, Piedrola conceded that "prophets are obligated to appear before their superiors and the judges who call them. If I have said anything wrong, such as the prediction that the Inquisition has no jurisdiction over me . . . I have only said it out of zeal and with the best of intentions." Thus, in the space of a few minutes Piedrola dismantled the religious authority he had taken years to construct. He further announced his total obedience to the Church.

By the time of his last audience with the inquisitors, Piedrola's confession went even further. Now he presented himself as a contrite sinner and, still hoping to avoid serious punishment, announced himself as a complete fraud. Describing himself an "illiterate idiot" who was also "soft in the head," Piedrola claimed never to have had the gift of prophecy at all. "[A]ll of what I've said I've said according to human knowledge and then embellished with some sayings from the writings of the prophets." At other moments, he shifted the blame for his prophecies to "His Holiness, the Cardinals, the Inquisitors General, His Majesty, and the rest of His Majesty's servants, ministers, and counselors, both clerical and lay," who did not disabuse Piedrola of his error years ago, when they first had the opportunity.

After begging the tribunal to show mercy and pardon him because of his "noble blood" and good intentions, Piedrola made one last-ditch effort to circumvent the inquisitors' power over him and chose his own punishment: "I beg God, if He hears me, to make me my own judge as He did with Jonah when they asked Jonah what sentence he wanted to give himself when the fates turned against him. He said, 'Take me and throw me into the sea.' I say to you, take me and put me in an insane asylum for however long you think is necessary."

Surprisingly, the inquisitors agreed. With the help of several prominent Toledo architects, the inquisitors made an exhaustive search of convents and monasteries that might serve as a suitably isolated residence for Piedrola. Eventually they settled on the fortress of Guadamur, located in a small village six miles west of Toledo, where they imprisoned Piedrola for two years. In addition, they banished him from the court in Madrid for the remainder of his life.

In the view of Sotocameño, the Inquisition prosecutor, Piedrola's punishment—long-term isolation from human contact and permanent expulsion from Madrid—fit the soldier-prophet's crimes. He saw Piedrola as a "disturber of peace in the republic . . . seditious, . . . a con man . . . subject neither to His Holiness [the pope] nor to His Majesty in Earthly things." Sotocameño's invention of new categories of heresy tailored to fit Piedrola's crimes reflects the degree to which secular and sacred authority were connected in early modern Spain, and the degree to which Piedrola's prophecies threatened both. More directly related to a traditional notion of heresy, but still unique to Piedrola's case, was Sotocameño's accusation that the soldier-prophet was a "usurper of divine and celestial authority." Among the quotidian charges that Sotocameño leveled against the prisoner were illicit pacts with the Devil, necromancy (a form of sorcery), and "Lutheran" heresies (the catch-all inquisitorial term for Protestantism).

While Piedrola's visions themselves were provocative, he teetered on the edge of heresy with his claim that the clergy had no supervisory authority over his supernatural powers. Similarly, Piedrola's appropriation of religious rhetoric for political ends was not, in itself, incongruous, outwardly criminal, or even heretical. In fact, the Cortes's recommendation that he be considered for the office of Royal Prophet is in itself a good indication of the degree to which spiritual and political discourse intertwined. However, Piedrola's appropriation of religious rhetoric to threaten the lives and safety of the king and his family did constitute a crime—that of *lèse-majesté*—worthy of arrest and punishment.

Piedrola's visions challenged the authority of the Holy Office, the Church, and the monarchy. But Piedrola was no revolutionary. His aim was not to overturn the existing structures of power within Spanish society but rather to manipulate them in ways designed to help him worm his way into the uppermost echelons of the royal court. In view of his background—commoner, tinker, foot soldier—Piedrola could never have expected to enter that privileged world. To do so, he needed a new identity, one that could bring him the notoriety necessary to command the attention of the king and his councillors. It was in the persona of a prophet, "neither holy or false," that Piedrola found the identity he needed to make such a leap. But the soldier-prophet miscalculated, and in the end he barely escaped the fate—death on suspicion of sedition and heresy, permanent exile, or years of galley service—that awaited so many who harbored similar aspirations.

FURTHER READING

The best biography of King Philip II is Geoffrey Parker, *Philip II* (Chicago: Open Court, 1995), although it should be supplemented with his *Grand Strategy of Philip II* (Cambridge:

Cambridge University Press, 1998). Spain's Mediterranean policy can be approached through Fernand Braudel, *The Mediterranean and the Mediterranean World in the Age of Philip II* (New York: Harper and Row, 1972); as well as Andrew Hess, *The Forgotten Frontier: A History of the Sixteenth-Century Ibero-African Frontier* (Chicago: University of Chicago Press, 1978).

More information on politics and prophecy in early modern Spain can be found in Richard L. Kagan, *Lucrecia's Dreams: Politics and Prophecy in Sixteenth-Century Spain* (Berkeley: University of California Press, 1990). See also Ottavia Niccoli, *Prophecy and the People in Renaissance Italy,* trans. Lydia G. Cochrane (Princeton, NJ: Princeton University Press, 1990). On popular culture and religion in the early modern world, the classic text remains Keith Thomas, *Religion and the Decline of Magic* (Oxford: Oxford University Press, 1997).

CHAPTER FOUR

The Price of Conversion

Francisco de San Antonio and Mariana de los Reyes

Abram or Abraham Rubén was a Jew from Fez, a thriving North African city with a long-established Jewish community. In 1603, at the age of approximately twenty-five, Abram Rubén left his native land. He headed first to the eastern Mediterranean, where he worked as an itinerant rabbi, performing a variety of ritual practices for small groups of Jews with whom he came into contact. Rubén then traveled to the Netherlands, where he placed himself in the care of a Catholic priest and in 1616 he converted to Christianity, taking the baptismal name of Francisco de San Antonio. Soon, however, he moved to Lisbon, a city with a large community of conversos, many of whom were "secret Jews" lacking basic instruction in Hebrew and the tenets of Judaism. Once in contact with this community, San Antonio returned to his ancestral faith and resumed his work as a rabbi, but in doing so he attracted the attention of the Portuguese Inquisition, which, like its Spanish counterpart, prosecuted baptized Christians suspected of heresy. The Portuguese Inquisition arrested San Antonio—twice—for his "Judaizing" and subsequently banished him from Portugal for life.

In 1621 San Antonio was on his way out of Portugal when, in the town of Santarem, he befriended María González, a young Old Christian who had recently been abandoned by her husband. Together the couple left Santarem and headed for Madrid as Francisco hatched a creative money-making scheme. María would pretend to be an unmarried Jewish woman with a sincere desire to convert to Christianity and marry Francisco de San Antonio. Francisco would bring her case to the attention of Spain's zealously Catholic King Philip IV, who would then favor the couple with a royal gift. Everything went according to plan. María was baptized in a grand ceremony in the Royal Chapel of Madrid and took as her baptismal name Mariana de los Reyes ("of the kings"). Her wedding to Francisco de San Antonio took place that same day. For their contribution to the One True Faith, Philip IV rewarded the newlyweds with a pension in La Coruña, a city in northwestern Spain.

Francisco resumed work as a clandestine rabbi, this time in Madrid. Everything went as they had planned for another three years, more or less, until Francisco and Mariana both fell ill. Teetering on the brink of death in Madrid's Antón Martin Hospital, Mariana de los Reyes confessed her sins to the hospital's priest. Bailiffs from the Spanish Inquisition's Tribunal of Toledo arrested Francisco de San Antonio upon his release from the hospital, 22 November 1624. They arrested Mariana four months later. In keeping with inquisitorial practice, the two were tried separately, he on charges of Judaizing and she on charges of bigamy and taking the baptismal sacrament in vain. These are their cases.

Francisco de San Antonio

First Audience

In the morning audience of the Holy Office of the Inquisition of Toledo, on this, the twenty-third day of the month of November of the year sixteen hundred and twenty four, are present the Lord Inquisitors Gutierre Bernardo de Quieroz and don Fernando Oras.[1] The Lord Inquisitors ordered a man brought from jail from whom they received an oath in its proper form. In it, the man promised to tell the truth in this audience as in any others they may have with him until his case is resolved, and promised to keep secret all he may see and experience here.

Asked what his name is, where he was born, what his profession is, and how long it has been since he was arrested, he answered, "My name is Francisco de

1. This translation is based upon the original trial transcript in the Archivo Histórico Nacional, Madrid (AHN), Sección Inquisición (Inq.), Tribunal de Toledo, leg. 134, exp. 18.

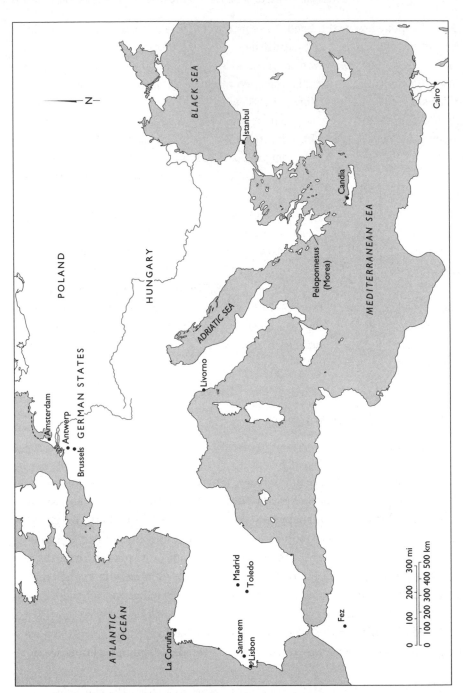

5. *Travels of Francisco de San Antonio*

San Antonio. I was born in Fez and I am of the Hebrew Nation.[2] I'm forty-five years old and a soldier. I've been in this Holy Office's secret jail since the afternoon of the twenty-second of this month, after lunch."

He gave his genealogy in the following fashion:

Parents: He said, "My father's name is Moysen.[3] He was a merchant and was born in Fez. . . . All my relatives are there except for one of my brothers, who's a soldier in Lisbon and whose name is Felipe Correa da Silba. He's married to a hosier, whose name I don't know." He later said, "Her name is María, but I don't know her last name, or whether or not they have children."

Wife and Children: He said, "I'm married to María de los Reyes,[4] who's from Santarem, Portugal. We got married three years ago in Madrid and have no children."

Asked if he was a baptized and confirmed Christian and if he confessed and partook of the Eucharist as the Holy Mother Church commands, he said, "I am a baptized Christian. I was baptized in 1616 in Amberes [Antwerp] by the bishop of that city. I'm not confirmed, but from [the day of my baptism] since, I hear Mass, confess, and partake of the Eucharist as the Holy Mother Church commands. My last confession was this year on All Saints' Day, in the hospital of the parish of Saint Martín. I made my confession to the rector, and in that hospital I received the holy sacrament of the Eucharist."

He crossed himself but he did not know how to bless himself. He said the four prayers,[5] the [Ten] Commandments, and the Articles [of the Faith], and said them well.

Asked if he knew how to read and write, and if he had studied at University, he said, "I know how to read and write, though I can't do either well in Castilian. In Hebrew, I can read and write well. I haven't studied at any university and I have no degrees at all."

Asked for his life story, he said, "I was born in Fez, where I lived with my parents until I was twenty-five. It was at that time that I learned to read and

2. In this scribe's transcription, both Francisco de San Antonio and the inquisitors refer to those who practice Judaism, openly or clandestinely, as "of the Hebrew Nation" or followers of "the Law of Moses."

3. Moysen: A Spanish variant of "Moses," a first name common among preexpulsion and diaspora Jews, though not among Christians.

4. Francisco, his wife, and the Inquisition scribe are inconsistent about his wife's first name. Originally María González, Francisco's wife took the baptismal name Mariana de los Reyes just before they were married. She is referred to in his trial and hers both as María and as Mariana.

5. To check up on prisoners' knowledge of Catholic doctrine, the inquisitors asked them to recite four prayers: the Our Father (the Lord's Prayer), the Hail Mary, the Salve Regina, and the Credo.

write in Hebrew. From there, I went to Livorno [?] in Italy, where I lived for three months. I went from there to Constantinople, where I stayed for three years, working as a merchant. From there, I went to the great [city of] Cairo, where I was for a few days and returned to Constantinople to purchase some merchandise. From there I went to Candia [Crete] with merchandise and from there to Canoto [?], which belongs to the Republic of Venice. From there, I went with some merchandise to the Morea in Turkey, and from there to the river in the land of Hungary [the Danube?]. From there, I went to Poland and from Poland to the land of the Germans *[Tudesca]* and from there to the city of Amsterdam, where I stayed for three to four years. It was there that I instructed the Portuguese in the Law of Moses, for which they paid me five hundred florins a year. But, after I had read the Bible in Hebrew a great deal, God enlightened me and I decided to get baptized and become Christian. Because of this decision, in 1616 I went to the city of Antwerp, where I was put in the care of Father don Pedro Fernando Paio [inquisitorial marginalia: he was baptized in 1616 in Antwerp], so that he might teach me the ways of our Holy Catholic Faith. . . .

"I was baptized by the bishop of the city, as I have said. Afterward, I went to Brussels with the friar who had taught me and then took up a post as a soldier, with an extra salary of four escudos, in the regiment commanded by Captain don Iñigo de Borja. After having been there for nine months, I set off for Spain in a Portuguese ship in the port of Aviana [?] that was going to Portugal.

Heading toward Madrid from the town of Santarem,[6] I ran into the afore-mentioned Mariana de los Reyes, my wife, who was traveling in the company of a student from Santarem, called Diego Noguera. We traveled together toward the port, and on the way, Maria de los Reyes told me how the student had taken her from her parents' home and how she did not dare go back[7] and how, if I would take her to Flanders with me, she would become my wife and would come with me. So I said yes.

"When we arrived at the port [Lisbon?], we stopped at an inn where we met

6. Francisco de San Antonio has omitted from his narration his two convictions by the Portuguese Inquisition and his sentence of expulsion, which set him en route to Madrid, via Santarem, a port located upstream from Lisbon on the banks of the Tagus River.

7. In Francisco's version of the story, which does not match his wife's, he presents Mariana as a "seduced" woman, too ashamed to return to her parents' home after having been deflowered by the student.

an important man, a *regidor*[8] of the town of Aveiro whose name I don't recall. María de los Reyes and I made marriage promises to each other in front of him.[9] A few hours later, we set out for to Madrid. There, I sent a note [to the king?] on behalf of my wife, explaining that she was my wife and a Hebrew. Even though I knew she was Christian, [I wrote that] she had a desire to be baptized. His Majesty forwarded the note to the Patriarch of the Indies,[10] who, believing that María de los Reyes was Hebrew, as I had written in the note, baptized her in the Royal Chapel on Saint James's Day[11] in the year 1621. As her baptismal name, they gave her Mariana [de los Reyes], since I had told them that she was previously known as Cafira.[12]

"I then returned, with my wife, to Flanders, having been married by the aforementioned Patriarch of the Indies who had baptized her. We were in Antwerp until 17 May 1621 [?],[13] at which point I repented for what I had done in Madrid, [that is,] for having baptized María de los Reyes when she was already [baptized]. I confessed this to my confessor, who took me to the papal nuncio in Brussels, who absolved me. After being absolved, I came back to Spain with my wife. As we left the port, we were robbed by a couple of Dutchmen who took all our papers, among them the absolution the Nuncio had given me the previous September [1622?].[14]

"About two years ago, my wife and I arrived in Madrid. I was sent to Galicia to serve as a soldier, but wasn't taken on, so I came back to Madrid, where I've been [until this point]. Last month, my wife and I became ill, and the Hospital

8. A municipal councillor.

9. Through such promises, otherwise known as a betrothal, Francisco and Mariana signaled their intention to be married in a church ceremony. Although such promises no longer constituted a valid and binding marriage after the Council of Trent, they constituted a contract that carried legal weight and in popular religious practice entitled the participants to cohabit and engage in sexual relations.

10. A title held by the royal chaplain.

11. Saint James was Spain's patron saint and is associated with Christian Spain's victory over Muslim Spain. That Mariana's baptism was held on Saint James' Day, 25 July, suggests that it was a major event.

12. The name the Inquisition notary transcribed as "Cafira" and "Cafera" (in Mariana's testimony) does not exist in Hebrew. However, it is similar to the Hebrew word for "female friend," or "girlfriend," "C[h]avera." Was Francisco de San Antonio taking a subtle jab at the Spanish monarchy when he told his female companion to say that her Hebrew name was "girlfriend"?

13. The chronology is confusing, either because of a recording error by the inquisitorial scribe or because San Antonio was inventing the account of the visit to Antwerp.

14. The chronology remains confusing. Francisco may have been telling the truth, or he may have tried to wriggle out of inquisitorial charges of heresy by explaining that the papal nuncio in Brussels had already absolved him of guilt for his heretical act but that proof of the absolution had been stolen.

of Antón Martín took us in. It was there, I think, that my wife confessed to the priest that she had been baptized twice.[15] When I left the hospital, the Holy Office arrested me on the fourteenth of this [month]."[16]

Asked if he knew or presumed the reason why he had been arrested and brought before this Holy Office,[17] he said, "I presume it's for having baptized my wife, María de los Reyes, saying she was Hebrew. I don't know any other reason why I've been arrested."

He was asked what made him, knowing that María de los Reyes was a Christian, baptized and born in Spain,[18] say that she was a Hebrew who wanted to be baptized. Did he think that one could be baptized twice or that such was necessary for baptism to be effective?[19] He said, "What made me do it was an understanding that they wouldn't want me to marry María de los Reyes, since she's a Spanish Christian and I'm a Hebrew.[20] It was because of this that María de los Reyes told me that she would pretend to be born a Hebrew and say she wanted to be baptized. I told her she should call herself "Cafira." I also did this because I am not at all learned in the Holy Catholic Faith and understood that it was not a sin to baptize María twice, as I have said, and as I confessed in Antwerp. My confessor, as I said, led me out of ignorance. I beg you to be merciful with me, since I did not sin out of malice."

He was told that this Holy Office was not accustomed to arresting people without having sufficient information that they had said, done, and committed, or seen or overheard others commit something that was, or appeared to be, an offense against God and against the Holy Roman Catholic Faith, or

15. Mariana de los Reyes may have thought she was dying and wanted to unburden her guilty conscience through confession. Mariana's testimony makes no mention of her illness or alleged confession.

16. Francisco de San Antonio had previously mentioned that he was jailed on the twenty-second. The two statements are not incompatible, as prisoners were not always imprisoned at the time they were arrested.

17. Prisoners were not informed of the charges against them. They were, instead, asked what they thought they had done wrong. This process often caused prisoners to incriminate themselves further, by confessing to crimes with which the inquisitors had not yet thought to charge them.

18. "Born in Spain": Mariana de los Reyes was born in what is now Portugal, but the inquisitors' statement is not inaccurate. The Crowns of Spain and Portugal were united from 1580 to 1659.

19. The inquisitors are trying to determine whether or not Francisco de San Antonio harbors the "Lutheran" (Protestant) heresy that baptism is not a sacrament, or that it is ineffective, or that, to be effective, it must be performed upon consenting adults, rather than infants.

20. Francisco de San Antonio is referring to laws that prohibit intermarriage between Jews and Christians, which had existed in Spain since the Middle Ages. His wife, however, later testifies that Francisco de San Antonio's motives were other, and that he, in fact, had her masquerade as a potential convert to Christianity in order to win a land grant from the king.

against the free and right exercise of the Holy Office. He thus should believe that, because of such information, he has been brought here. Because of this, and out of reverence for Our Lord and His glorious and blessed Mother, Our Lady the Virgin Mary, he is warned and charged to search his memory and to tell and confess the whole truth about whatever he feels guilty of or whatever he knows others to be guilty of, without hiding anything or protecting anyone, or giving false testimony. Instead, he should unburden his conscience as a Catholic Christian and save his soul, and his case will be resolved with all the brevity and mercy that Justice allows.

He said, "The same day the Holy Office arrested me, Luis de Fuentes, a scribe, . . . [asked if] I would give him Hebrew lessons, since he understood that I taught [Hebrew]. He also asked to borrow a Greek alphabet I had, so that if I ever went back to Flanders he could teach [Greek]. [When they arrested me,] they took the aforementioned alphabet, along with the papers they found in my trunk.[21] I have nothing more to say, and for everything I've done I ask for God's pardon and the mercy of this Holy Office."

Warned that he should think well [on what he had done] and tell the whole truth, he was ordered to return to jail. The bailiff took him away and he signed[22]

> This passed before me
> [signed] Francisco de San Antonio
> [signed] don Francisco Giron de Loaysa

Second Audience

In the morning audience of the Holy Office of the Inquisition of Toledo, on the twenty-seventh day of the month of November of sixteen hundred and twenty-four, are present the Lord Inquisitors Gutierre Bernardo de Quieroz and don Fernando de Oras. They ordered that Francisco de San Antonio be brought from his cell. The defendant, still under the oath he had sworn, was told to tell what he had remembered about these affairs.

He said, "I have nothing more to say than that which I have already said."

He was told that he knew how, in the previous audience, he was warned on

21. Inquisitors confiscated a Hebrew alphabet from Francisco de San Antonio, not a Greek alphabet. Was Francisco hoping that the inquisitors would not be able to tell the difference between Greek and (contraband) Hebrew?

22. The Inquisition read the prisoners' testimony back to them at the end of each audience and prisoners signed (or, if illiterate, had the notary sign for them) the transcript to indicate that it was a faithful rendering of their words.

behalf of God our Lord and His glorious and blessed Mother, Our Lady the Virgin Mary, to search his memory and unburden his conscience, telling the whole truth about everything he had done or said, or had seen done or said by other people, which might be an offense against God Our Lord and His Holy, Evangelical Catholic Law, which the Holy Mother Roman Catholic Church holds and teaches, or against the right and free exercise of the Holy Office, without hiding anything, or giving false testimony. For the second time, he is warned and charged with the same, to think on why he has been brought here and to tell the reasons as a Catholic and a Christian, and his case will be resolved with all the brevity and mercy that justice permits.

He said, "I have nothing more to say other than what I've said. This Holy Office may do [what it likes?], but as a baptized Christian, I have nothing more to say."

Warned to think well [on what he has done], he was ordered to go back to jail. The bailiff took him away. All of this passed before me.

[signed] Francisco Giron de Loaysa

[Francisco de San Antonio continued to insist, in his third audience with the inquisitors, that he had "nothing more to say." Witnesses against him, however, whom the Inquisition interviewed before his arrest, implicated Francisco in an expansive list of secret Jewish activities, which the prosecutor enumerated (below) in his official accusation against the defendant.]

I, Doctor Juan Rincón Romero,[23] prosecutor for this Holy Office, in the proper form, appear before your Lordships and, given the necessary [evidence], accuse Francisco de San Antonio of criminal behavior. Francisco de San Antonio, who is of the Hebrew Nation, who was born in Fez and lives in Madrid, and who is a prisoner in the secret jails of this Inquisition, and who is present here, is charged with heresy, perjury, apostasy, being an excommunicated maker and shielder of heretics. As a baptized Christian, commonly understood and reputed as such, enjoying the privileges and exemptions conceded to other faithful Catholics, putting aside the fear of God and fear for the salvation of his soul, causing scandal in the Christian religion and community, he has made himself into a heretic and become an apostate of our holy Catholic and Evangelical faith. He has gone over, instead, to the dead Law of Moses,

23. The prosecutor's statement is in the first person in the original Spanish.

the observance of which he has done and committed, and has resulted in the case against him. In particular:

1. On one occasion when the defendant came upon two other people discussing the Law of Moses, one of those people told him he had arrived at just the right moment, since that person had a great desire to learn about said Law. He said, "God must have brought you here at this good time. Since you know the sacrifices and ceremonies [of the Law], would you teach me?"[24] This person also asked [Francisco de San Antonio] to circumcise him, to which the defendant responded that he would do so soon enough. [The defendant then] asked the person where he was from, what his name was, and what his father's name was. When this person had told him where he was from and what his father's name was, this defendant replied that he knew [this person's father] well, and that he had wanted to speak with him but a dog had prevented it. By *dog* he meant one of the Christians who believes in the Evangelical Law.

2. Also, later on in this same conversation, the defendant said that [this person] should come over to his house so that they could go together to an out-of-the-way place, where they could hide from the world and where no one would notice them. He told this person to come after dark and that [in the meantime], this defendant would look for a little book of Hebrew letters that he could use to teach this person. [In exchange?] the defendant asked this person to bring him something he could use to put another person under his power.[25]

3. Also, a few days later, in the church where the defendant had gone with the aforementioned person and exchanged the book as he had offered, this defendant said that he had checked around and found that the wife of the person to whom he had rented the book for thirty reales a month still had a very important page of it. So the defendant went with this person to the house to get the page, and this person saw that it was a page with little letters written in columns on both sides. The defendant

---

24. Iberian communities of crypto-Jews, having lost contact with openly practicing Jewish communities, were often unable to perform some of the major Jewish rituals (such as circumcision) for fear of discovery. In addition, these communities tended to lose knowledge and full understanding of Jewish prayers and practices.

25. In medieval and early modern European culture, Jews and Jewish rituals were often associated with sorcery. This charge against Francisco may have arisen from his wife's testimony that Francisco had given her a potion to drink that made her do his bidding.

said that this was a [Hebrew] alphabet, and he said the names of the letters in Hebrew.[26] He said that the rest of the little writing was the ceremonies and sacrifices of the Law of Moses, and he made a few sounds, which this person swore he was unable to understand. I ask that this paper be shown to the defendant so that he may read it and tell us very specifically and carefully what it contains, explaining each thing, one at a time.

4. Also, after that, the defendant went with a certain person, persuading her to come to his house to take lessons with him on the third day [Wednesday?]. When she arrived, she saw another of his nation, with whom [the defendant] had been talking. After she and the defendant had left his house, they met another person of his nation. The defendant said that this man would give half his estate to see dead or strangled a certain person who is now a prisoner [of the Holy Office], implying that the prisoner knew that the man was Jewish and kept the Law of Moses and other things.

5. Also, having arrived at a certain place with this person, the defendant said some prayers in Hebrew and performed several ceremonies according to the Law of Moses so that this person would know what [prayers] to say upon eating, going to bed, and getting up. When this person told the defendant that he knew a prayer that was good for any time of day, the defendant asked him to say it. He said, "God is come and God will come. God made me and God will save me."[27] To this, the defendant responded, "God is come—what idiocy is this? God hasn't come, and the prayers one must say are as follows." The defendant then said the prayers in Hebrew. I ask that the defendant be made to tell what they contain.

6. Also, this defendant told a certain person that he was married to an Old Christian from Santarem to whom, in a few days, he would say, "My dear, go with God. Cursed be those who do not join my nation."[28]

---

26. The inquisitors found this document when they searched Francisco de San Antonio's house and inventoried his possessions. It is preserved in his case file.

27. This prayer rhymes in the original Spanish, "Dios es benido y dios bendrá, dios me hiço y dios me salbará." This is not a Jewish prayer. Rather, it incorporates two major themes that Christianity does not share with Judaism: the notion of salvation ("God will save me") and the idea that the First Coming has already occurred ("God is come"). This prayer may indicate the "corrupted" forms of worship that the secret Jewish communities adopted.

28. The fear that Jews would attempt to convert Christians by force was common in medieval and early modern Spanish culture and is recorded in the Expulsion Charter of 1492.

7. Also, on another occasion, the defendant said that in Madrid there were
    several Portuguese merchants,[29] and he named a few, who were trying
    very hard to free a certain person who was imprisoned [by the Holy
    Office], for fear that [the Holy Office] would discover the great network
    of Portuguese of the Nation [in Madrid].[30]

8. Also, speaking of the Ceremonies of the Law, the defendant mentioned
    that in one place he had lived they had given him so many florins to
    slaughter birds and cows and other animals that these people could eat,
    and that these people often went hungry because they didn't know how
    to slaughter animals according to the Laws of how to do it.[31]

9. Also, as a dogmatizing, apostatizing heretic, this defendant induced
    and persuaded a certain Catholic to pretend and dissemble that she was
    of the Hebrew Nation and that she wanted to convert to our Holy
    Catholic Faith and Evangelical Law. [He also persuaded her] that she
    should undergo public baptism, knowing that she was already bap-
    tized. He did all of this out of disrespect for the holy sacrament of
    baptism.

10. Also, he has committed more and less grave offenses similar to these, of
    keeping and observing the law of Moses, and he knows of several other
    people who have likewise done and committed the same.[32] As an en-
    abler and shielder of heretics, he has kept quiet and covered things up
    so that they do not attract the notice of the Holy Office. . . . I accuse him
    of having perjured himself in spite of having been warned several times
    to unburden his conscience and tell the truth. For these reasons I beg
    Your Lordships to . . . declare Francisco de San Antonio a heretical
    apostate, enabler and shielder of heretics. For his crimes may he incur a
    sentence of excommunication and other punishments and instructions
    as established by the Holy Office. May the Holy Office command that
    these be inflicted upon his body and goods, handing him over to the
    Justice of the Secular Arm in proper form,[33] applying what good he

29. Most of the crypto-Jews living in seventeenth-century Madrid were merchants of Portuguese
extraction.

30. The fear of informants among Madrid's crypto-Jewish community was ever present.

31. The shohet, or ritual slaughterer, is an esteemed figure in Jewish communities. It is his job to
slaughter animals in accordance with the Jewish rules of food preparation known as kashrut. Food
not prepared according to these rules is considered unfit to eat.

32. This "catchall clause" is formulaic.

33. The prosecutor is asking for the death penalty, a formulaic request included in nearly all cases
of "major heresies" such as Judaizing. Because the Holy Office did not have the power to execute those
it found guilty, inquisitors would "relax" (hand over) such prisoners to the authorities of the royal

may have to His Majesty's Royal Council, as a punishment to the prisoner and an example to others. . . . I also ask that . . . the prisoner be put to torture[34] and that torture be inflicted upon his body as many times as the law will allow, until the entire truth is known."

[signed] Doctor Juan Rincón

[Juan Rincón Romero convicted Francisco de San Antonio partly on the basis of witness testimony, partly on information gleaned from the Lisbon Tribunal, and partly on the basis of Mariana de los Reyes's testimony against him.

The Inquisition had originally arrested Mariana for her participation in the sham baptism, which the Inquisition understood as a violation of the baptismal sacrament. Mariana's life story, far shorter than her husband's, was less expertly told. Francisco, experienced in the inquisitors' ways, omitted incriminating details. Mariana narrated them with blithe ignorance of their ramifications.]

Mariana de los Reyes[35]

First Audience

On the sixth day of the month of May in the year sixteen hundred and twenty-five, [in the morning audience of the Inquisition of the Holy Office of Toledo?] is present the Lord Inquisitor Licenciado Gutierre Bernardo de Quieroz, who, for the time being, is alone. He commanded that a woman be brought from jail, from whom an oath was taken in the proper form. She swore and promised to tell the truth in this audience as in any others she may have until her case is resolved and she promised to keep secret [the contents of these proceedings]. She was asked the following questions:

Asked what her name is, where she is from, how old she is, and how long it has been since she was arrested, she said, "My name is Mariana de los Reyes,[36] wife of Francisco de San Antonio, who lives in Madrid. I'm from Santarem,

---

("secular") justice system, the "secular arm," who would then execute the prisoners by burning them at the stake.

34. The prosecutor's request for torture was formulaic and included in nearly all cases of "major heresies" such as Judaizing.

35. AHN: Inq., Tribunal de Toledo, leg. 25, exp. 18.

36. As Mariana de los Reyes was a native Portuguese speaker, it is possible that her audiences with the inquisitors were conducted in Portuguese even though the Inquisition's notary recorded them in Spanish.

Portugal, and I am more than twenty-six-years old.[37] I was arrested on the fifth of this month."

She gave her genealogy in the following fashion:

Parents: "Pedro González, muleteer, from Valença do Minho, Portugal. María Fernández, from the same place."

Paternal Grandparents: "I've never met them and don't know their names."

Maternal Grandparents: "I've never met them and don't know their names."

Father's Siblings: "I've never met them and don't know their names."

Mother's Siblings: "I had an uncle on my mother's side, but I don't know his name or where he lives."

Defendant's Siblings: "Manuel, Beatriz, Catalina, and Dominga, who are all of marriageable age and who were all born in Santarem."

Husband: "I'm married, as I've said, to Francisco de San Antonio. I married him about four or five years ago in the Royal Chapel in Madrid. Before that, about six years ago, I had been married in Santarem to Pedro Ribero, a field worker.[38] We were married in Santarem, in the Santisimo Milagro Church, by the priest, or prior, of that church, whose name I don't know. My godparents were Geronima Jorge, who is dead, and her husband, whose name I don't remember.[39] There were other people there, too, but I don't know their names.

"Pedro Ribero and I lived as man and wife for about two years, during which time we had a son we named Amaro. I don't know if he's alive, since I left him in Santarem with a young lady named doña Paula. At the end of those two years, Pedro Ribero left Santarem. I don't know where he went. About four months after that, Francisco de San Antonio came to the city and persuaded me to go with him to this Kingdom of Castile. So we went together to the town of Madrid.[40] In Madrid, I met a washerwoman called Beatriz, who's Portuguese and who lives next to Panaderos Street. She told me that doña Paula

---

37. Mariana's uncertainty about her exact age had less to with sensitivity about the aging process than with the fact that many individuals in early modern Europe did not keep regular track of the passage of time.

38. It was at this point in Mariana's testimony that the inquisitors realized she was a bigamist, in addition to being twice baptized. According to the notes at the front of her case file, which comprise the initial investigation and "qualification" of her case (approval for it to move forward), Mariana was originally arrested only for her participation in the sham baptism.

39. Iberian husbands and wives did not share the same last name. Both males and females tended to retain their patronymics throughout their lives.

40. Although Madrid was home to the Spanish monarchy, it was (and is), in legal parlance, not a city but a town.

had written to her to tell her that Pedro Ribero was dead.[41] Beatriz is an older woman who's tall and skinny and fair skinned.[42] She does her washing in the washing shed in Leganitos, here in town. When we heard this, Francisco de San Antonio asked me to marry him. Before we married, he persuaded me to say that I was also of the Hebrew Nation and that I wasn't baptized. And I did, since Francisco de San Antonio told me that [if I did] the king would give him money and, even better, a pension [*merced*]. They baptized me about three years ago, more or less, in the Royal Chapel. The baptism was done by the Patriarch and my sponsors were the Count of Castrillo and doña Ana María de Cordova, lady in waiting to Our Lady the Queen.[43] The Patriarch was also the one who joined my hand in marriage to Francisco de San Antonio.

"For being baptized a second time, having been baptized already, I ask your pardon and mercy. I did it because Francisco de San Antonio persuaded me and tricked me into doing it. I didn't realize that I was doing anything wrong, because Francisco de San Antonio gave me something to drink. [After I drank it,] it seemed to me, if he'd told me to jump into a well, I would have done it."[44]

Asked of what race and generation were her parents and the other relatives she'd mentioned, and if she, or any of them, had been a prisoner of, penanced by, or reconciled [to the Church] by the Holy Office of the Inquisition, she said, "Everyone I've mentioned is an Old Christian. None of them has been arrested or punished by the Holy Office, and neither have I."

Asked if she is Old Christian, baptized and confirmed, she said, "I hear Mass and confess and partake of the Eucharist at the times the Holy Mother Church demands. As I've said, I was baptized in Valença do Minho and was confirmed in Santarem, by the archbishop in the Santisimo Milagro Church, when I was about fourteen. After that, as I've said, I was baptized a second time in the Royal Chapel, and I hear Mass and confess and partake of the Eucharist. My last confession was in Madrid in the Church of San Martin, where I also partook of the Eucharist this past Easter."

41. Flimsy evidence of a first spouse's death is typical of testimony provided by individuals who were charged with bigamy. In order to permit remarriage, the Catholic church required substantive, generally documentary proof of the death of the first spouse.

42. This information may have been given in response to an unrecorded question regarding the physical description of Beatriz (presumably so that Inquisition investigators could find her and question her).

43. The count was Bernardino de Avellaneda y Delgadillo, a member of the powerful Council of State. Ana María de Cordova was his wife.

44. Mariana's accusation resonates with two medieval/early modern stereotypes: Jews as sorcerers and Jews as poisoners.

She crossed and blessed herself and said the four prayers. Asked if she knows how to read and write, she said, "No."

Asked for the story of her life, she said, "As I've said, I was born in Valença do Minho, where I lived with my parents for about two years until they took me to Santarem, where we [settled]. I was married to Pedro Ribero until about four or five years ago, when Francisco de San Antonio came to the city. I went with him to the town of Madrid, where we lived for about two years. From there, we went together to the castle in Brussels, where we stayed for about ten months. From there we came back to Madrid, where we stayed for about a year and a half. Since His Majesty gave us a pension in La Coruña,[45] we went to live there. We stayed in La Coruña for about four months, then came back to Madrid, where I've been ever since."

Asked if she knew, presumed, or suspected the reasons why she had been arrested and brought to the secret jails of the Holy Office, she said, "I presume I've been arrested because I was baptized a second time having already been baptized once before, as I've said, which I did as a weak and ignorant woman."

Asked if she knew that one could not be baptized a second time, having been baptized before, and that it was a sin to do so, she said, "I'm so stupid that when they baptized me the second time, I didn't realize what it meant. Now I know well that I've done wrong and erred. I beg you to have pity on me."

Asked if when she got married the second time, to Francisco de San Antonio, she told [the Patriarch] that she had been married to Pedro Ribero, she said, "I didn't tell him because he didn't ask."[46]

Asked if she knew that one could not marry two or more times, if one's first husband was still alive, she said, "I know this well, but since Beatriz told me that Pedro Ribero was dead, I didn't think it was necessary to make further inquiries. So I remarried, which I did as an ignorant woman of little learning. If I've erred in this, I ask for your pardon and mercy."

She was told that this Holy Office was not used to arresting people without

---

45. A port city located in northwestern Spain, in the former kingdom of Galicia.

46. Because the Patriarch believed Mariana de los Reyes to be Jewish, he may have skipped the protocols designed to ensure that marriages performed between Catholics were legitimate and valid. According to the Council of Trent, Catholic clergy asked to perform a marriage must make several inquiries about the couple, a process that lasted several weeks. The inquiries, which included questions about the couple's previous marital status, were meant to determine whether or not there were impediments to the marriage such as consanguinity (close blood ties between the potential spouses) or the existence of a previous legitimate marriage that had not been annulled or dissolved by the death of the other partner.

sufficient information that they had said, done, and committed, or seen others say or commit anything that could be against our Holy Catholic Church and Faith or against something our Holy Roman Catholic Church preaches, follows, and teaches, or against the right exercise of the Holy Office. Thus, she must believe that she has been arrested based on such information. Out of reverence for the Lord Our God and His glorious and blessed Mother Our Lady the Virgin Mary, she is warned and charged to search her memory and tell and confess the whole truth. She said:

"I have nothing more to say other than what I've said already."

She was warned, and ordered to go back to jail.

[signed] Licenciado B. de Quieros

Second Audience

In the morning audience of the Holy Office of the Inquisition of Toledo, present the Lord Inquisitors, Licenciados Gutierre Bernardo de Quieroz and don Francisco de Valde y Llano, bishop elect of Teruel, they ordered that Mariana de los Reyes be brought from jail. . . . They asked her what she had remembered about her case, [reminding her] that she was still under oath. She said, "I remember that when the aforementioned Francisco de San Antonio, my husband, told me to be baptized, he told me to say that my name was Cafera, so I did. When I was baptized, they gave me the name Mariana de los Reyes.[47] My real name is María González and, as I've said, I'm the daughter of Pedro González . . . who, because he's fair, was called Redbeard.

"I also remembered that Beatriz, the washerwoman who told me that my first husband was dead, works in the washing shed in Leganitos. I don't remember anything else."

[Mariana was warned a second time but insisted that she couldn't remember anything else. She was ordered to return to jail. The inquisitor's prosecutor, Juan Rincón Romero, who also prosecuted her husband's case, charged Mariana de los Reyes with disrespect for the marriage sacrament (bigamy), disrespect for the sacrament of baptism, and perjury. Her defense against those charges consisted largely of casting herself as a "weak and ignorant woman" and blaming her husband for having led her astray.]

---

47. "De los Reyes" literally means "of the Kings" or "of the Monarchs." Since Mariana was baptized with the king's blessing in the Royal Chapel, and sponsored by members of the royal court, the name was particularly fitting.

Defense

1. "Francisco de San Antonio persuaded me to be baptized and to marry him, even though I told him, 'Look, it's a sin to be baptized and to marry twice, since my first husband is still alive.' Francisco de San Antonio told me to be quiet, that [the second marriage] didn't matter at all because of the baptism. . . . [I did this] as a fragile and ignorant woman who believes too easily what she's told.

2. "Francisco de San Antonio told me that with the baptism and the marriage, the king would give us a reward and a benefice, as he had done for others, and that we would go to Flanders, where no one would know [what we had done]. With that, Francisco de San Antonio tricked me. As a weak and helpless woman I gave in and did what he persuaded me to do. For it, I am very repentant. I ask you to be merciful with me."

[The Tribunal of Toledo confirmed its suspicion that Mariana was a bigamist by writing to the Lisbon tribunal of the Inquisition to have it inquire about her marital status and the status of her husband. A return letter explained, in Portuguese, that Mariana's husband was alive and well and that her first marriage was indeed still valid. In its letter the Lisbon tribunal enclosed additional information on Francisco de San Antonio, informing the tribunal of Toledo that Francisco had been arrested in Lisbon twice before for Judaizing, the first time receiving a light sentence of appearance in an *auto de fe* and the second time being banished from Portugal.

Francisco responded in his own defense that he had "never intended to stray from our Holy Faith" and that his second arrest by the Portuguese Inquisition had been on trumped-up charges. Francisco insisted that he was a good Christian whose only deviations from orthodox Catholicism were made out of ignorance, the fault of his confessor, or under the influence of his wife, whom he blamed for instigating the baptismal scandal.

Francisco's Lisbon arrests made him a *relapso* (repeat offender), who could, according to inquisitorial law, have been "relaxed to the secular arm of justice." Instead, the tribunal gave him six years of galley slavery, which was a de facto death sentence, one more protracted than burning at the stake.

The inquisitors found Mariana de los Reyes guilty of all charges against her and sentenced her to appear in an *auto de fe,* abjure *de levi,* receive two hundred lashes, be shamed "along the customary streets," and be banished from Madrid, Toledo, and their environs for eight years. Although Spanish secular law did recognize women as the "weaker sex" and placed women under the legal guardianship of their husbands, the Catholic Church and the Spanish Inquisition held all Catholics, male and female, accountable for their own heresies. The question of the legitimacy of her marriage to Francisco de San Antonio was remitted to the ecclesiastical courts.]

At the moment when Francisco de San Antonio and Mariana de los Reyes chose to settle in Madrid, the town was experiencing dramatic change. As home to the royal court, Madrid was caught up in the euphoria that accompanied Philip IV's accession to the monarchy in March 1621. Its population, which already exceeded one hundred thousand, was growing rapidly as men and women from all parts of the monarchy, drawn by the allure of riches promised by the royal court, immigrated there in search of a job, royal patronage, or both. The decision of Francisco and Mariana to join this tide is therefore not surprising. But questions remain. Why would a Jew choose to settle in Madrid, so close to the center of royal power and an inquisitorial tribunal? And why would the Spanish monarchy let him in?

The answers to these questions can partly be attributed to the dramatic political changes that occurred at the very start of the reign of Philip IV (1621–65). The new monarch, ably assisted by his energetic confidant and minister, the count-duke of Olivares, had embarked upon an ambitious program of reform designed to revitalize the kingdom's economy, streamline its governance, and bolster the monarchy's reputation, both at home and abroad. Educational and social reform was also on the agenda, and while many of the monarch's proposed changes met stiff resistance, none was more controversial than his decision to alter the Crown's long-standing policy toward conversos.

For more than a century, Spain's Habsburg monarchs had backed every effort to exclude conversos from the mainstream of Spanish society. Toward this end, the monarchy gave the Inquisition unwavering support and abetted the spread of "blood purity" statutes designed to keep conversos out of cathedral chapters, religious orders, universities, and a variety of public offices. These statutes required individuals seeking entry to these and other institutions to submit both written and oral proofs attesting to their Old Christian lineage for several generations. From the start there were those, churchmen included, who questioned the legitimacy and efficacy of these statutes, and by the seventeenth century many recognized that the requirements had done more harm than good. Contemporaries also recognized that the proofs required by the statutes had resulted in countless lies, perjuries, and slanders, not to mention personal distress. At one point, even the inquisitor general questioned the wisdom of this policy, and in 1618, during the proceedings of the Castilian Cortes gathered in Madrid, several representatives proposed the relaxation of the entire "blood purity" system.

Initially, the monarchy was reluctant to embrace such proposals, but Philip III (1598–1621), notwithstanding his controversial order expelling the moriscos from Spain in 1609 (see chapter 5), proved far more flexible on the issue of both Jews and conversos than any of his predecessors. He even reversed the century-long policy of excluding all Jews from Spain when, starting around 1603, he granted residence permits to Moroccan Jews of Sephardic origin who, fleeing North Africa, brought with them strategic information of vital interest to the Spanish Crown. The Inquisition looked askance at this new policy, as it provided an opportunity for several Jews, known as *judíos de permiso* (licensed Jews) to take up residence in Madrid.[48]

The reign of Philip III also marked the beginnings of change in the monarchy's converso policy. At the start of the seventeenth century, Spain's economy, practically exhausted after generations of almost continuous warfare, slipped into a period of protracted decline, and the monarchy, teetering on the edge of financial ruin, was desperate to tap new sources of revenue. One source that looked especially promising was Lisbon's wealthy community of converso merchants, many of whom traced their origins to Spain. Following King Philip II's annexation of Portugal (1580–82), these New Christians were legally vassals of the Spanish Crown, and many were anxious to repatriate. They were also eager to obtain a share of Spain's lucrative trade with the Indies. Some, taking advantage of a law, promulgated in November 1492, that allowed for the repatriation of former Jews who had converted to Christianity, found their way to Seville and established themselves there as merchants. More arrived in 1604 when, in exchange for a large gift of money, Philip III persuaded the pope to issue a general pardon allowing New Christians to live and trade in other cities and, starting in 1606, the Indies as well.[49] Did other possibilities exist for tapping the expertise and capital of these New Christians for the benefit of the Crown? One who thought so was Martín González de Cellorigo, a one-time Inquisi-

---

48. For more on these changes in the Crown's converso policy and the *judíos de permiso,* see Mercedes García-Arenal and Gerard Wiegers, *Man of Three Worlds: Samuel Pallache, A Moroccan Jew in Catholic and Protestant Europe,* trans. Martin Beagles (Baltimore: Johns Hopkins University Press, 2003).

49. See Antonio Domínguez Ortiz, *Política y hacienda de Felipe IV* (Madrid: Editorial del Derecho Financiero, 1960), 128.

tion lawyer who, in 1619, advocated that the Crown soften its policy toward the conversos in order to take advantage of their wealth.

Such arguments did not win universal approval, but the count-duke of Olivares, Philip IV's closest adviser, embraced them as his own. With assistance from a certain Jacob Cansino, a Jew from Oran who had received special royal license to journey to Madrid, Olivares learned about the international workings of Portugal's conversos, and he granted them immunity from inquisitorial harassment in an effort to persuade them to settle in Madrid. By August 1626 Olivares had even managed to put together a consortium of wealthy Portuguese conversos who had agreed to lend the king four hundred thousand escudos.[50] This move proved unpopular, but Olivares, justifying his actions on emergency grounds, was determined to marshal the resources of these conversos for the benefit of the Crown. By the mid-1620s, therefore, a small group of Portuguese converso businessman had converged on Madrid. Preceding them, however, were other, less prosperous conversos who were equally anxious to return to Spain and profit from the king's largesse.

Francisco de San Antonio

Among these conversos was Francisco de San Antonio. Lacking the financial resources to be a moneylender for the Crown, he arrived in the Spanish capital without the protection that Olivares offered to his wealthier brethren. But San Antonio, as his autobiography suggests, was an adventurer and something of a risk-taker as well. Born around 1578 in Fez, in what is now Morocco, as a child Abram Rubén formed part of that city's large and flourishing community of Jews. Some Jews in this community traced their roots back to the Middle Ages; others, Rubén's family presumably among them, were of Sephardic origin and had arrived in Fez following their expulsion from Spain in 1492. At the end of the sixteenth century, Morocco entered a prolonged period of civil war and political upheaval that sparked the emigration of many of these "Barbary Jews," many of whom, eager to return to their Iberian roots, settled in Portugal and converted, at least nominally.

Abram Rubén formed part of this diaspora. Like Luis de la Ysla before him (see chapter 1), Rubén initially found his way to Italy and then to the Ottoman Empire, where, by his own confession, he eked out a living as a merchant as well as an

50. For more on these negotiations, see ibid., 130–31; and James C. Boyajian, *Portuguese Bankers at the Court of Spain, 1626–1650* (New Brunswick, NJ: Rutgers University Press, 1983); and John H. Elliott, *The Count-Duke of Olivares: A Statesman in an Age of Decline* (New Haven, CT: Yale University Press, 1986), 117–20, 301–4.

itinerant rabbi, teaching the "Law of Moses" to Portuguese Jews he met along the way. Separated from many of their ancient traditions, some of these Jews had even forgotten Jewish dietary laws and paid Rubén fifty florins to become their ritual slaughterer so that "these people could eat, and . . . these people often went hungry because they didn't know how to slaughter animals according to the Laws of how to do it."

In 1616 Rubén traveled to Flanders, converted to Christianity, and adopted the name Francisco de San Antonio. He then became a soldier and was en route to Italy when he decided to stay in Portugal. There he presumably made contact with other Barbary Jews and resumed his work as a rabbi. The Lisbon tribunal of the Inquisition first became suspicious of San Antonio's activities in December 1617. He was arrested and apparently tortured the following year, but released, at which point he resumed his work as a rabbi. Two years later, however, the Inquisition again arrested San Antonio on charges of Judaizing and sentenced him to appear at the *auto de fe* held in Lisbon on 5 April 1620. The tribunal's records further indicate that San Antonio appeared in another *auto* held on 2 June 1621. On this occasion the punishment was exile, but on his way out of the kingdom, in the town of Santerem, San Antonio, age forty-two or forty-three, met María González. This peasant girl was almost half his age, but having been recently abandoned by her husband, she was apparently eager to escape her native town. Evidently taken with San Antonio's physique—he is described at one point as a man with "pale skin, blond hair, red beard and a 'good body' "[51]—she joined up with him. Soon they became engaged to be married and, apparently aware of the Spanish monarch's changing attitude toward conversos, headed for Madrid.

Along the way to the Spanish capital, San Antonio devised a scheme centered on the sacrament of baptism, which aimed at using this ritual to turn a handsome profit. He convinced his wife to pretend that she was a Jew eager for conversion, a scenario designed to ease their way into Spanish society. The monarchy took the bait and arranged for a high-profile baptism performed in the chapel of the royal palace in a special ceremony on 25 July 1621—Saint James's Day, which was in honor of Spain's patron saint!—that was presided over by the king and queen and Diego de Guzmán, the royal chaplain, who also held the title of Patriarch of the Indies. The ceremony took place at 6 P.M., with the count of Castrillo, the king's majordomo, and his wife, Ana María de Córdoba, serving as Francisco's and Mariana's sponsors, and is tersely

---

51. See AHN: Inq., Tribunal de Toledo, leg. 134, exp. 18, fols. 9v, 15, for details about San Antonio's dealings with the Inquisition in Lisbon as well as his physique.

recorded in the chapel's registers as follows: "I, Diego de Guzmán, royal chaplain . . . baptized and married Francisco de San Antonio, of the Hebrew nation, with a red beard, thin face with a scar over his right eyebrow and a mole next to his ear, and Mariana de los Reyes, of the Hebrew nation, pale and blond, and of medium stature."[52] Once the ceremony was over, Philip IV, eager to celebrate this high-profile conversion and marriage, rewarded San Antonio with a land grant and a small pension.

San Antonio's scheme was such that it might easily win him a place in the rogue's gallery of early modern Europe. Clearly, it served to precipitate his arrest by the Holy Office in November 1624, but his trial transcript suggests that his judges were less interested in his fraudulent baptism than in his Judaizing, and especially his relations with the Portuguese New Christian community then forming in Madrid. In comparison with relapsing from the Faith into the Law of Moses, conning the king of Spain was but a minor offense.

San Antonio's trial is of particular importance because of the window it provides into the inner workings of the still somewhat nebulous world of Madrid's emergent community of Portuguese conversos. Many in Madrid, the clergy in particular, harbored suspicions about the orthodoxy of these New Christians, and testimony gathered in the course of San Antonio's trial suggests that their suspicions were not totally unfounded. The inquisitors learned, for example, that some of these conversos, San Antonio among them, gathered regularly in the courtyard of the royal palace to gossip, to exchange useful bits of information, and above all, to warn their brethren about the precariousness of their situation in Madrid. As one of these New Christians, Juan Alvarez, was alleged to remark, "the dogs of the Inquisition would like to burn us alive." Alvarez further warned his brethren to be careful about what they said and did because "even the plants and stones are listening."[53]

Despite such dangers, San Antonio, following his return from Flanders, did not hesitate to resume his work as a rabbi tending to this community's spiritual needs. Using his converso status as a cover, San Antonio provided these "Portuguese merchants" a variety of services that ranged from circumcisions to the ritual (kosher) slaughter of "birds and cows and other animals." Tomás Lorenzo, a cloth merchant, even claimed that San Antonio taught him "the [kosher] way of slaughtering cattle by beheading them." In addition, the "gran rabi" as San Antonio was called, offered

52. Ibid., fol. 15.
53. Ibid., fol. 9v.

these New Christians basic instruction in Hebrew, for which purpose he employed a special primer that he had evidently brought with him from Portugal. The trial further suggested that some members of this community were so ignorant of traditional Hebrew rites and practices that San Antonio appeared as a heaven-sent gift. "God must have brought you here at this good time," one New Christian reportedly told San Antonio; "since you know the sacrifices and ceremonies [of the Law], would you teach me?" San Antonio proved a willing and able teacher and for about two or three years earned a living in Madrid by tending to the spiritual and religious needs of this community. However, the trial failed to turn up information about the names of many of his clients, largely because San Antonio managed to keep their names secret, presumably to protect them from the Inquisition.

San Antonio's efforts to withhold certain key bits of information from his inquisitors highlights the kind of judicial strategy he employed. A veteran of several earlier inquisitorial inquiries, San Antonio aimed to reveal as little as possible about his Judaizing and the identities of his friends and associates. Instead he directed the judges' attention to what he surely knew was the lesser crime of the sham baptism he had engineered in the royal chapel. He therefore readily confessed to the heresy of "taking the sacrament of baptism in vain," but in doing so, he sought to use his status as a recent convert to his own advantage by explaining that "I am not at all learned in the Holy Catholic Faith and understood that it was not a sin to baptize María twice." His realization that this was an error came only later, at which point, like a penitent Christian, he confessed his sin to the papal nuncio in Brussels, who absolved him and "led me out of ignorance." (The nuncio's certificate of absolution had, conveniently, been stolen by "a couple of Dutchmen" just before San Antonio returned to Madrid.) He had sinned, San Antonio claimed, not out of malice but out of ignorance, and he pleaded for mercy.

The inquisitors expressed little interest in this defense. Rather, they focused on San Antonio's rabbinical activities, evidently with an eye toward unmasking the true beliefs of the Portuguese New Christians residing in Madrid. The papal nuncio in Madrid had already expressed doubts about the orthodoxy of these *marranos* (or *pigs*, a derogatory term referring to conversos), and in general most inquisitors were opposed to the Crown's policy of allowing Portuguese conversos (let alone Jews!) to settle in Madrid. Therefore, any information they managed to extract from San Antonio could be used to help galvanize opposition to Olivares's pro-converso policy. That policy, alarmingly in the view of most churchmen, smacked of the "reason of state" doctrines associated with the sixteenth-century Florentine thinker

Machiavelli, who had advised princes to implement policies designed to enhance their power and prerogatives and, equally importantly, to do so without regard to moral and religious concerns.

Lurking in the background of San Antonio's trial, therefore, was the Inquisition's determination to reverse the monarchy's policy of allowing Portuguese New Christians to reside at the Spanish court. Olivares sought to grant these conversos full access to Spanish society and, in doing so, marshal their financial resources for the benefit of the Crown, but this policy ran contrary to the popular notions of conversos as fundamentally untrustworthy and unreliable. Xenophobia also played its part. Castilians in the 1620s feared that Portuguese merchants and bankers were rapidly gaining a stranglehold on royal finances and enriching themselves in the process. Resentments of this sort surfaced soon after Portuguese New Christians made their first appearance in Madrid, but Olivares managed to hold them in check, thanks in part to the support of Inquisitor General Andrés Pacheco, a Jesuit who was sympathetic to the idea that conversos, Portuguese or otherwise, merited full acceptance into Spanish society. By the early 1630s, however, opposition to this policy had mushroomed to the point where Olivares finally had to give way. A new, tougher inquisitor general, Antonio de Sotomayor, was appointed following the death of Pacheco in 1631, and starting almost immediately, the Holy Office targeted the Portuguese New Christians residing in Madrid, arresting many of its most prominent members. These persecutions culminated in the great *auto de fe* staged in Madrid's Plaza Mayor in 1632 that sentenced seventeen *judaizantes*, all Portuguese, to be burned at the stake. This *auto*, personally attended by both Olivares and the king, represented the symbolic end of the Crown's pro-converso policy and, concomitantly, the triumph of a particular kind of Castilian nationalism in which anti-Machiavellianism, popular xenophobia, and anti-Semitism all intertwined.

Independently of the doctrinal issues involved, these issues figured in the trial of San Antonio and, to a lesser degree, that of his wife. Starting in 1621 Olivares had managed to influence the general drift of inquisitorial policy, and with help of Andrés Pacheco, the inquisitor general, he persuaded members of the Suprema to support his views on conversos. But Olivares was unable to control the general shift of public opinion, let alone the inquisitorial rank and file, many of whom were staunchly opposed to his pro-converso policy and determined to persecute conversos whenever and wherever they could. In this respect, the Holy Office expressed divergent views on conversos, and these internal divisions—largely unnoticed by many historians who have written about the Inquisition—help to explain why Francisco de San

Antonio was arrested on charges of heresy in 1624, whereas a privileged coterie of prominent New Christian bankers enjoyed both monarchical protection and support.

In the course of the ensuing trial, the judges who confronted San Antonio saw him as nothing less than a pernicious and dangerous Judaizer: a baptized Christian who secretly fomented Jewish heresy among communities of converts. The prosecutor Juan Rincón Romero stated the Inquisition's position when he asserted that San Antonio was a "maker and shielder of heretics," a "dogmatizing, apostatizing heretic" who, in addition to being a heretic himself, had instructed conversos in the tenets of Judaism, performed circumcisions, and prepared food according to Jewish dietary laws. Rincón Romero also accused San Antonio of a series of "stereotypically Jewish" crimes typical of those commonly attributed to Jews in the Middle Ages. These included charges of sorcery (using potions to "put another person under his power" and thus having "induced and persuaded" Mariana to undergo a second baptism), insulting Christians by calling them "dogs," forcibly converting Old Christians to Judaism (a reference to the conversion of his wife, Mariana), and conspiring with other secret Jews to subvert the Inquisition.

As San Antonio awaited his third and final audience, the Inquisition learned about his previous arrests in Lisbon. Witnesses had also provided them with a detailed list of his rabbinical services, many of which appeared in the final list of charges the prosecutor drew up against him, and further information was obtained from the testimony of his wife, Mariana de los Reyes. Once the prosecutor had made his formal accusation, Francisco showed contrition and confessed fully and openly to the charges he had just heard, undoubtedly cognizant that public confession of guilt was the key to avoid the death sentence. The Inquisition, in its own words, aimed to "reconcile" repentant prisoners with the Church and consequently framed its punishments as spiritual and physical penance designed to purify the prisoner's soul. Unrepentant or "relapsed" (recidivist) heretics were usually burned at the stake, whereas those who proved contrite generally managed to get off with punishment of a lesser sort. Including the two trials in Lisbon, this was Francisco's third or fourth appearance before the Holy Office, and his apparent familiarity with its doctrines and procedures probably saved his life. However, he did wind up as galley slave, which was practically a death sentence in its own right and a punishment far worse than he probably expected. His previous experience with the Inquisition in Lisbon had seemingly taught him that the Inquisition was likely to treat Judaizers relatively leniently, and he is probably assumed that, in the event he was arrested on charges of Judaizing in Madrid, the Inquisition there would do the same. If such was his thinking, San Antonio had clearly misjudged the intensity of anti-converso, anti-Portuguese sentiment at the Spanish court.

So what motivated San Antonio to go to Madrid without the kind of personal protection that Olivares offered to wealthy New Christians? Why would he make a show of publicly converting to Catholicism but then continue to work as a secret rabbi? Did he have some kind of particular religious calling, a burning desire to help New Christians return to or at least maintain interest in and acknowledge their ancestral faith? Or did he simply misjudge the precariousness of his situation in the Spanish capital? Whatever the precise calculus San Antonio employed, some combination of faith, profiteering, and a perverse sense of adventure seemingly led him to leave his home in Morocco to become a traveling merchant, a soldier, and a con man who endeavored to defraud the king of Spain. Above all, San Antonio was a rabbi, a teacher whose knowledge of the basic precepts of Judaism, while not especially remarkable, represented a scarce commodity within the New Christian communities of Lisbon and Madrid. Among his fellow conversos, such knowledge brought him a small income in addition to a modicum of social prestige, but it also attracted the attention of the Holy Office and the inquisitorial prisons in Toledo, and it eventually led to six somewhat grizzly years as a galley slave in the Spanish fleet.

María González, aka Mariana de los Reyes

The circumstances leading to Mariana de los Reyes's arrest were no less remarkable. Christened María González, she was the eldest in an Old Christian family of five sisters born to Pedro González, a muleteer, and María Fernández, living in Santarem, a small Portuguese town just north of Lisbon. Around 1619, at the age of twenty, María married Pedro de Ribero, a field hand, also living in Santarem. Soon she was pregnant, but for reasons that María never adequately explained in her testimony, Pedro abandoned her shortly after the birth of their child, a boy. It was at this crucial juncture that Francisco de San Antonio, a North African converso running from the Portuguese Inquisition, came into her life. Leaving her child in the care of a woman named doña Isabel, presumably a relative, María left with Francisco en route to Madrid. Within a matter of weeks, María González became Mariana de los Reyes, a twice-baptized bigamist married to a converted Jew. A few years later she found herself, along with her new husband, in the secret prisons of the Toledo Inquisition.

The fragmentary life of Mariana de los Reyes recounted to the inquisitors during her first audience was short on detail and touched on few of the key issues in her case. Yet her other testimony reveals that she was prepared to manipulate popular stereotypes of women and of Jews to her own advantage. In addition, by readily admitting to a series of lesser of crimes, bigamy among them, she managed to sidestep the issue of her husband's Judaizing and thus avoid possible charges of guilt by association.

As it turned out, Judaizing played only a minor role in Mariana's trial, and in general the Inquisition's prosecutor, Juan Rincón Romero, did not press her on this issue. As he saw it, Mariana had violated two of the central pillars of Roman Catholic doctrine: the sacrament of baptism and the sacrament of marriage. At the Council of Trent (1546–63), the special assembly that was gathered to address the challenges posed by the Protestant Reformation to orthodox Christian belief, the Roman Catholic Church had reaffirmed the sanctity of these and other sacraments. That of marriage was of particular importance, and in the course of the late sixteenth century, the Church, partly in an effort to prevent clandestine unions and other forms of cohabitation, upheld the notion of marriage as a permanent, binding, and sacred union that could only be administered by a priest. As if to emphasize the point, bigamy, tantamount to a "violation of the marriage sacrament," became a new object of inquisitorial prosecution in the late sixteenth century. By the 1580s, for example, bigamy accounted for approximately 10 percent of arrests by the Inquisition's Tribunal of Toledo. Nonetheless, those who had committed this sin tended to get off rather lightly, generally with no more than an *abjuración de levi* and a minimal punishment.[54]

In contrast with her husband, Mariana apparently did not realize that the story of her life was an opportunity to incriminate herself further. Mariana took the bait and included in her autobiography her marriage to Pedro Ribero. She explained her situation simply, in the second sentence of the one-paragraph version of her life story. "I was married to Pedro Ribero until about four or five years ago, when Francisco de San Antonio came to the city." Later, when questioned further about her second marriage, her defense was straightforward but weak: a claim to have heard rumors of her first husband's death. It proved ineffective, as a letter from a priest in Santarem explained to the inquisitors that Pedro Ribero was still alive. This was all the proof the judges needed to ascertain Mariana's guilt. Mariana may not have been as familiar with inquisitorial procedures as her husband was, but he had undoubtedly

54. The kinds and number of cases tried by this tribunal are the subject of Jean-Pierre Dedieu, *L'administration de la foi: L'Inquisition du Tolède, XVIe–XVIIIe siècle* (Madrid: Casa de Velázquez, 1989).

briefed her on what he knew about the Holy Office during his previous arrests. She was therefore probably aware that a confession of violating the baptismal sacrament, a relatively minor sin, might allow her to avoid punishment for a more serious one.

The charge of "taking the sacrament of baptism in vain" was unusual. Catholic doctrine maintained that the seal of baptism, like the sacrament of marriage, was permanent and everlasting. Thus any attempt to renew it for religious purposes smacked of heresy as it suggested that the efficacy of the original baptism was in doubt. Equally problematical was Mariana's attempt to use baptism for material gain, in this case, a land grant from the king. Confined in the San Martín Hospital, Mariana had told a priest about her second (and illegal) baptism, and she must have known that it was the reason for her arrest. There was no reason, therefore, to obfuscate and risk even more intensive inquisitorial inquiry into her activities in Madrid. Contrition represented a better tactic, and so, without any prompting, Mariana openly confessed to "having been baptized a second time," and in doing so she begged her inquisitors for their "pardon and mercy."

Like her husband, therefore, Mariana confessed to minor sins while pleading ignorance with regard to others. Another part of her trial strategy was to capitalize on stereotypical gender roles and to deploy what might be called the "weak woman defense." The legal, medical, religious, and political culture of early modern Iberia (indeed, all of Europe) deemed women to be "naturally" ignorant and therefore incapable of understanding complex doctrinal and theological issues.[55] Women were also expected to be subservient and generally expected to do what men asked them to do. Capitalizing on such values, Mariana explained that she finally understood that she had "done wrong and erred" by allowing herself to be baptized a second time, but she quickly added that she was "a weak and ignorant woman," too "stupid" to realize that the second baptism was heretical. She further insisted that she had remarried without verifying rumors of her first husband's death because she was an "ignorant woman of little learning."

Stereotypes of another sort also figured in Mariana's other defensive tactic: the "victim of Jewish sorcery" defense. Since the Middle Ages, Jews had frequently been depicted as malevolent magicians who utilized potions, powders, and other concoctions to befuddle, confuse, and, in certain instances, to maim and even to murder Christians. As noted earlier, the notion of the Jewish sorcerer figured in the list of charges that Rincón Romero drew up against Francisco de San Antonio. It was also

---

55. Early modern ideas about the fragile nature of womanhood are explored in Ian Maclean, *The Renaissance Notion of Women* (Cambridge: Cambridge University Press, 1983).

one that Mariana used in her own defense. San Antonio, she confessed, "persuaded and tricked" her into the second baptism by means of a magic potion. "I didn't realize that I was doing anything wrong [at the second baptism], because Francisco de San Antonio gave me something to drink. [After I drank it,] it seemed to me, if he'd told me to jump into a well, I would have done it." Mariana's strategy was imaginative, but it did not work. The inquisitors, though generally receptive to the idea that Jews by their nature were out to trick Christians whenever they could, ultimately judged Mariana guilty of both charges that the prosecutor Rincón had levied against her: bigamy and violation of the sacrament of baptism. Stereotypes of Jews might be useful in helping to incriminate conversos, but in this case at least, they did little to get Old Christians off the hook.

Could Francisco and Mariana's get-rich-quick scheme have possibly worked? Probably not. Mariana's illness and hospital-bed confession helps to explain the timing of their arrests, but by November 1624 the Inquisition was already on the lookout for *judaizantes* among the growing contingent of Portuguese New Christians in Madrid. In addition, Francisco's activities as a clandestine rabbi made him a relatively easy target, one almost certain to draw inquisitorial fire. Indeed, given the fact that he was a relapsed Judaizer, it is surprising that San Antonio managed to escape the death sentence. Confession and contrition were keys to surviving the inquisitorial arrest, and Francisco played his part correctly and ultimately avoided death by immolation. Mariana, too, confessed and repented while simultaneously attempting to shift blame onto her spouse. The Holy Office used Mariana's testimony as ammunition against Francisco but convicted Mariana of heresy all the same. For violations of the baptismal and marriage sacraments, Mariana de los Reyes was to receive two hundred lashes, a public shaming, and banishment from Madrid, Toledo, and their environs for eight years. Perhaps she returned to her family in Santarem, where she would have had a lot of explaining to do when she ran into Pedro de Ribero, but information about that portion of her life has yet to be found.

FURTHER READING

The definitive study of the Spain of Philip IV is John H. Elliott, *The Count-Duke of Olivares: The Statesman in an Age of Decline* (New Haven, CT: Yale University Press, 1986).

The Portuguese New Christian community in Madrid may be approached through James C. Boyajian, *Portuguese Bankers at the Court of Spain, 1626-1650* (New Brunswick, NJ:

Rutgers University Press, 1983); as well as Yosef H. Yerushalmi, *From Spanish Court to Italian Ghetto: Isaac Cardoso: A Study in Seventeenth-Century Marranism and Jewish Apologetics* (New York: Columbia University Press, 1971). For Jews in seventeenth-century Madrid, see Mercedes García-Arenal and Gerard Wiegers, *A Man of Three Worlds: Samuel Pallache, A Moroccan Jew in Catholic and Protestant Europe,* trans. Martin Beagles (Baltimore: Johns Hopkins University Press, 2003).

Issues relating to the appearance of women before the Inquisition are examined in Mary E. Giles, ed., *Women and the Inquisition: Spain and the New World* (Baltimore: Johns Hopkins University Press, 1999). An interesting case study of bigamy in early modern Spain can be found in Alexandra Parma Cook and Nobel David Cook, *Good Faith and Truthful Ignorance: A Case of Transatlantic Bigamy* (Durham, NC: Duke University Press, 1991).

CHAPTER FIVE

A Captive's Tale

Diego Díaz

In 1609 Diego Díaz and his family were expelled, together with all other converted Muslims (moriscos), from Spain. Diego (then approximately twenty-seven years old), his father and brothers, and thousands of others crossed the Pyrenees to exile in southern France. Fifteen days later Diego Díaz, unwilling to live in exile, crossed back into Spain and eventually returned to Daimiel, his former hometown.

Ten months later, Díaz came to the attention of the town's authorities, who ordered his arrest and deportation. Subsequently transported to the port of Cartagena, Díaz soon found himself on a ship bound for "Christian lands." Deporting Christians (even morisco Christians) to Muslim territories, where they would surely be enslaved and converted to Islam, was illegal. However, it was a highly profitable enterprise for unscrupulous ships' captains, including the captain carrying Díaz, to transport their prisoners to North Africa and sell them into slavery. The ship carrying Díaz thus found its way to Algiers, where, as he tells it, he was taken captive and enslaved along with his fellow prisoners.

Díaz maintained that shortly after his captivity, he was involuntarily circumcised and forced to convert to Islam. He reported, however, that although he dressed as a Muslim, he continued to practice Christianity secretly throughout his captivity,

6. Travels of Diego Díaz

confessing his sins to a fellow captive who was a friar while the two played cards to hide the true nature of their activity. At the friar's suggestion, Diego learned the Algerian dialect of Arabic, found work at the docks, and befriended some local fishermen. Six months after he was taken captive, Díaz talked (or paid) his way onto one of the fishing boats headed north into the Mediterranean, jumped overboard when the boat neared the Spanish coastline, and swam to shore.

Back in Spain, Díaz learned the trade of meat-cutter and settled near the city of Cuenca. There he married Magdalena del Castillo and with her had three children. In 1632, thirteen years after his escape from Algiers, the Spanish Inquisition detained Díaz and Magdalena del Castillo on the grounds that they were secretly practicing Islam.

Confession of Diego Díaz, resident of Belmonte[1]

In the city of Cuenca, on the sixth day of the month of November of sixteen hundred twenty-two,[2] Diego Díaz, resident of Belmonte, appears before me, the notary, to give his confession in this case. I received his oath, which he made to God our Lord, to tell the truth regarding all he may be asked. He made his confession as follows:

Asked to say and declare what his name was, where he was born, who were his parents, and in what city, town, or place he was baptized, and what, at present, were his employment, age, and [marital] status, he said, "My name is Diego Díaz. I was born in the town of Daimiel[3] and baptized in the parish of Santa María in the same town. I am the legitimate son of Andrés de Solis and Teresa de Torres, who are now dead. At present I live in the town of Belmonte, [where I've lived] for the past ten years. I work as a meat-cutter in the butcher shops of that town, am fifty years old and a married man." This was his answer.

Asked to say and declare how it was that he said and declared himself born in the town of Daimiel since on other occasions that have arisen he had said publicly that he was from De Valle and other times from Orihuela, he said, "I

---

1. This translation is based upon the trial record in Archivo Diocesano, Cuenca: leg. 437, número 6169. It is referenced in Mercedes García-Arenal, *Inquisición y moriscos: Los procesos del Tribunal de Cuenca* (Madrid: Siglo Veintiuno Editores, 1978), 140–50.

Belmonte is a town near Cuenca, the city where Díaz's trial was conducted.

2. This is the scribe's mistake. All other documents in the case file suggest that Diego Díaz's trial began in the year 1632.

3. A town near Ciudad Real, in New Castile. Its Muslim population had converted en masse in 1502.

deny it. I said no such thing. What I'd said about being from Orihuela was that I'd learned my trade in that city." This was his answer.

Asked to say and declare where he was born and where his parents were from, he said, "My parents were born in the town of Daimiel." This was his answer.

Asked to declare if he was descended from Moors or moriscos or from any other bad sect reproved by our Holy Catholic faith, and if on different occasions some people who were disgusted with him had called him "Moor" and this defendant did not respond, make a scene, or defend himself at all, he said, "I deny it. [text missing, trapped in the book binding] No one has said such words to me, nor [illeg.] has there been cause for them. If someone had said this, I would have known to defend myself and would have defended myself, since I do not come from any bad sect of Moors or moriscos or of those reproved [by the Holy Office]."[4] This was his answer.

He was asked to say and declare why, if it was true that he was not descended from moriscos or Moors or from any other bad sect and was not of a bad sect himself, he had participated in and witnessed ceremonies of the moriscos. Why has he not heard Mass on Sundays or festivals of obligation? Why has he eaten meat and fish together on Fridays and fast days, shaved his head, and forbidden lard and pork from touching his stew pot? Why has he cooked his food with oil and said things in foreign languages? Why has he not made sure his children are instructed in Christian doctrine or in reciting the prayers or in using the rosary to this end? He said, "I am a good Christian, fearful of God our Lord and of my conscience. If in the past some things have obliged me to eat meat during fasts, it has been in public and with permission from my doctor and confessor because I was ill with 'salty phlegm.' It has not been for any other reason. This past summer I was ill with . . . a cough for which I was bled twice. When the barber[-surgeon] saw that the bleeding wasn't working, he told me to shave my head, which I did. This is why I shaved my head, and not for any other reason. I have taught Christian doctrine to my children, as is my duty." This was his answer. He said it was the truth, by the oath he swore. He did not sign because he does not know how to write.

Before me

[signed] Baltassar Iriguoien y Alamona

---

4. Failure to defend one's honor in response to an epithet was taken as evidence in early modern Spain that the epithet was true.

[On 13 November of the same year, the Holy Office interviewed Díaz's wife Magdalena del Castillo. She too claimed to be an Old Christian and denied all charges of "Mohammedizing."[5] The next letter in the case file, dated 13 November 1632, Cuenca, was from Juan Miguel Aguilera, a lawyer whom Diego Díaz appears to have hired privately. In this letter the lawyer asked that Díaz be set free and that his goods, confiscated by the Holy Office, be returned. Judging from the dates of the communications, it is probable that Díaz was released in November 1632 per his lawyer's request but rearrested in August 1633. A second letter from Juan Miguel Aguilera asked the Tribunal of Cuenca to release Magdalena del Castillo, Diego Díaz's wife, because she was ill and "about to give birth." The Holy Office did interrogate pregnant women, though its statutes expressly prohibited torturing them. In this case the inquisitors treated Castillo quite leniently. After having midwives verify her pregnancy and her illness, the judges released her from prison. There is no record that they proceeded against her after she had given birth.

Following testimony from several witnesses regarding Diego Díaz's conduct and a warrant for his rearrest, notaries prepared an inventory of his household possessions that included (apart from a somewhat modest assemblage of clothing, kitchenware, and household furnishings), several devotional items, among them "one small silver cross," "one very little silver- and gold-plated Christ," "one little silver Lamb of God," and "one little Christ on an ebony cross." Yet these artifacts of Christian identity were not enough to dispel the Inquisition's supposition that Diego Díaz was a Mohammedizer and a heretic.]

First Audience

In the Cuenca Inquisition, morning audience, twenty-sixth of August, sixteen hundred and thirty-three, the Lord Inquisitors doctors Enrique de Peralta y Cárdenas and don Tomás Rodríguez y Mo[lina?] commanded that a man be brought from the secret jails. From that man they received an oath in the proper form. He was sworn in and he promised to tell the truth in this audience as in any others he may have until the outcome of his case is determined. He was charged with keeping secret all he may see, hear, and learn, and all that may happen to him.

5. The term the Holy Office applied to those who committed Islamic heresies. It indicated a misunderstanding on the part of the Holy Office of the role of the Prophet Muhammad in Islam. By using the term *Mohammedizer* (rather than *Islamicizer*, for example) the Holy Office mistakenly paralleled Muhammad, who was a prophet in Islam but not a deity, with Jesus, who in Christianity is divine.

Asked what his name was, where he lived, how old he was, what he worked as, and how long it had been since he came to this Holy Office, he said, "My name is Diego Díaz. For the past ten years I've been a resident in the town of Belmonte. In that town I work as a meat-cutter. I'm fifty years old and arrived as a prisoner of this Holy Office yesterday, Thursday, in the morning, just after daybreak. I was born in the town of Daimiel in the archbishopric of Toledo."
He gave his genealogy as follows:
Parents: "Andrés de Solis and Teresa de Torres, deceased, farmers by profession. Residents of Daimiel."
Paternal Grandparents: He said, "I never met them but I've heard it said that my grandfather Francisco Vallestero was a farmhand and native of Daimiel."
Maternal Grandparents: He said, "I never met them and haven't heard anything about them."
Aunts and Uncles on his Father's side: He said, "I never met any of them and don't know if there are any."[6]
Aunts and Uncles on his Mother's side: He said, "My mother had the following siblings:

— Francisco de Dueñas, deceased, resident and native of Daimiel, a farmer, who was married but I don't know his wife's name or her origins. She's dead. They left one daughter called Isabel, but I don't know if she's dead or alive, or whether she's married or where she is.
— Diego de Dueñas, resident and native of Daimiel, farmhand, who is dead and was married but I don't know to whom. He had no children.
— Juan Dueñas, resident and native of Daimiel, deceased, a farmer. I don't know if he married, since it has been a long time since I've been in Daimiel.
— I have no other aunts and uncles on my mother's side."

Brothers and Sisters:

— "Francisco Vallestero, resident of Daimiel, farmer, married to a woman called La Morena. I don't know her real name. They have a sixteen- or seventeen-year-old son, but I don't know his name. He's a bachelor.

6. It would not have been unusual for Diego to be distant from his extended family to the point of not knowing their names or whereabouts, but it would also not have been unusual for Diego, as an Inquisition prisoner, to use strategic silences as a way of protecting members of his family.

— Juan de Solis, resident of Villarrubia de los Dios [?] [illeg.], who makes pitchers and who is married there in Daimiel. I don't know his wife's name, but they have a son called Domingo who is about seventeen and a bachelor.

— Andrés de Solis, deceased, who used to live in Daimiel. He was a shoemaker and was married. I don't know his wife's name, but I do know she was rich. He left behind two or three children, but I never met them and don't know their names.

— Alfonso Vallestero, who died a long time ago, was a resident of Daimiel and a farmhand. He never married.

— And María Solis, who died very young."

Wife and Children: He said, "I am married to Magdalena del Castillo. We married about eight years ago. She's the daughter of Juan del Castillo and Magdalena Hernández, both born in Murcia, as I understand it, who live in Espinardo, near Murcia." He said he had the following children: "Teresa, six years old, María, three years old, Isabel, three months old. I've never been married to any other woman and I have no other children."

Asked what caste and lineage he thought his parents, grandparents, and other relatives were from, and if any of them or if he himself had been a prisoner, reconciled, penanced, or [otherwise] punished by the Holy Office of the Inquisition. He said, "We're old [moriscos][7] from . . . Castile. We came here three hundred years ago to serve the monarchs of Castile. After the expulsion of the *granadinos*,[8] they wanted to throw [my family] out, and they did. But by virtue of an order from His Majesty that allowed us to live in these kingdoms and work at whatever offices we pleased, we came back later to live and work in those towns and returned to our former houses. I don't know if my parents, grandparents, or other relatives I've mentioned have been punished, arrested, penanced, or reconciled by the Holy Office of the Inquisition. I haven't,[9] until now, when I was taken prisoner."

7. Diego Díaz is referring here to *moriscos antiguos,* that is, moriscos whose families converted to Christianity before the forced conversion of 1502. See the commentary that follows.

8. Moriscos from Granada who were forcibly converted to Christianity in 1502 and subsequently resettled in New Castile following the rebellion known as the War of the Alpujarras of 1568–70. Díaz uses the term to distinguish these "new" moriscos from "old" moriscos such as himself who belonged to Muslim families who converted before 1502. In 1609 King Philip III exempted "old moriscos" living in Daimiel and four other towns in the southern part of New Castile from the general order expelling moriscos from the Crown of Castile. Some of these "old moriscos" left the peninsula along with the *granadinos,* while others, like Díaz, after abandoning the kingdom, decided to return.

9. Diego appears to have forgotten that he had been detained, briefly, the previous November.

Asked if he was a baptized and confirmed Christian, and if he went to Mass, confessed, and partook of the Eucharist at the times the Holy Mother Church commands, he said, "I am a baptized, confirmed Christian. I was baptized in the town of Daimiel, parish of Santa María. Father Perceda, a Christian who [works?] with this Holy Office, has my baptismal certificate. I don't know if I'm confirmed.[10] I hear Mass, confess, and partake of the Eucharist on the days and times the Holy Mother Church commands. The last time I confessed and partook of the Eucharist was in the town of Villa de la Mota [del Cuervo], with a friar from the [monastery of the] Holy Trinity. I don't know his name. Father don Juan de Ca[illeg.] gave me the Eucharist on the last festival of obligation." He made the sign of the cross and blessed himself and said the Our Father, the Hail Mary, the Credo, and the Salve Regina, the commandments of the Law of God, and the [Articles of] Confession in Spanish. He said them well. He didn't say the Articles of Divinity and what they had to say to humanity, but even though he didn't say them, he said he knew them very well.

Asked if he knew how to read and write and if he had had any schooling, he said, "I went to school in the Kingdom of France in Bayonne. [I was in school] in San Juan de la Luz [St. Jean de Luz] at the time of the expulsion, and then not again until 1609.[11] [Marginalia: The expulsion took place after 1609.][12] I was in France for about fifteen days, along with others who'd been expelled. I was also in Algiers for about six months in the company of other foreigners whose names I don't remember."

Asked for the story of his life, he said, "I was born in the town of Daimiel, as I've said, in my parents' house, where I lived until I was sixteen or seventeen." [Later he said, "or maybe twenty."] "During that time I worked as a farmhand, until the expulsion. Then I went to France, where I was for the time I've said. From there, I came back to Daimiel, where I was caught and put in prison for two months. They took me with other prisoners to Cartagena and they put us on a ship to take us out of Spain. We put into port in Algiers, where I was for six months. After that, I got onto another boat, a fishing boat. When I saw the Spanish coastline, I jumped into the water and swam to shore at Tortosa. From there, I went to Valencia, where I learned my trade. I learned meat-cutting

10. It would have been unusual to forget whether or not one was confirmed. Díaz may have preferred another strategic silence to an admission that his record as a Catholic was less than perfect.

11. This is the first of various conflicting chronologies that Díaz gives of his life before and after the expulsion. In this narrative he had left his hometown to go to school in San Jean de Luz before the expulsion. Below, he says he worked as a farmhand, presumably in Daimiel, until the expulsion.

12. Here Díaz refers to the 1609 expulsion of the moriscos from Spain. He mixed up his dates, as the scribe noted in the margin of the transcript.

from a man I was with for six years who is called Pedro de Casas y Hera, who lives in Albatera, in the Kingdom of Valencia. From there I went to the city of Orihuela and lived with a mallorquín[13] called Procenio, who was a fishmonger. Things were good with him, and I worked as a field hand. From there I went to Manzanares, where I worked for two years as a meat-cutter. After that I went to Belmonte, where I was a meat-cutter for nine or ten years, and after that I went to La Mota [del Cuervo] in Cuenca, where I've been working at the meat-cutter's trade since last Lent, until I was arrested by the ministers of this Holy Office."

Asked if he knew, presumed, or suspected the reasons he had been arrested and taken to the jail of this Holy Office, he said, "Here and now I do not know, nor can I presume to know the cause of my imprisonment."

First Warning

He was told that this Holy Office was not accustomed to arresting people without sufficient information that they had said, done, and committed, or had seen, heard, or [witnessed] others commit something that was or appeared to be against our Holy Catholic, evangelic faith, which enjoins us to follow and teach the holy mother Roman Catholic Church, or against the free and right exercise of the Holy Office. Therefore, he should believe that because of such information he has been taken prisoner. Out of reverence for the Lord our God and his Glorious and Blessed Mother Our Lady the Virgin Mary, he is warned and charged to search his memory and to tell and present the truth in full regarding that for which he is guilty or of which he knows others to be guilty. . . .

He said, "There was a rumor I'd heard in Belmonte, threatening that I was going to have an encounter with this Holy Office. I spoke with the servants of the Lord Inquisitor who presides over this tribunal. It was a really cold day and the servants gave me a brazier to warm myself. They asked me why I'd come. I told them it was to check with the Holy Office about some threats that had been made against me, so that, if I were guilty, the Holy Office could punish me.[14] The servants told me that their master said I should go with God's blessing."

13. Mallorquín means a person from Mallorca, one of the Balearic Islands located near Spain's Mediterranean coast.

14. Trying to circumvent an inquisitorial investigation by checking privately with an inquisitor to see whether or not one was under suspicion was highly unusual and obviously did not work for Diego Díaz.

Asked to tell what threats were made against him in Belmonte and regarding what, he said, "The threat was from Juan de Rivera, who lives in Belmonte, who told me, 'Get out of here, I'm in a worse trouble than you are.' "

Asked about what he was referring to and what the said person [Rivera] had meant when he said he was in worse trouble, he said, "I'm involved in a criminal case in the ecclesiastical tribunal[15] in which they accused me last year of eating meat, cheese, fish, sardines, and tuna all together on fast days. Juan de Rivera didn't tell me what he meant by worse business."

Asked if he presumed, when he heard the aforementioned Juan de Rivera talk about a worse business, to know what that business was, he said, "It couldn't be anything other than being accused before this Holy Office."

Asked to state why he presumed, and feared, accusation before the Holy Office, he said, "Because they would charge me with being a morisco, since I shaved my head with a knife. It is true that I shaved my head with a knife, because Bernardo Gómez, barber of Belmonte, told me after he'd bled me twice that it was important [to shave my head] because of the sores I had on my head and also because of my salty phlegm. He also told me that it was important for me to put on a clean shirt on Fridays.[16] It is true that this is the day I put on a clean shirt to go settle accounts with my bosses, because Fridays are the day I rest from work. I change my shirt on Fridays for no other reason, and with no bad intention, other than what I have said."

He said he told the truth by the oath he had sworn. His testimony was read back to him and he said, "It is well-written and correct." He was warned again in the usual way and ordered to be taken back to his cell. Because he did not know how to sign, the Lord Inquisitor signed for him.

> [signed] don Enrique de Peralta y Cárdenas
> Before me, B. de Gov. Luviano

[Diego Díaz 's second audience with the tribunal took place on 30 August 1633. It was a brief session in which he divulged no new information to the inquisitors. However, the inquisitors' second formulaic warning prompted Díaz

---

15. Ecclesiastical tribunals (run by the Church, with lesser courts at the parish level and higher courts that followed the canonical hierarchy, they dealt with infractions committed by clerics and religious infractions that were sins but not heresies) were not part of the inquisitorial justice system (run by the Spanish state; prosecuted heresy only). In this case, the ecclesiastical tribunal would have interpreted Diego's fast-breaking as a sin (no intent to violate Church doctrine), while the Inquisition would later interpret the same act as a heresy (intentional violation of Church doctrine).

16. The shirt referred to was a *camisa,* a long undergarment, worn every day and as sleepwear. Diego Díaz and his wife and children appear to have had two each, one to wear during the workweek and the other to wear on holidays and days off. Note that Friday is the Muslim Holy Day.

to recite a list of his charitable donations in order to prove his fidelity to the Church. "I have made donations secretly and publicly. You may ask Anabella, my neighbor's daughter, who lives on the middle [floor] of my building, and . . . the other neighbors in the neighborhood. . . . Vicar Andrés Martínez and Vicar Mortalla can tell you how I made donations to the army and to Reguillo the miller . . . and to Iñigo to give to the poor." Diego Díaz's list of charitable giving, like his collection of miniature crosses and crucifixes, appears to have had little impact on the inquisitors. They ordered him back to his cell and then recalled him on the afternoon of 3 September 1633 for a third audience. On this occasion, after having noted that Díaz had "nothing more to say than what he'd already said," they again warned him to confess the entire truth.]

First Prosecutorial Accusation [undated]:

I, the prosecutor, put before Your Lordship an accusation against Diego Díaz, meat-cutter, resident of Belmonte. Being a baptized Christian and enjoying the exemptions and prerogatives faithful and Catholic Christians enjoy, he has, without fear of God or of the Justice of this Holy Inquisition, with great scandal to the Christian nation, hereticated himself and apostatized from our holy Catholic faith and evangelical law of Our Lord and Redeemer Jesus Christ. He has crossed over into the perverse sect of Muhammad, the sect to which the ancestors of Diego Díaz adhered and in which they believed and whose ceremonies they conducted, believing that in this sect they would be saved and knowing that it was contrary to our holy Catholic faith.

—Also, he was not able to hide what he had in his heart. In anger, on some occasions he has said, "I cursed him who does not serve in Algiers, because in Algiers there are no taxes nor duties.[17] When asked what this meant, he would reply that he had been there many times and that he had the territory measured pace by pace. I ask that he be made to declare which two times he was in Algiers, why he went, if he went with any other person who is now within these kingdoms [of Spain], and whom he was with. [He should also be made to declare] why he went to Algiers during the six months he has declared in his testimony and in what garb.[18] He was also asked to state whether he spoke with Christians there and in what law he told the Moors he lived. Also, living in the

---

17. Díaz, who is evidently conceiving of Muslim Algiers as some kind of tax haven, is seemingly complaining about the high taxes in Castile.

18. The prosecutor wants to know whether Diego Díaz dressed as a Christian or as a Muslim during his time in Algiers. The inquisitors were likely to have regarded Muslim dress as the equivalent of a "cultural heresy" if not an actual sign of conversion to Islam.

Law of Muhammad, he has taken and takes as a joke the precepts and obser-vances of the Law of Jesus Christ. Therefore, he does not regularly hear Mass on Sundays and feasts of obligation. It is well known that he goes on those days to the butcher shop and that when he comes back, he lies down and does not leave his house until one or later. On some occasions he has told his servants to stay in the house all morning when it is a feast day and that their chores are more important than Mass. If once or twice he has heard Mass, it has been to dissimulate and conceal [his true faith].

—Also, on Fridays, vigils, fasts, and other such days of abstinence, he has eaten and ordinarily eats meat. He has also made the others in his household, children and wife, eat it, even though they were all healthy and not ill enough to do so. Being healthy, with malicious intent, on those same days and some-times at the same meal they ate fish, tuna, cheese, and other things noxious to [one's] health and even more noxious for [those who are] ill.[19]

—Also, it is assumed that he never prays Christian prayers and that he has not taught them to his children and does not have a rosary. If he does [have a rosary], I ask that he show it, and that he be made to state whether or not he has taught his children the prayers.

—Also, he has sheltered certain moriscos in his house, and has shut himself up in a room with them and spoken in an unknown language. I ask that he be made to declare the content of their conversation and whether the language was *algarvesía*,[20] and if he knows how to speak and understand it, and where he learned it.

—Also, it is to be assumed that he has performed and performs other ceremonies of the sect of Muhammad, and that he has continued to perform them over the whole course of his life at any time he could without attracting attention. It is also to be presumed that he knows other people who are Moors by caste and in their hearts, and that as his accomplices they have concealed his deeds so that they will not be punished. In particular, it is known that he has concealed a certain person who is related to him whom he knows is an ad-herent of the aforementioned sect.[21] I accuse him of these deeds. [illeg.]

19. In other words, if Díaz and his family were so ill as to be allowed to eat meat during fast days, they should not have been eating, at the same meal, foods such as fish and cheese that were commonly considered prejudicial to one's health.

20. The dialect of the moriscos. Speaking *algarvesía* was another cultural heresy, indicative of a preference for Islam over Christianity.

21. The prosecutor may be referring to Díaz's wife, Magdalena, who was arrested on charges of Mohammedizing and then released from jail because of illness and pregnancy. Records do not show

—Also, knowing that what is contained in this accusation is true, and having sworn to tell the truth in all of his audiences, he has not done so. For this he has been gravely warned and [in spite of this] it appears he has said things that bear little resemblance to the truth, such as the statement that he threw himself overboard from a fishing boat to swim to shore in Spain. It is not believable that [an Algerian] fishing boat should be able to get so close to enemy territory. I demand that he declare if he was also a fisherman or for what reason the fishermen brought him in their boat.

For all of this I ask and beg Your Lordship to accept my report as true and . . . well proven, and to accept Diego Díaz as the author of the aforementioned deeds and as a Mohammedizing heretic, pernicious apostate, and fomenter and concealer of other Mohammedizers. For this, may he incur the penalty of excommunication, and may the loss of all his goods go along with this, said goods to be applied to the chamber and treasury of His Majesty. May the person of Diego Díaz be handed over to the secular arm of justice.[22] May he and his descendants incur the prohibitions and other penalties established by law in these kingdoms as the legitimate customs [for dealing with] apostatizing heretics. May these penalties be carried out against his person and his goods with all possible rigor so that he may be punished and may serve as an example to others.

—Also, if necessary to prove my accusations, I ask that the aforementioned Diego Díaz be tortured, that the torture be applied and withdrawn as many times as is necessary until he has fully confessed to his crimes and the crimes of others. Above all, I ask that justice be done in all things. I swear that I do not enter this accusation out of malice.

[signed] Doctor Alonso de Vallejo

This accusation was read and shown, under oath and in the proper form, to Diego Díaz and his lawyer.[23] We ask him to respond in truth to the content of

---

that Magdalena was rearrested at any time before or after she gave birth. No other potential Mohammedizers among Díaz's relatives are ever mentioned in his trial transcripts or the fragments that remain of his wife's trial.

22. The prosecutor is asking that Díaz be burned at the stake by the royal justice system. A prosecutorial request for "relaxation to the secular arm of justice" was pro forma in most cases.

23. Diego Díaz's defense statement shows evidence of expert legal advice. Records do not indicate whether Diego had consulted the Inquisition-appointed defense attorney, the lawyer Diego had hired privately to help get himself and his wife out of prison when they were first arrested, or both.

the aforementioned accusation, which he has in his possession, to read charge by charge and respond to each of the accusations in turn.

Introduction: This is the aforementioned Diego Díaz, who was a resident of the town of Belmonte and at present lives in Mota del Cuervo. He is a baptized Christian but does not know if he is confirmed.

To the First Charge: He said, "I've been in Belmonte for about ten years, more or less, and haven't left there unless it was during Lent or for some task associated with my trade. Thursday nights, because that's when I had to settle accounts with my boss, I put on a good shirt. Friday nights I take it off again because that's when I have to cut the meat. Sometimes in summer, I change my shirt two or three times in the same week. . . . My wife and children have never changed their shirts on Thursday nights. My wife can sometimes go three weeks without changing her shirt, because she is ill with pain, as my neighbors will attest. Whenever the washerwomen come to the house, I change my shirt without stopping to notice whether it's Friday or some other day of the week."

To the Second Charge: He said, "My neighbors will testify to the fact that my wife and children and I have eaten pork from our stew pot, as will Mari Múñoz, the pork seller."

To the Third Charge: He said, "I don't recall having said people should go to Algiers, for in Algiers there are neither taxes nor duties, nor having said that I had been there many times. I was in Algiers only once, as I said in my first audience. None of those who went with me to Algiers is currently in Spain. Neither are any of those I saw while I was there. In the six months I spent in Algiers I dressed in Moorish garb in order to get closer to the boats. I asked for work at the docks, which I obtained. . . . I spoke in Algerian with some of the Christians, whose names I don't know. One said he was from Toledo and the other from Granada.[24] So much time has passed that I don't remember any of them well. I confessed to a friar, and to hide what we were doing we pretended to be playing cards. I don't know what order he was from since he wasn't wearing his habit, and I don't know his name or where he was from except that he was a captive. In all the time I was there no one asked me what law I lived under, and I didn't tell anyone what law I lived under, except for the confessor." [inquisitorial marginalia: not being asked what law he lives under might be

---

24. The city of Algiers harbored a large number of Christians from Spain, France, Italy, and other countries who had been taken prisoner by Muslim corsairs, enslaved, and forced to work in various capacities. Why Díaz spoke to these Spanish "Christians" in "Algerian"—presumably, some variant of Arabic—as opposed to Castilian is mysterious.

true, since here everyone knows; but in daily intercourse, not saying whether one is Moor or Christian is improbable.]

To the Fourth Charge: He said, "I have heard many masses on Sundays and feast days without missing any except for when I was sick and on some days when I had to work, as Father Sanchuelo, Father Hoz, and the sacristan of [the church of] San Francisco in Belmonte, all natives of this city, will tell you. . . ."

To the Fifth Charge: He said, "I have eaten meat on some of the prohibited days because of the illness I had. Because I couldn't eat it, I would ask if there was any fish and they would give me a little and I would eat it with the meat. My wife has been and still is so ill that she can only eat meat, but even so, she never ate it on the prohibited days. Of my children, the oldest is six now and the next one, four. They ate meat sometimes, but I don't remember when I gave it to them."

To the Sixth Charge: He said, "I never recite any prayers other than the Christian ones. I don't know any others. I have taught them to my children, and I do have a rosary that I left just now in my jail cell. Every suit of clothes I have has one."

To the Seventh Charge: He said, "The people I spoke to were from Valencia. Since I had lived in the Kingdom of Valencia, I spoke with them in that language.[25] They were very old. . . ."

To the Eighth Charge: He said, "I have not committed any crime, neither do I know of any person who has sinned by keeping the Law of Muhammad."

To the Ninth Charge: He said, "I have told the truth and have not perjured myself. If I had followed and kept the Law of Muhammad I could be in Algiers right now, since it is a land of plenty and full of vice. When I got there, they wanted to marry me off, but because I follow the law of Our Lord Jesus Christ I returned to Spain in a fishing boat. . . ."

[Diego Díaz now affirmed, in a formulaic statement, that all he had said in his own defense was true.]

Voluntary Audience

In the city of Cuenca in the Holy Office of the Inquisition on the ninth day of the month of September in the year sixteen hundred and thirty-three, morning audience, Lord Inquisitors Doctors Sebastián de Frías, don Enrique de Peralta y Cárdenas, and don Tomás Rodríguez presiding. They ordered

---

25. Presumably, Díaz spoke to these people in *valenciano,* a variant of the Catalan language.

Diego Díaz to be brought from his cell. When he was present, they . . . asked him why he had requested an audience and [admonished] him to tell the truth by the oath he had sworn.

He said, "It is true that I asked for an audience. I asked for the audience to beg your lordship to send a judge to see me so that I may speak with him alone about something I haven't mentioned. I want to talk about a sin I confessed in Avignon, which was pardoned by a certificate from Aurelino Sánchez, N[otarius?] V[aticvanus?], from the episcopal audience where the certificate was brought. The sin is that, during the expulsion of the moriscos, I left with the others. When we disembarked in Algiers, the Turks in that city came and took us into the city and put us in the *atarazanas*,[26] which are large, royal arsenals where arms and artillery are stored. When we got there, they inspected all the men and went around cutting off the skin end (*pellejo* or foreskin) of their shameful parts. [Inquisitorial marginalia: They circumcised them.]

"When I responded to the [prosecutor's] accusation, I forgot to say that it is not true that I told the maid to do her chores instead of going to Mass. What I said was that she should only go if she didn't go to Mass in Belmonte, where there are many masses. There was a time we sent her to Mass and she didn't come back until three in the afternoon because she'd been going from tavern to tavern, getting drunk. . . .

"I also wanted to ask your lordship if one can be a Moor without knowing any of the Moorish ceremonies, because I don't know them and haven't had anyone to teach them to me. Even though I was expelled from Spain as a Moor, I did not arrive in Algiers as one, in spite of the accusations made against me there."

He was told to state the accusations that had been made against him there [i.e., during his time in Algiers]. He said, "I went into a building where there were two or three hundred young Turkish men. . . . I saw that when they needed to urinate they lowered their trousers and pulled their shirts up and squatted like women. Then they took their shameful parts and hit them several times against the walls to clean the urine off. They say that if even one drop of urine gets on their shirt, they will go to hell. Then they put their trousers under their shirts, and then another shirt and pair of trousers over them. These

---

26. The scribe here copied Díaz's word as "taraçanas," a variant of "atarazanas," the Spanish term (albeit of Arabic origin) for shipyard or arsenal.

Moors bought boy slaves to sleep with them.[27] Look, my lord, this is turpitude! Why would anyone want to be a Moor?

"I dare say there are, in Algiers, more than six thousand *granadinos*,[28] who are Christians, and that the moriscos from Aragon and Valencia who went there were Christians. If any one of those *granadinos* in Algiers has a son, he does not dare let go of his hand until he is twenty years old, out of fear that the Moors of Algiers will take him to make bad use of him, as I have said."

Asked if the Moors rest on Holy Thursday and if he was a Moor, [he said], "I do not rest as they have accused me many times, on Holy Thursday. In this city I've confessed twice, once with a Franciscan friar, whose name I don't know, and the second time with Father Lerma. I told him to take a donation I'd given him to the house of a woman who lived across the street from Holy Christ [Church]. That's when they brought me to [the Inquisition in] Cuenca. . . . I beg your lordship—the voice of the people is the voice of Heaven—seeing as my whole nation has acquired a bad reputation, to go at once to Belmonte.[29] There you will find more than two hundred people, not only these but the whole town, who will attest to my life and habits. Any of those who have testified to the contrary are foreigners and men who let their wives do what they will.[30] . . . I beg your lordship . . . to make the inquiries quickly, so that I may see my wife and children and return to live as a married man. In all my life I've never known Moorish ceremonies, or anything about them."

He was asked to state what words the Moors spoke at the time he was circumcised in Algiers, and to state if the man who circumcised him was dressed differently from the others, and which ceremonies they performed, and how many people they circumcised in one day, and at what time. He said, "The day they circumcised me there were four or five barbers in the armory I mentioned. Also present were the justices and ministers of justice because they suspected that the *granadinos* were Christians. The barbers went around circumcising us without saying a word. We moriscos didn't say anything either. As they cut the foreskin, the barbers cured us . . . and bandaged us. That day they circumcised about a hundred people. After they'd finished, they gave us all a big meal, the kind you would have in Spain on a wedding day."

27. Male-male homosexual acts in early modern Spain constituted the capital crime, and the sin, of sodomy. Christians often attributed the vice of sodomy to Muslims.

28. *Granadinos* in this context refers to moriscos originally from Granada.

29. The "nation" Díaz refers to here is the "nation of moriscos."

30. Cuckolds were considered vile, dishonorable, and therefore not credible witnesses.

Asked if he consented to this, and if he was willingly circumcised, he said, "It is true that I understood this ceremony to be a sin and against the law of Our Lord Jesus Christ. That's why I went to confess it to a friar, who was deputized by the bishop and nuncio, when I was in Avignon. The friar was from Vitoria and understood Spanish, and had been in Úbeda. I confessed to him that they had circumcised me, and he absolved me. I confessed that it had been against my will and only out of fear that they would kill me that I let myself be circumcised."

Asked if they made him perform, or if he performed, other Moorish ceremonies or if there were ceremonies at meals, he said, "They did not make me perform any ceremonies. Neither did I witness anything at meals except that the feast they made for us was on the floor on benches with tablecloths over them. Only the circumcised men attended, but I didn't see that they said anything during the meal, or before it or after. The Moors walk around with shoes that have no uppers[31] and do everything backward from the way it's done in Spain. Women walk around with their faces covered so no one can see them."

He was asked to state if, on these occasions in Algiers, he doubted whether the law of the Christians was the true law and that it is the only one in which men may be saved. And he was asked to state if he judged the law of the Moors to be good and thought he could be saved in it, and if he believed it in his heart and found it good. He said, "I have never doubted that the law in which men will be saved is that of Our Lord Jesus Christ, and that only those who receive the baptismal waters may go to heaven, having done good works. I have never believed that the law of the Moors was good, or that men can be saved in it."

He was told that if he were as good a Christian as he says, he would not have let himself be circumcised, an act manifestly contrary to the faith of Our Lord Jesus Christ. Rather, he should have suffered a thousand deaths before he let himself be circumcised. It is the same as if he had, with words, denied the faith of Our Lord Jesus Christ, since he did so in deed. He said, "It was never, in any way, my intention to deny the law of Our Lord Jesus Christ. My intention was to confess it, in case it was a sin."

Asked if before they were circumcised the Moors made any threats about what would happen to them if they did not let themselves be circumcised, he said, "On the tenth day after we'd disembarked in the marina, there came a

---

31. Díaz describes a part of a shoe he calls the "oreja," literally, "ear."

company of Turkish soldiers with a mandate to give us aid, comfort, and food. They did not mistreat us, so we went with them to the armory where they gave us refreshments. Then one day, without saying anything, they came in and circumcised us. . . . God, my heart is grieved."

He swore by the oath he had made that this was the truth. It was read back to him and he said it was well written. The Lord Inquisitor signed.

[signed] Doctor Sebastián de Frías

Before me Bal. De Villaviciosa

Second Accusation

I, the prosecutor, enter before Your Lordship a second accusation against Diego Díaz, meat-cutter, resident in La Mota del Cuervo. In addition to the ceremonies of the law of Muhammad outlined in my first accusation, he has performed others which are clearer manifestations that he prays the prayers of the Moors and believes that he will be saved by them. At the time of the expulsion of the moriscos, when he was in Algiers, he was circumcised. To exculpate himself he said he confessed the incident, but this is not to be believed, because it is known that the Moors, like other nations, do not force anyone to receive their laws who does not want them.[32] Thus, we must believe that in order to become a Moor, or because he was a Moor, he asked to be circumcised. If they had circumcised everyone, not just those who asked for circumcision, they would not have circumcised only one hundred men, but all those who were there. . . .

In Algiers, Moorish garb is different from the garb of the Christians who live there. He went around the whole time he was there in the garb of a Moor, a deed that is almost like professing that the sect of Muhammad is the one that he has in his heart. I ask that he state whether the Moors with whom he had contact thought he was a Moor and to which law he said he belonged when he first arrived in Algiers. He should say whether or not, while he was there, he entered a mosque, or Moorish temple, and if he was present during the prayers or ceremonies of the Moors, or if he performed them himself. . . .

Also, I ask him to state why it took him so long to confess after he had been circumcised, since the seal on the certificate of confession from the friar [in

---

32. The prosecutor's statement is misleading, since it was known that the Moors in the North Africa did occasionally "force" conversions to Islam. On the whole, however, most Christian captives who converted to Islam did so voluntarily. On this point, see Bartolomé and Lucile Bennassar, *Los cristianos de Alá: La fascinante aventura de los renegados* (Madrid: Nerea, 1989).

Avignon] is dated the twelfth of September of 1618. Why did he spend that whole year in Avignon, which is in France, keeping quiet? And why did he not say anything to Your Lordship when asked for his life story? . . .

For all these reasons I ask and beg Your Lordship to accept my report as true. . . . I swear that I do not enter this accusation out of malice, but for Your Lordship.

[signed] Doctor Alonso de Vallejo

Defense

I, Diego Díaz[33] from the town of Belmonte, prisoner in the jails of this Holy Office, respond to the charges and accusations made by the prosecutor of this Holy Office, which ask that I be punished for saying that I have abandoned the faith of Our Lord Jesus Christ and professed the law of the false and perfidious Muhammad, and which state that to this end I have not heard Mass on Sundays or on festivals of obligation, have eaten meat on Fridays and fast days, have changed my shirt on Fridays, and have done other superstitious things in diminution of our holy Catholic faith. To these and all the other things contained in his complaint and accusation I respond:

Your Lordship's servant, I ask that Justice be served by setting me free and condemning my accuser to the cost of my trial, for the following reasons.[34] First, because the lack of information regarding time, place, and specificity of action and other substantive details other than those stated in the complaint and accusation lack any relation to the truth. Thus, I deny them, for they are prejudicial. I affirm what I have already said and stated in my confession, which should count in my favor. As I have said to your Lordship many times, I always go to Mass on Sunday and festivals of obligation and weekdays, when I am able, except for the times I have been ill. Not only have I heard Mass, but I have made many charitable donations to monks and clerics so that they would say masses for my soul, my health, and my success, and I have done other charitable good works as a good and faithful Christian. I deny that I ate meat on Fridays and fast days. If I did, it was only because of the attacks I get of

33. The original version of this text is written in the first person.

34. Here Diego Díaz shows his familiarity with the ecclesiastical and secular justice systems, in which, in case of a not-guilty verdict, the accuser was often made to pay for the cost of the trial. What Díaz did not realize was that the Inquisition worked differently. Those who denounced heresies to the Inquisition were not penalized in any way if the accused turned out to be innocent.

[coughing?] and sores on my head and neck. And then I only [ate meat] with license from the surgeon and barber. I deny having changed my shirt on Fridays for bad reasons. I did so because on those days I don't work. As for the rest that I have said in my confession, I repeat it here as evidence in my favor. . . . I said in my confession that when I was in Moorish lands they violently and forcibly circumcised me and other moriscos, which they did because they knew we were Christians. What consoled me at that time was knowing that in my soul I had not abandoned the faith of Our Lord Jesus Christ, as I had not. Rather, I suffered. If we had not submitted [to circumcision] they would have killed us.

Your Lordship will find that all the witnesses against me disagree [among themselves] or are sole witnesses.[35] They do not agree as to time, place, or circumstances. Many have not ratified their testimony, and therefore their testimony may not be taken as proof. They testify against me because they are my sworn enemies. Because of their hatred for me they have made depositions against the truth. I therefore discount them[36] and contradict their testimony with my oath and the necessary protestations. The only thing that hurts my case is the disgrace of my nation and my ancestors.

Most of all, I suspect Antonio Malo and Maria Laguna his wife,[37] who threatened me . . . because I had a tavern next to theirs.[38] Mine had a good reputation for treating customers well. Theirs had a bad reputation for their bad treatment, which consisted of dispossessing guests of their goods by playing card games with them with marked decks, and swindling them in other ways. His wife drinks. Thus, because they are criminals and because of the aforementioned exception, their witness testimony is invalid.[39] I also suspect Ana, Antonio Malo's maid, who used to be my maid. Out of hatred and rancor she would speak out against me. While she was still a servant in my house, I

35. By this point, the Inquisition had provided Diego with a copy of the witness testimony against him. The copy listed the witnesses by number, but not by name.

36. Discounting witnesses (putting them on a list of *tachas*) was common procedure in the Inquisition, which did not accept testimony from sworn enemies of the defendants. While witnesses and "denouncers" remained anonymous, a smart defendant could get his or her testimony discounted by naming all possible denouncers and unfavorable witnesses as enemies.

37. Here begins Díaz's list of "tachas."

38. It would not have been unusual for an early modern Spaniard to be engaged in multiple small enterprises (meat-cutting and tavern owning, in this case).

39. The aforementioned exception would be the "mortal enemies" or *tachas* clause that discounts testimony of sworn enemies.

went one night to look for her. I found her in the Vrejona House, where they sell *aguardiente*.[40] There she was, drunk, stretched out on the floor. I threw a jug of water over her to wake her from her stupor. From that day on, she has not returned to my house."

[At this point in the trial, Díaz continued to discredit witnesses by using the "tachas" or "strike-out" clause, which enabled prisoners to invalidate the testimony of persons known to be their "sworn enemies." In this case Díaz did so by correctly guessing who the witnesses were and then by identifying almost all of them by name.]

Audience Succeeding the Second Accusation

In the city of Cuenca in the Holy Office of the Inquisition, on the twentieth day of the month of September in the year sixteen hundred and thirty-three, afternoon audience, the Lord Inquisitors Doctors Sebastián de Frías, don Enrique de Peralta y Cárdenas, and don Ramón Rodríguez de Embarray presiding. They commanded that Diego Díaz be brought from his cell. When the prisoner was present, they asked him what he had remembered regarding his case, and charged him to say it in order to unburden his conscience and to comply with the oath he had made, and that it would have no ill effect on his case. He said, "I have nothing more to say other than what I've already said."

He was asked to state what year it was when he, as he said, arrived in Algiers and he and the other Spanish moriscos were circumcised and he did not consent to it with his will because he always remained a Christian and, so as not to be discovered, confessed to a Catholic friar. And he was asked to state what questions of faith he discussed with the friar and if, in particular, he confessed to the sin of circumcision. He said, "I don't remember at all the year or time of year of the expulsion. I think that about two years after the granadine moriscos left Spain they took me to Avignon for the first time, and I had a public trial, but I don't remember when. From there, I came back to Spain but was caught, along with Francisco Moreno, also from Daimiel, who is now dead, in the town of Haro. A cleric from the Prebend caught us and turned us over to the ecclesiastical justices, who kept us prisoner for three months and then returned us to Avignon to the General Prebend.[41] From there I went to San Juan de Luz, where my father was. I stayed there for about six

---

40. *Eau de vie*, a clear distilled spirit similar to brandy and which is made from grape must.

41. *Prebend* here probably signifies a cathedral chapter, which is traditionally comprised of canons (or prebendaries). The "general prebend" may be some kind of ecclesiastical court.

months and then came back to Spain, to Madrid and then to Daimiel, where I worked as a servant for a *familiar*[42] of the Inquisition named Orozco. I was with him for eight or ten months. Then a royal judge, Madera, arrested me in that town, along with many other prisoners, and took us to Cartagena, where we were for some days until the mayor, Cabrera, took charge of a group of moriscos and us. He gathered us up and the bailiff Madera put us on a boat and ordered us to be disembarked in Christian lands. But the boat took us to North Africa [*Berbería*] instead, and we disembarked on a beach in a tiny town called Sarjel, three or four leagues from Algiers. We all started to walk toward Algiers, but halfway there, there came a troop of soldiers, more than a hundred strong, from Algiers, to intercept us. They took us to that city, treating us well and letting those of us who couldn't walk ride on horseback. They gave the best horses to the wives of those [moriscos] who had been expelled from Spain. Two or three days later they circumcised us, as I've said, with two Algerians grabbing one man, holding his arms, lowering his trousers and then circumcising him—all without saying a word. I don't know exactly when I confessed with the friar, or priest, exactly as we [pretended] to play [cards], but I confessed to him that it weighed upon my conscience to be there and that they had circumcised me. [Inquisitorial marginalia: It is improbable that they did so violently.]"[43]

Asked to state how many days it was after he was circumcised that he confessed to the friar what had happened, he said, "I think it was about two or three months after the circumcision, because it was then that two or three granadine Muslim saddle-makers, whose names I don't know, told me there was a Christian cleric captive with them and that they had confessed to him. They asked me if I wanted to go confess with them. . . ."

Asked to state how much time had elapsed between when he confessed and when he left Algiers and [when he arrived in Spain,] when and regarding what his first confession was, he said, "The same confessor who [asked] me if I spoke Arabic advised me to go to Oran and from there to Spain, and that I should make friends with some of the Algerian moriscos who are boat captains, and then go out in their boats and escape. He said other things, too. I had the

---

42. *Familiares* were associates but not employees of the Inquisition. They were not necessarily the spies that tradition has made them out to be.

43. The Inquisition's prosecutor, who had just called for Diego Díaz to be tortured and burned at the stake, was probably correct when he speculated that the circumcision was more voluntary than involuntary.

chance to get onto the boat of one of the morisco captains from Aragon. When we got close to the coast between Aragon and Catalonia, I jumped into the water and went to that town [Tortosa?]. From there I went to Zaragoza, where I was ill and in the hospital. I confessed [my sins] before entering. [Inquisitorial marginalia: He left all this out of the story of his life.] From there I went to France to San Juan de la Luz, in search of my father and brothers. I found out that some of them had died and others had returned to Spain. From there I went to Avignon in France, where I confessed."

Asked to state who advised him to go to Avignon in France and whether there was anyone there who could absolve him of this sort of thing, he said, "I had planned to go to Rome to confess my sin. On my way to Avignon I ran into two Franciscan clerics before I arrived in the city. I told them I was going to Rome to be absolved of a sin reserved [for Rome's jurisdiction], without mentioning what that sin was. They told me that here there was a bishop and nuncio who could absolve reserved sins. They bought me a drink so I would go with them, and I stayed with them there for a few days. [Inquisitorial marginalia: He who is circumcised violently and by force does not sin, neither does he need absolution. He who does so fearing for his life, though he commits a grave sin, is not a heretic, and the sin is not reserved, for in his heart he kept faith. Thus, if the defendant had a reserved sin, he was a heretic.] I went to talk with the bishop and nuncio, but they wouldn't see me. Instead, they sent me to see if I could find a priest who spoke my language. The priests sent me to a friar from Vitoria who had lived in Toledo for thirteen years. He counseled me and absolved me. From there I went . . . to Perpignan, then Alicante then Albatera [a small town near Orihuela], where I lodged with a licensed meat-cutter and learned my trade. What I have said is true by the oath I swore." He did not sign. The Inquisitor signed

> [signature illegible]
> Before me
> [signed] Ba. De Villaviciosa

Eighteenth day of January, of 1634: Votes and Sentencing: Let the prisoner be gravely reprimanded in the hall of the audience.[44] Let him abjure *"de levi"*

---

44. Being reprimanded privately, that is, in the Inquisition's hall of audiences, was a far less serious punishment than being reprimanded publicly in an *auto de fe*. It is possible that the tribunal, rather than desiring to punish Díaz less severely, elected to announce his sentence in private because it sought to avoid publicity. Unfortunately, Díaz's case file does not include a detailed record of the rationale behind this decision.

and swear that from now on he will abstain from saying or doing things similar to those of which he has been accused.

In a Spain supposedly free of moriscos, Diego Díaz was one. Arrested on suspicion of "Mohammedizing," Díaz, in order to prove his innocence, had to convince the Inquisition that he could be both a morisco and an orthodox Spanish Catholic. The heart of Díaz's defense flew in the face of a relatively new legal convention. Following the expulsion of 1609, moriscos had no official place in Spain. The self-identity Díaz needed in order to establish his innocence was legally impossible. Yet he managed to escape from the Inquisition without serious punishment. How was he able to do so? And why did the inquisitors let him off so easily?

These questions have no easy answers, but part of the response surely lies in the ambiguous zone that straddled seventeenth-century Spanish notions of ethnicity and nationality. Most Spaniards of the period linked nationality (i.e., Spanishness, whether Catalan, Castilian, Basque, etc.) with religion, that is, Christianity. To be a Spaniard was to be a Christian, and anyone who professed any other religion or who respected something other than the Sunday Sabbath was, by definition, a foreigner, in most instances a Muslim or a Jew. Individuals who maintained dietary customs and practices different from those practiced by most Catholics were similarly suspect, and for males, something as mundane as having a circumcised penis symbolized difference. Yet these categories, however rigid, blurred with respect to moriscos, conversos, and other individuals who straddled the ethnic-national frontier. Such persons found themselves in a liminal status, one akin to mestizos, mixed-bloods and their descendants, in other cultures. Mestizo culture is by definition an amalgam, containing within it, sometimes confusingly so, elements derived from divergent backgrounds.[45]

Diego Díaz was no mestizo. By his own admission, he was an "old" morisco. But as a morisco living in Christian Spain, he and his family apparently maintained certain traditions—such as wearing clean shirts on Fridays, the Muslim holy day—that other Spaniards would have regarded as strange, unusual, even "foreign." We do not know what meaning this custom had for Díaz—wearing a clean shirt on Fridays was not standard Islamic practice. It is also possible that the custom had lost all religious meaning for him, but the opposite is equally plausible. What is certain is that Díaz's case for innocence centered on the repudiation of what others regarded as

45. On mestizo culture, see Serge Gruzinski, *The Mestizo Mind: The Intellectual Dynamics of Colonization and Globalization,* trans. Deke Dusinberre (New York: Routledge, 2002).

the foreign elements in his religious life. He further defended himself with arguments specifically tailored to appeal to the ethnic and religious prejudices of Spain's Old Christian majority. To this end he represented himself as a wholly orthodox Catholic who was appalled by the barbarous customs and sexual practices of the *moros* living in North Africa. Consequently, his life story—as revealed piecemeal in a series of question and answer sessions with the Inquisition—serves to illuminate some of the ways in which individuals were able to twist and otherwise manipulate standards of orthodox behavior within a culture that historians have generally construed as one of the most rigidly conformist in early modern Europe. Díaz understood the rules of Spanish society, and he worked within them, constructing an autobiography that would serve as his defense.

Diego Díaz belonged to a family of old moriscos, or moriscos who had converted to Christianity before the royal edict of 1502, which required all Muslims living in Castile to convert. These *moriscos antiguos* enjoyed certain privileges, among them exemption from a tax, the *farda,* that other, more recent converts were required to pay. Old moriscos lived throughout Castile, but they settled primarily in the southern part of New Castile known as the Campo de Calatrava. There, in towns such as Almagro and Daimiel—Díaz's birthplace—they lived, somewhat separated from the rest of the population, in districts known as *alhamas,* which had once been entirely Muslim. These old moriscos retained some of their traditional religious practices, but with the passage of time, some of these religious practices evolved into inherited cultural practices largely devoid of spiritual meaning. In addition, old moriscos gradually adopted many of the cultural customs of their Christian neighbors, married into Christian families, and integrated well into the local society.

Such was not the case for the "new" moriscos, those moriscos—and their descendants—who had converted after the royal edict of 1502. Most of these moriscos came from the Kingdom of Granada or of Valencia, and for the most part they converted to Christianity under duress. Poorly integrated into Christian society, these new converts, especially the ones residing in rural areas of both Granada and Valencia, retained their language, their traditional costumes and culture, and, in some instances, their religion.

During the reign of Charles V (1516–56), Spain's first Habsburg ruler, the monarchy attempted to legislate the assimilation of these new moriscos into Spanish society. It initiated several attempts at proselytization, but, compared to the resources invested in the campaign to convert the native population of the Americas to Christianity, this was a definitely half-hearted effort, and it met with only limited success. In addition, the Crown issued decrees outlawing Muslim dress, the practice of women's veiling, and even the use of *algaruesía*, the Spanish Muslim dialect of Arabic. These measures, haphazardly enforced, accomplished little. Most new moriscos remained Christians in name alone.

Starting in 1567, the situation changed. Spain's new monarch, Philip II (1556–98), a ruler who was far more doctrinaire in religious matters than his father, was determined not only to root all traces of Protestantism in Spain but also to resolve what was coming to be known as the "morisco problem." In 1566 Philip issued new restrictions on moriscos living in Granada and, ignoring the pleas of those who argued that these decrees were certain to precipitate a rebellion, ordered them to be rigidly enforced. As predicted, the rising occurred the following year and quickly mushroomed into a broader conflict known as the Second War of the Alpujarras (1568-70).[46] After two years of steady fighting, the army commanded by Juan de Austria managed to crush the revolt. This military victory, however, did little to resolve the "morisco problem"; at least from the monarchy's perspective, it made things even worse. In essence, all that the war accomplished was to transform what had been an ethnoreligious minority into enemies of the Spanish state. A growing number of Spaniards now saw moriscos as a "fifth column," in league with their fellow Muslims, the Ottoman Turks, against whom King Philip II was fighting a protracted war.

Philip II's response to this new situation was to initiate, starting in the 1570s, a policy that bears an uncanny resemblance to what is now called ethnic cleansing. Hoping to remove the surviving population of granadine moriscos from coastal regions where they might possibly assist Ottoman invaders, the king and his advisers decided to evict them from their traditional homes and scatter them, in small groups, throughout northern and central Spain. Underlying this policy was the idea that the *granadinos*, divided and separated, would mix with Old Christians, as well as *moriscos antiguos* such as Díaz, and, in so doing, would embrace Christianity and other aspects of Spanish life.

For the moriscos, this policy of forced resettlement led to little more than suffering and resentment. Christians did not consider it a success either, as it led, at least from Inquisition's perspective, to sharp increases in the number of "Mohammedizing" heresies. Spanish churchmen and royal officials soon began to debate the ultimate fate of the moriscos. Could they ever assimilate to Christian culture? How much of a threat did they constitute to Spain's religious purity? Ethnic purity? National security?

---

46. Miguel Angel de Bunes Ibarra, *Los moriscos en el pensamiento histórico: Historiografía de un grupo marginado* (Madrid: Catédra, 1983), 22-25, 30.

If the moriscos were a threat to any of these, what was the more effective solution, assimilation or expulsion? Before the seventeenth century, answers to these questions were decidedly mixed, since some clergy still believed that, through a mixture of education, proselytization, and time, the moriscos might someday assimilate. Most Spaniards, however, took the opposite stance and tended to lump moriscos, both old and new, into a single undifferentiated, decidedly inferior, and potentially dangerous social group. Some clergy even equated the moriscos with false Christians incapable of ever assimilating into the culture of Catholic Spain. "The best known crimes of the moriscos in Spain," one seventeenth-century commentator explained, "are heresy, apostasy and proselytizing, because they still follow the bad sect [of Islam]."[47]

Such beliefs contributed directly to King Philip III's decision in 1609 to order the expulsion of all moriscos from Spain. The royal decree was controversial, but it had widespread support. "Through this just expulsion," wrote one chronicler, "our kingdoms are purified and made clean."[48] Despite such claims, the "purification" this chronicler alluded to was by no means complete. Clergymen throughout Spain argued that those moriscos regarded as "good Christians" should receive exemptions from the expulsion decree.[49] Thus, with the help of their parish priests and by means of other strategies, many of the old moriscos living in the Campo de Calatrava managed to remain in Spain. Nevertheless, in the postexpulsion era, even old moriscos could no longer consider their position within Spanish society to be secure. Many of their neighbors, not to mention secular and religious authorities, now viewed them as Mohammedizers, Turkish sympathizers, or, as the Trinitarian father Diego de Haedo put it, "the worst and cruelest enemies of Christians."[50] So when the Holy Office arrested Diego Díaz for the second time (in 1633) and discovered his morisco ancestry and his residence in North Africa, it is not surprising that the inquisitors in Cuenca viewed him as a dangerous heretic, as well as a *renegado*, or

47. Jaime Bleda, *Coronica de los moriscos de España* (1618), as cited in Bunes Ibarra, *Los moriscos,* 13. The original reads: "Los delitos de los *Moriscos* en España mas sabidos, y conocidos de todos eran como se ha dicho, heregía, apostasía, y dogmatización, porque la mala secta que entre ellos guardaba." For more on the image of Muslims and moriscos in early modern Spain, see Miguel Angel de Bunes Ibarra, *La imagen de los musulmanes y del norte de Africa en los siglos xvi y xvii* (Madrid: CSIC, 1989).

48. Marcos de Guadalajara y Javier, "Predicción y destierro de los m*oriscos,*" as cited in Bunes Ibarra, *Los moriscos,* 40. The original reads: "Con esta justa Expulsion . . . quedan purificados y limpios todos nuestros Reynos."

49. For the arguments employed on behalf of these moriscos, see James B. Tueller, "Good and Faithful Christians: Moriscos and Catholicism in Early Modern Spain" (Ph.D. diss., Columbia University, 1997), chap. 7.

50. *Topographia e historia de Argel* (Valladolid, 1612), 8. Haedo is generally regarded as the pseudonym of Alonso de Sosa.

renegade, the term applied to Catholics who had voluntarily surrendered their faith and converted to Islam.

In the course of his trial, Díaz, an illiterate meat-cutter, elaborated various defensive strategies. The first, common to other savvy Inquisition prisoners, involved the manipulation of inquisitorial trial procedures, specifically, the *tacha* or "cross-out" clause, which allowed prisoners to discount testimony against them given by individuals whom they could identify as mortal enemies. When the inquisitors presented Díaz with a copy of the testimonials against him—a copy specially made for the accused, with the witnesses' names left out—Díaz correctly guessed the identities of his denouncers and cited them as enemies. Through this strategy, he successfully eliminated the minor charges of cultural "Mohammedizing" (his refusal to eat pork or his habit of changing his shirt on Thursday evenings, for example) that certain individuals claimed to have witnessed.[51]

The *tachas* clause allowed Díaz to evade these minor charges, but how could he disprove the inquisitors' suspicion that, during his stay in Algiers, he had converted to Islam and become a renegade? Diego de Haedo, in an influential book on Algiers first published in 1612, had described such conversions in considerable detail. He included detailed information concerning the ceremonies surrounding the ritual circumcision of converts, much of which was identical with the circumcision story provided by Díaz.[52] For the inquisitors, Diego's circumcised penis constituted irrefutable evidence of conversion and therefore of heresy.

Díaz, not surprisingly, saw it in a different light. He accepted the circumcision as proof of wrongdoing, but wrongdoing that had nothing to do with heresy. He openly admitted that his circumscribed member was shameful and a marker of sin but repeatedly claimed that his circumcision was forced. Recent studies, however, suggest that few of the Christian captives held in Muslim Algiers were circumcised under duress and in the manner Díaz described. Rather, the vast majority of the male captives known to have been circumcised in North Africa only experienced this rite following a *voluntary* conversion to Islam.[53] It was also at this point, and as a way of

51. On the criminalization of cultural practices that did not run counter to Christian doctrine, see Ronald E. Surtz, "Maurofilia y maurofobia en los procesos inquisitoriales de Cristóbal Duarte Ballester," in *Mélanges,* ed. Luce López-Baralt, ser. 9, vol. 2 (Zaghovan, Tunisia: Fondtion Temimi, 2001), 711–22; Julio Caro Baroja, *Los moriscos del reino de Granada: Ensayo de historia social* (Madrid: Itsmo, 1976), 124–25; García-Arenal, *Inquisición y moriscos,* 46.

52. *Topografía,* 9v–10.

53. For the conversion and circumcision of these captives, see Bennassar and Bennassar, *Los cristianos de Alá,* esp. chap. 4. For more on the way Spaniards viewed North Africa and its culture, see Mercedes García-Arenal, *Los españoles y el norte de África, siglos XV–XVIII* (Madrid: Ediciones Mapfre, 1992).

celebrating this rite of passage, that the newly circumcised convert was feted in the way Díaz recounted. The inquisitor's prosecutor therefore had good reason to doubt the veracity of Díaz's story, but he did not have the evidence to prove it. In the meantime, Díaz, playing upon inquisitorial sympathies, claims to have felt so bad about his mutilated member that he sought out confession—and thus absolution—at the very first opportunity.

In making this argument, Díaz also displayed a rather sophisticated understanding of the difference between heresy—a religious crime subject to punishment by the Holy Office—and sin, which was not. According to canon law, heresy implied the willful denial of and separation from Catholic doctrine, whereas sin carried with it notions of error arising either from ignorance of doctrine or situations in which believers engaged in practices that they knew to be wrong. How Díaz, a meat-cutter by trade, learned about this difference is by no means clear, but in an effort to appeal to the inquisitors' understanding of this issue, he foregrounded it in his testimony concerning his circumcision.

> I said in my confession that when I was in Moorish lands they violently and forcibly circumcised me and other moriscos, which they did because they knew we were Christians. What consoled me at that time was knowing that in my soul I had not abandoned the faith of Our Lord Jesus Christ, as I had not. Rather, I suffered. If we had not submitted [to circumcision] they would have killed us. It was never, in any way, my intention to deny the law of Our Lord Jesus Christ. My intention was to confess it, in case it was a sin.

By admitting to the circumcision as a sin but denying it as a willful heretical act, Díaz offered his inquisitors a way to understand it as a nonheretical act.

The third element of Díaz's defense was possibly the most difficult for him to construct. Unlike the first, in which he used inquisitorial procedure to his own advantage, or the second, in which he used canon law to support his innocence with respect to his circumcised penis, Díaz had little to support his argument that he could be a Christian, a Spaniard, and a morisco at the same time. On this issue he reminded the inquisitors that Muslims considered him a faithful Christian and had consequently mistreated him. ("They violently and forcibly circumcised me and other moriscos, which they did because they knew we were Christians.") In making this argument, he played off the idea, fairly current at the time, that Muslims perceived moriscos as Christians or, at the very least, as individuals whose customs and religious practices were very different from their own. One Spanish commander in the Alpujarras war had observed that "among the Christians [moriscos] were treated as and believed to be Moors, and were despised. Among Moors, [they were taken] for Christians, so that they were not believed or aided."[54] Similarly, Diego de Haedo had distinguished between moriscos originating from Spain and *moros,* or Muslims, indigenous to North Africa.[55]

Also integral to Díaz's effort to separate himself from the *moros* was his effort to define Algerian Muslims as a totally alien people with whom he had nothing in common. Algerians, he asserted, "do everything backward from the way it's done in Spain." Algerian women "walk around with their faces covered so no one can see them." Men, "when they needed to urinate . . . lowered their trousers . . . and squatted like women." They were also sodomites who would buy boy slaves and kidnap the sons of morisco captives and "make bad use" of them, an assertion that echoed Haedo's account of "sodomía" as a widespread practice in Algiers.[56] "Look, my lord, this is turpitude!" Díaz exclaimed, "Why would anyone want to be a Moor?"[57]

Díaz went on to argue that morisco lineage did not offer sufficient proof of heresy. "The only thing that hurts my case is the disgrace of my nation and my ancestors." And while he admitted that moriscos in general had a "bad reputation," he claimed that two hundred of his neighbors could attest to his clean living and good habits and to the fact that "in all my life I've never known Moorish ceremonies, or anything about them." Then, shifting gears, he asked the following rhetorical question: "I also wanted to ask your lordship," he said, "if one can be a Moor without knowing any of the Moorish ceremonies, because I don't know them and haven't had anyone to teach them to me."

Diego Díaz's case proceeded to its end, and the inquisitors met to render judgment. The inquisitors, as usual, did not leave behind a detailed written account of their decision-making process. However, if the case's eventual outcome—*abjuración ad levi* in a private as opposed to a public *auto de fe,* offers any indication of the judges' reasoning, Díaz's arguments appear to have worked. The inquisitors voted unanimously to let him go with minimal punishment. "Let the prisoner be gravely

---

54. Diego Hurtado de Mendoza, *Guerra de Granada,* cited in Bunes Ibarra, *Los Moriscos,* 25. Modern historians have voiced the same perception. See Francisco Márquez Villanueva, *El problema morisco (desde otras laderas)* (Madrid: Librarias Poduhufi, 1991), 6.

55. *Topografía,* 8.

56. Ibid., 9.

57. Suspicions of Muslims as sodomites appear in Inquisition trial transcripts of morisco defendants. See Surtz, "Maurofilia y maurofobia," 714; and William Monter, *Frontiers of Heresy: The Spanish Inquisition from the Basque Lands to Sicily* (Cambridge: Cambridge University Press, 1990), 189–230, 276–99.

reprimanded in the hall of the audience. Let him be declared lightly suspect [of heresy] and swear that from now on he will abstain from saying or doing things similar to those of which he has been accused." This sentence, the lightest possible, was very close to absolution, the inquisitorial equivalent of not guilty.

What is interesting in this case is that the Inquisition did not subject Díaz to either physical or pecuniary punishment, nor did it publicly humiliate him or declare him a heretic. Neither did it hand him over to the secular justice, either to have him deported from Spain as a morisco or to have him serve for a number of what would have been truly terrible years as an oarsman in Spain's galley fleet. Working in Díaz's favor was the fact that he was an old morisco from the Campo de Calatrava and therefore fairly well integrated into Spanish life. There is also evidence that other moriscos from this same region had had recourse to the secular courts to escape the Expulsion Order and to remain where they were. Díaz, in contrast, did not go to the law. Rather, he left Spain for France, later returning to La Mancha, a region adjacent to his homeland, where he could, thanks in part to his skills as a meat-cutter, re-integrate himself into Spanish life. In the end, therefore, his inquisitorial trial, however disruptive or disturbing in the short run, was something of a nonevent and thus a victory for Díaz. Through skillful manipulation of inquisitorial procedures and a life story that included lucid arguments especially tailored for inquisitorial ears, Diego Díaz overcame the legal oxymora of his ethnicity, his religion, and his nationality. In so doing, he circumvented the king's Expulsion Order and defended himself against the Inquisition.

However, in light of evidence suggesting that most of the Christian captives in North Africa who converted to Islam were in fact renegades, we, as modern readers, ought to remain somewhat skeptical about the veracity of Díaz's story. Unless new documents pertaining to his case appear, we probably will never know for certain whether this old morisco was, deep in his heart of hearts, a Christian, a Muslim, or, as is equally likely, some unusual combination of these two traditions.

FURTHER READING

Available literature in English on the history of the moriscos in Spain is somewhat limited. The classic treatment of the subject is that of Henry C. Lea, *The Moriscos of Spain: Their Conversion and Expulsion* (New York, 1901); but that work should be supplemented by Anwar G. Chejne, *Islam and the West: The Moriscos, a Cultural and Social History* (Albany, NY: SUNY Press, 1983). Readers of Spanish should also consult Antonio Domínguez Ortiz and Bernard

Vincent, *Historia de los moriscos: Vida y tragedia de una minoría* (Madrid: Revista de Occidente, 1978), and, with specific reference to Cuenca, Mercedes García-Arenal, *Inquisición y moriscos: Los procesos del Tribunal de Cuenca* (Madrid: Siglo Veintiuno Editores, 1978). See also David Coleman, *Creating Christian Granada: Society and Religious Culture in an Old-World Frontier City, 1492–1600* (Ithaca, NY: Cornell University Press, 2003), esp. chap. 4.

On renegades, see Ellen G. Friedman, *Spanish Captives in North Africa in the Early Modern Age* (Madison: University of Wisconsin Press, 1983); and María Antonio Garcés, *Cervantes in Algiers: A Captive's Tale* (Nashville, TN: Vanderbilt University Press, 2002); although the best overall study is Bartolomé Bennassar and Lucile Bennassar, *Los cristianos de Alá: La fascinante aventura de los renegados,* trans. José Luis Gil Aristu (Madrid: Nera, 1989).

On religious issues in Cuenca and its diocese, see Sara T. Nalle, *God in La Mancha: Religious Reform and the People of Cuenca, 1500–1650* (Baltimore: Johns Hopkins University Press, 1992).

CHAPTER SIX

Keeping the Faith

Doña Blanca Méndez de Rivera

Blanca Méndez de Rivera, born in Seville about 1590, was orphaned as a child. Raised initially by a cousin and later educated in a convent, at the age of fifteen Blanca married Diego López Ribero, a Portuguese merchant. A year later Blanca's cousin instructed her to reject the Christian doctrine she had learned in the convent and embrace the "Law of Moses" instead. Blanca obeyed. Between 1606 and 1621 she had five daughters and introduced them to Judaic rituals and practices. Then, following the arrest of several of her friends and relatives on charges of Judaizing, Blanca and her family emigrated to Mexico City, the capital of New Spain.

Once in the New World, Blanca and daughters—known collectively as the Blancas—joined other crypto-Jews, the majority of whom were of Portuguese origin, residing in Mexico City. As they provided their brethren with a variety of religious services, the Blancas emerged as prominent members of the crypto-Jewish community, which was protected by the viceroy and generally ignored by the Inquisition. Yet this situation was not destined to last. In 1641 a new viceroy, together with the Inquisition, initiated a crackdown on the city's crypto-Jewish community with the help of specially recruited spies, one of whom, Gaspar de Robles, was Blanca's relative. Soon the Holy Office was ready to pounce, and on 17 May 1642 the Blancas found themselves in the inquisitorial prison.

The Blancas suspected they might have been turned in by one of their own who was an Inquisition spy. They discussed the possibility out loud in their prison cells. What they did not realize was that the Holy Office in Mexico City, contrary to inquisitorial regulations, stocked its prisons with spies who nightly prowled the hallways in woolen slippers, recording the prisoners' unguarded conversations and reporting them to the inquisitors. This is the life story of Blanca Méndez de Rivera, as she told it on and off the record.

Criminal trial record of doña Blanca Méndez de Rivera,[1] widow of Diego López Ribero of Seville, observer of the Law of Moses . . . Imprisoned from 17 May [16]42 to 16 April 1646, when she went to the *auto.*

First Audience

Asked what her name was, where she was from, how old she was, what profession she practiced, and when she was arrested, she said, "My name is doña Blanca de Rivera.[2] I am fifty years old, more or less, and make my living as a seamstress. I was arrested by this Holy Office last Saturday, the seventeenth of this month and year. I am a native of the city of Seville, born on Dados Street and baptized in San Salvador parish."

She gave her genealogy as follows:

Parents: "Enrique Rodríguez Obregón, from Llerena, Extremadura, and doña Margarita López, from Seville. They are dead. My father was a slave trader who carried blacks from Angola to New Spain."[3]

Paternal Grandparents: "I never met them and don't know their names."[4]

---

1. The trial transcript (Archivo General de la Nación, Mexico City [AGN]: Sección de Inquisición [Inq.], vol. 1530, exp. 3), along with expert advice on how to read and interpret it, was generously provided to us by Professor Robert Ferry of the University of Colorado, Boulder. Blanca and her daughters, collectively known as "Las Blancas," are the centerpiece of Ferry's forthcoming book on women's social networks in seventeenth-century Mexico.

2. The honorific *doña* was a status marker that denoted membership in the untitled nobility *(hidalguía).* By identifying herself as "doña," Blanca is making a claim for high social status, which she may have hoped would protect her from the Inquisition. Such status (membership in the titled or untitled nobility) was an advantage in secular court proceedings but was not taken into account in the inquisitorial justice system.

3. The Spanish colony of New Spain encompassed today's Mexico, Central America, and southwestern United States. The Spanish term Blanca used to refer to her father's occupation was *cargador de negros.*

4. Contrary to our assumptions about the stasis of early modern Europeans, many were highly mobile. Secret Jews, especially, tended to be mobile, moving from city to city either to escape inquisitorial persecution or to escape the notoriety of having been, or being related to, an Inquisition

Maternal Grandparents: "I never met them, don't know their names, and never heard anyone talk about them. I never knew my father, since he died when I was four or five years old. My mother died soon after."

Paternal Aunts and Uncles: "I don't have any and have never met any."

Maternal Aunts and Uncles: "I don't have any of those, either, and don't know of any."

Siblings: "Doña Catalina de Rivera is the oldest. She got married in Cartagena de Indias, to Capitan Luis de Mena. I don't know whether they're alive, but I did hear it said that they had a son, Laureano Maldonado de Rivera, who, they say, died in Peru. Luis López, [my brother], as far as I know, is in Maracayo, but I'm not in touch with him and don't write to him. I don't know if he's married, alive, or dead."

Husband and Children: "Diego López de Ribero, native of Castelobranco in the Kingdom of Portugal, who died eleven years ago here in Mexico City. He's buried in this city's Holy Cathedral. We married in the city of Seville and lived together as man and wife for more than twenty years. During our marriage we had the following children: María, Margarita, Catalina, Clara, and Isabel,[5] all of whom were born in Seville on Dados Street and were baptized in the parish of San Salvador. María[6] married her cousin Manuel de Granada, a native of Seville, after receiving a dispensation from His Holiness.[7] Manuel

---

prisoner. And despite current notions about the stability and closeness of the early modern family, historians have found that many early modern Europeans did not maintain close contacts with extended family. Blanca's claims not to know any of her relatives because her parents died when she was young, however, are false: she later admits to being raised by a cousin and to knowing other relatives in Seville. By claiming not to know any of her relatives, Blanca may have been protecting them so they would not be tainted with heresy by association and fall under the scrutiny of the Inquisition themselves. She was also protecting herself from guilt by association. The inquisitors later discover that she fled Seville after her cousin and other associates were arrested as Judaizers by that city's Holy Office.

5. Blanca lists her daughters in birth order. At the time of their arrests, the oldest daughter, María, was about thirty-five years old. The youngest, Isabel, was twenty-one. See Robert Ferry, "The Blancas: Women, Honor, and the Jewish Community in Seventeenth-Century Mexico," unpublished paper, 8.

6. Members of Mexico City's secret Jewish community agreed that María was extremely bright and knowledgeable in matters of the faith. Isabel, they said, was "as smart as" her oldest sister. Catalina they called "timid," Margarita "clever," and Clara "simple, feeble-minded and crazy." See Boleslao Lewin, *Confidencias de dos criptojudíos en las cárceles del Santo Oficio (México, 1645–1646)* (Buenos Aires: Lewin, 1975), 97. Lewin's evidence comes from a jailhouse conversation between Juan Pacheco de León and Francisco Botello, recorded by Inquisition spy Gaspar de Alfar on 11 January 1646.

7. Blanca makes clear that her daughter's marriage to a first cousin was legitimate and under the auspices of the Catholic Church. Canon law prohibited first cousins from marrying without a special dispensation from the pope. In contrast, marriage between first cousins was both permissible in Judaism and frequent among Spanish secret Jews as a way of ensuring the family's security as well as the continuity of their clandestine faith. According to historian Stanley Hordes, 96 percent of marriages

died in China and left two sons behind, the older named Rafael, who is about fifteen years old and who studies in the College of Arts, and Gabriel de Granada, who goes to school. Margarita agreed to marry another cousin, Miguel Núñez, who left eleven years ago.[8] They say he's in Havana. He and Margarita have no children. Catalina is married to Diego Correa, native of Seville, who has a dry-goods shop in the Plaza. They have a son, Luisico,[9] who's four and a half. Clara[10] is married to Felipe López de Noroña, a native of Seville. They live in this city and have no children. Isabel is still unmarried."

"I never remarried, and was only married to Diego López Ribero. I have no other children, apart from those I've mentioned."

Asked what caste and lineage were her parents and grandparents, aunts and uncles, and other relatives, and if they, or any of them, or this confessant, had been penanced or reconciled or condemned by the Holy Office of the Inquisition, she said, "I know about my parents and my paternal grandparents, but I don't know about my maternal grandparents. My paternal grandparents and parents, I'm quite certain, are, by caste and lineage, Portuguese, from the Kingdom of Portugal.[11] They are known as Old Christians, and neither they nor my husband, nor my children, nor I have been a prisoner or a convict of,

---

among the secret Jews of New Spain were endogamous, that is, with other members of the same community, who were often blood relatives. Stanley Hordes, "The Crypto Jewish Community of New Spain, 1620–1649" (Ph.D. diss., Tulane University, 1980), 210, as cited in Solange Alberro, *Inquisition et société au Mexique, 1571–1700* (Mexico City: Centre des études Mexicaines et Centraméricaines, 1988), 434.

8. In other words, Margarita and her cousin exchanged promises to marry (similar to getting engaged) but did not go through with the wedding itself. In the seventeenth century, Catholics like Margarita de Rivera who exchanged marriage promises but did not then marry their betrothed were left in a state of connubial limbo. Their fiancés were not obligated to follow through on the marriage promise, but neither member of the betrothed couple was able to marry anyone else until and unless a priest gave the couple a dispensation that allowed them to break the promise.

9. Luisico is a diminutive of Luis.

10. From the moment of their arrest, Clara's mother and sisters feared that she, the "simple, feeble-minded and crazy" sister, would talk easily, which she did when the inquisitors insinuated that if she told all they would let her see her husband, whom Clara loved very much, in spite of his reputation for being "feeble-minded and savage." Clara never saw her husband again. She died in prison. See Lewin, *Confidencias*, 97.

11. At the time of Blanca's arrest, the Portuguese were fighting the Castilian Crown. They had rebelled in 1640 in an effort to establish their independence after having been absorbed into Habsburg monarchy in 1582. Historians have argued that Castilians, even Castilians in Colonial Mexico, may have been hostile toward Portuguese. It did not help Blanca's case that many of the Portuguese immigrants to Castile and Castilian colonies, including New Spain (Mexico), were conversos and actively practicing secret Jews. The connection between Portuguese immigrants in Castile and conversos was so strong as to make the terms synonymous in common usage. To be "of the Portuguese nation" meant to be of converso descent.

or punished by, the Holy Office of the Inquisition. This I also know to be true of my husband and his many relatives, parents, grandparents, and many other relations in the city of Seville."

Because it was very late the audience ended. Advised that she think it over well and tell the truth, she was warned in the correct fashion and ordered to return to her cell. Having read back to her all she said in this audience, she said it was the truth and well written. She affirmed it and ratified it with her signature, and I with mine. If she is married, [the signature] is invalid.[12]

> Before me [scribe's signature illeg.]
> [signed] doña Blanca de Rivera

Second Audience

In Mexico City, Tuesday, the twentieth of May in the year sixteen hundred and forty-two, afternoon audience, Inquisitors Domingo Veles de Asas y Argos, and Doctor don Bartolomé González Soltero, Bishop Elect of Guatemala presiding. They commanded that Blanca de Rivera, widow, prisoner in the secret prisons, be brought before them so that they might conduct the aforementioned audience. Once present, she was asked if she had remembered anything in relation to her case, and was told to tell it and, by the oath she had sworn, to tell the whole truth.

She said, "Even though I've searched my memory, I have nothing to say other than what I have already said."

Asked if she was a baptized, confirmed Christian and if she heard Mass, confessed, and partook of the Eucharist when the Holy Mother Church commands, she said, "I am a Christian, baptized in San Salvador parish in Seville. Bishop don Juan de Lasal, Auxiliary Bishop [of Seville], during the archbishopric of don Pedro de Castro y Quiñones, confirmed me. I hear Mass on Sundays and festivals of obligation.[13] I confess and partake of the Eucharist on Holy Thursday.[14] The last time I confessed was the Holy Thursday before Easter this year. I confessed in the Mexico City cathedral with a Carmelite father who was fat and old, but I don't know his name. I partook of the Eucharist that same day in the sanctuary. All of my daughters confessed and

---

12. Blanca is widowed, so, unlike a married woman, whose legal authority would have passed to her husband, she could ratify her own legal documents.

13. Holidays on which the Church requires the faithful to hear Mass.

14. Seventeenth-century Catholics were required to confess once a year at Easter. Holy Thursday is the Thursday before Easter Sunday.

partook of the Eucharist as well, and we all have our seals of confession and communion."

She crossed and blessed herself and said the Our Father, the Ave Maria, the Creed, the Salve Regina, the [Ten] Commandments, the Law of God, and [the Law] of the Church; the Articles of the Faith and [the Articles] of General Confession, the sacraments, the seven mortal sins, and the other prayers of the Christian doctrine, and said them all well.[15]

Asked if she knows how to read and write, she said, "I do. I was taught to read and write in the Convent of the [Immaculate] Conception of San Miguel in Seville, where I was from the age of ten until they took me out to marry me to Diego López Ribero, who is now dead."[16]

Asked if she had ever traveled outside of these Kingdoms of Castile and the Indies, where to, and with whom, she said, "I haven't been outside of Spain except to come to this kingdom [of the Indies] with my husband and daughters. We came in General Fernando de Sosa's flotilla, on Captain Balthasar Ome's boat, along with one of the captain's brothers, Melchior Ome. I think the year was 1621. The Marques of Leves and the Marques of Veracruz were also in the flotilla. We all came to this city, where we've lived without leaving until 1629, when because of the flood we left the city.[17] I went with my husband and daughters and two sons-in-law to the mining town of San Luis Potosí, where my other two sons-in-law, Manuel de Granada (now dead) and Miguel Núñes de Huerta, were living. We stayed there in that town for about two years. Then we came back to Mexico City, where my husband died. Since then I haven't left the city, and neither have my daughters, to go anywhere at all."

Story of Her Life

She was asked for the story of her life. She said, "I was born, as I've said, in the city of Seville, which is where my parents died when I was five or six years old. I was raised by my widowed aunt doña Isabel Núñez,[18] first cousin to my

15. This should not be surprising, given that doña Blanca was convent educated. Other secret Jews were not as well versed in Catholic doctrine. It was rumored that after the Blancas' arrest, other members of Mexico City's secret Jewish community panicked. Fearing imminent arrest, they spent hours poring over Catholic prayer books and catechisms, "cramming" for this part of the inquisitorial interrogation. See Alberro, *Inquisition et société*, 559.

16. Note the phrasing ("they took me out to marry me"). Blanca's was an arranged marriage, unlike the marriages of her daughters.

17. The flood of 1629 was a major catastrophe in Mexico City. Parts of the city were covered in up to six feet of water.

18. Blanca later gives the name of the cousin who raised her as Ana Enríquez, who had been pen-

father, Enrique Núñez.[19] She put me in the Convent of the Conception when I was about nine or ten years old. There, a nun named doña Isabel Duarte, who was the aunt of don Francisco Duarte, president of the Casa de Contratación,[20] taught me reading and writing and lots of other virtuous things. I stayed in the convent until they took me out to marry me to my husband Diego López Ribero. While I was in the convent, Rui Dias[21] de Lemos, a cousin on my mother's side, who was in Cartagena and was the uncle of Luis de Lemos, paid for my expenses and arranged my marriage [with the help of] García de Lucena and his wife doña María Gomes, who were my husband's kin. We got married and held our veiling,[22] as I've said, in San Salvador parish. My godparents were my husband's kinsmen García de Lucena and doña María Gomes, his wife. We lived together as man and wife in Seville until we came to this kingdom. In that time we had all of our daughters, who were born in the city of Seville. After we landed in Veracruz, we came to Mexico City. From there we went to San Luis Potosí, from whence we returned here, where I have remained until now and which is where everything I confessed in my first audience, which I remitted to you, happened." This was the story of her life.

Asked if she knew, presumed, or suspected the reasons she was arrested and had been brought to the prisons of this Holy Office, she said, "I know well. I presume that I've been arrested for having been and being an observer of the Law of Moses, and for having committed the crimes I've confessed."[23]

Asked when it was that she began to profess and keep the Law of Moses, who taught her, which rites and ceremonies she performed, and if she knew that [the Law of Moses] was contrary to that of Our Lord Jesus Christ, which she professed in holy baptism, and if she believed in the errors of the Law of

---

anced by the Inquisition of Seville for Judaizing. By changing her cousin's name to Isabel Núñez, Blanca may have been trying to protect her cousin from rearrest as a relapsed heretic. She may also have been trying to protect herself from guilt by association.

19. Blanca had previously given her father's last names as Rodríguez Obregón. In changing Ana Enríquez's name to shield her, Blanca compounded the lie and changed her father's name as well.

20. The Casa de Contratación (House of Trade) was established in Seville (in 1503) to regulate trade with Castile's American colonies. Blanca was in a convent for high-status women, as indicated by the presence of the president of the Casa de Contratación's aunt.

21. *Dias* (with an *s* as opposed to a *z*) may be a scribe's mistranscription of a Spanish last name. More likely, however, it represents a correct pronunciation and betrays the Portuguese origins of doña Blanca's relatives. Portuguese immigrants to Castile and the Indies were likely to be conversos. Historians have found that they were more likely than Spanish conversos to be crypto-Jews, a conclusion many early modern Spaniards shared.

22. *Velaron.* The veiling was a part of the early modern Catholic marriage ceremony.

23. Blanca had not yet confessed anything at this point.

Moses with all her heart, straying from the faith and inheritance of the law of Our Lord Jesus Christ, if she persisted in those errors, and if at present believed that in them she would be saved, she said, "I confess that about eleven years ago, more or less, Justa Méndez, now dead,[24] taught me and my daughters the Law of Moses while we were living in her house. She told me it was good and necessary for my salvation, that the Law of Jesus Christ Our Lord wasn't, and that I should perform fasts,[25] which I should carry out in deepest secrecy without telling anyone at all. If anyone were to find out about these fasts, it could turn out very badly for all of us, especially for her, since she had been a prisoner of the Holy Office and had been punished for observing the Law of Moses. If the Inquisition were to find out that she had taught the Law to me and my daughters, a great deal of harm and evil would come to her. I promised to keep it a secret and not to tell all of my daughters, just the older ones, María and Margarita, not the little ones, Clara and Isabel. I didn't say anything to my daughter Catalina until after we had left Justa Méndez's house.

"From the time Justa Méndez told me this, I, being weak and miserable, believed it. I believed that the Law of Moses was right and true and necessary for my salvation, and that the Law of Our Lord Jesus Christ was not. I strayed from the Law of Jesus Christ even though I knew the Law of Moses was contrary to it. But truly, the [Law of Jesus Christ] did not entirely leave my heart, and I didn't entirely cease to believe it. I was never really sure about the Law of Moses, because it always caused me remorse in my conscience and raised doubts in my mind about which was more right and true and necessary for my salvation, the Law of Moses or that of Our Lord Jesus Christ. Even though I performed all the fasts of the Law [of Moses], as I've confessed, and I kept the Law with my daughters from the day we were taught until the present day, in my soul I've always held and believed that the Law that was more right and necessary for my salvation was the Law of Our Lord Jesus Christ. So it was that when I fasted with my daughters, I had to force myself to do it. I told them

24. Justa Méndez was Blanca's first landlady when she and her family arrived in Mexico City. Blanca's plan, which she worked out with her daughters ahead of time, was to implicate only dead secret Jews in her testimony so as not to jeopardize living members of the community.

25. *Ayunos.* Ritual fasts are part of Jewish religious practice, but Blanca, her family, and Mexico City's other secret Jews appear to have adopted a syncretic fasting style that resembles Catholic penitential fasts. Mexico City's secret Jews would have been well acquainted with fasting as an efficacious religious practice, both from their own education as secret Jews and from the wider Catholic culture around them. Fasting may also have been a relatively invisible, if inaccurate, way of practicing Judaism, therefore a particularly appealing ritual for Mexico City's secret Jews to adopt.

many times and regularly that I wished to God I had never met Justa Méndez or taught [the Law] to all my daughters. Many times I'd made up my mind to come to this Holy Office with my daughters to ask for mercy and confess my guilt, as I've done, but the Devil impeded it through shame and fear. For this I am very repentant.

"After I was arrested, I asked for an audience so I could tell all, as I've done, and today, even though I am so afflicted, I am greatly consoled for having confessed my guilt. My errors tear at my heart and cause streams of tears. I am very repentant. I have truly erred [and strayed?] from a faith as good and plain as that of Our Lord Jesus Christ, which is the only good, true, and necessary faith for the salvation of my soul, and not any other faith, especially not the dead Law of Moses, which I kept and held so blindly, as did my daughters, until we were brought as prisoners to this Holy Office, for which I give many and infinite thanks and praise to Our Lord. Through this imprisonment He has delivered me from my errors and placed me and my daughters on the path to salvation."

Asked if in the sacramental confessions she made she confessed to her confessor that she had believed in the errors of the Law of Moses, and in keeping it had fasted and observed it, and if she received the holy sacrament [of confession] and in what form, she said, "I never confessed these errors to my confessors because Justa Méndez told me not to, so that no one would find out. I told my daughters not to confess for the same reason, which has been my misfortune. I confessed and received the holy sacrament because they took me for a Catholic Christian, even though I knew well that the confessions and communications were sinful and offensive to God because I hadn't confessed those errors."

[When asked with whom she practiced rites of the Law of Moses, Blanca gave the names of several deceased secret Jews, whom she and her daughters had agreed ahead of time to implicate so as not to endanger any living members of Mexico City's secret Jewish community. At this point, Blanca only reported having performed fasts, not any other rituals. The audience ended with another formulaic warning.

After Blanca's fourth audience, she and her daughters had a jailhouse conversation that Inquisition spies secretly recorded from outside the cells. Blanca and her daughters said insulting things about the inquisitors and plotted ways in which they could protect themselves and other members of the Mexico City secret Jewish community. This conversation is reproduced, in part, in the prosecutor's final accusation against Blanca (translated below, see pages 171–80). The day after this conversation, the inquisitors moved Blanca out of her cell and into the torture chamber.]

Act of Transfer of Cell

In Mexico City, Thursday, the fifth day of the month of June in the year sixteen hundred and forty-two, afternoon audience, Lord Inquisitors Doctor of Jurisprudence Domingo Veles de Asas y Argos and Doctor don Francisco de Estrada y Escovedo presiding. They said that, as per the information they received up to today regarding the prison conversations of doña Blanca Méndez y [sic] Rivera, contained in this file, she, along with doña María and doña Isabel de Rivera, her daughters, had broken the secrecy that they were warned to keep in their prison cells, and which they were obliged to keep. They have communicated very perniciously and imprudently and have arranged to conceal the truth of their crimes and of those of many other persons, their accomplices, whose identities they have maliciously kept secret and concealed. So that the aforesaid communications may cease and so that they may not result in any grave danger or harm if they were to continue, the Lord Inquisitors have commanded and command that said doña Blanca Méndez y [sic] Rivera be transferred from the cell in which she is at present, and be placed in the torture chamber, which they will use as a cell for lack of any other place to put her[26] so that they may be sure she does not communicate with her daughters. Thus, have the prison bailiff, Francisco Ruiz Marañón, remove the instruments [of torture] from the chamber and, during the time that doña Blanca Méndez o [sic] Rivera is having her audience, let him move her bed and clothing to the aforementioned chamber and cell, where she will be housed after the audience.

In response, the bailiff said he would do so . . . punctually as he had been commanded. The above was signed with a rubric.

> [signed with rubric]
> Before me, Doctor of Jurisprudence Enrique
> de Narváez

[In her fifth audience, held on the same day as the transfer of cell, Blanca claimed not to remember anything but begged to be let out of solitary confine-

---

26. One of the things the inquisitors learned from Blanca's prison conversation was that she was mortally afraid of torture. The inquisitors' claim that they moved Blanca into the torture chamber only because there were no other cells available may have been disingenuous.

ment in the torture chamber. She said, "I do not remember anything else I should say, even though I searched my memory. Last night I felt exhausted and ill and was unable to sleep. Today I've been unable to eat because of a headache and melancholy. Because of this I beg and plead that for the love of God you give me a cellmate so that I do not die alone inside four walls." The inquisitors gave Blanca her third formulaic warning, and she repeated that she had nothing else to say. They ended the audience by commanding that she return to her new cell, the torture chamber.

By Monday 7 July 1642, her sixth audience, Blanca had cracked and appeared suicidal. She had, at this point, spent four weeks in solitary confinement in the torture chamber. She broke down and confessed, implicating nearly every living member of Mexico City's secret Jewish community.]

In Mexico City, Monday, the seventh of July of the year sixteen hundred and forty-two, morning audience, the Lord Inquisitor Doctor don Francisco de Estrada y Escovedo was presiding by himself, due to the illness of the Lord Inquisitor Argos. Francisco Ruiz Marañón, bailiff of the secret prisons, appeared before him and told him that doña Blanca de Rivera had requested an audience. She was brought in. Once present, she was told that the bailiff had said she had requested an audience. She is now in one, and she should say why she requested it and tell the truth by the oath she swore.

She said, "I asked for this audience and want it so I can unburden my conscience and tell the truth, because God has made me see the light so that I may tell [the truth] and try to save my soul. I have been, and am, so afflicted in the cell where I am that the Devil has tempted me many times to hang myself or take my own life. I would have done it if God had not held me in His hand. Because of this I ask and beg that by His love you put me in some other cell and I will truly convert to God and tell the truth as I have promised.

"In keeping [with that promise], I know that doña Blanca Enríquez,[27] now dead, who was the wife of Antonio Rodrigues Arias, also dead, and her daugh-

---

27. Blanca Enríquez and her daughters, collectively known as "the Rubias," as Blanca and her daughters were known as "the Blancas," were the Blancas' patronesses. Blanca Enríquez had been arrested and tortured by the Inquisition in Seville. Blanca Méndez de Rivera and others in Mexico City's secret Jewish community had seen Blanca Enríquez's torture scars and admired her courage for not having talked during her interrogation. Blanca Méndez de Rivera had sought to emulate Blanca Enríquez's courage but had failed, cracking after a month in solitary confinement in the torture chamber. The fact that the first denunciation Blanca Méndez de Rivera made was against her patronesses is a testament to how frightened and lost she was at that point in her trial. Blanca Enríquez and Blanca Méndez de Rivera may also have been cousins. See Alberro, *Inquisition et société*, 445 n. 89; "Proceso contra Isabel Duarte, la de Atúnez (1642)," AGN: Inq., vol. 487, exp. 21, fols. 619v and 620.

ters, doña Juana, wife of Simón Váez Sevilla, and doña Catalina Enríquez and her husband Diego Finoco, dead, and doña Rafaela Enríquez, wife of Gaspar Suárez, and doña Beatriz Enríquez, wife of Tomas Núñes de Peralta, and doña Micaela, wife of Sebastián Cardoso, all of these women along with Diego Finoco, have been and are observers of the Law of Moses. Before me and all my daughters they have stated and state that they were, and my daughters and I have done the same before them. I know that they have fasted and do fast the fasts of the aforementioned Law, as my daughters and I have done. We kept the fasts in our houses in observance of that Law.

·"Also, I know that Simón Váez Sevilla is an observer of the Law of Moses because I heard it said that he is, although I don't know who said it. Once while I was walking along the pavement in the Plaza, I saw Simón Váez Sevilla pass by. A group of men (I don't know who they were or what their names are) said of Simón Váez Sevilla, 'There goes that big Jew *(Judiasso)*.[28] Everything he's earned and everything he has will go to the Holy Office.'[29] Because he's married to doña Juana Enríquez I'm certain that he is an observer of the Law of Moses like his wife and mother-in-law. . . .' "

[In the remainder of this audience, Blanca denounced several secret Jews, male and female. She also mentioned having seen the torture scars of her friend and patroness doña Blanca Enríquez, who had been arrested by the Inquisition in Seville. "Doña Blanca Enríquez, the deceased mother-in-law of Simón Váez Sevilla, was penanced and a prisoner of the Inquisition in Seville. She told me they tortured her and she showed me the scars of the wounds on her arms that the cords [of the rack] had left. I tell you this to show that I'm telling the truth. Also, Juana Rodríguez, deceased, mother of doña Blanca Enríquez, was penanced twice, once by the Holy Office of Granada and once in Seville, according to what doña Blanca Enríquez told me while she was alive." Blanca de Rivera continued to denounce members of the Mexican secret Jewish community in her seventh audience. In the eighth, she gave the true story of her indoctrination into secret Judaism, which was not performed by Justa Méndez eleven years before in Seville, as Blanca previously stated.]

In Mexico City, Friday, eleventh of July in the year sixteen hundred and

---

28. Simón Váez Sevilla, a merchant of Portuguese extraction and a leader of Mexico City's converso community, is the subject of Eva A. Uchmany, "Simón Váez Sevilla," in *Michael: Journal of the Jews in the Diaspora* 8 (1983): 126–61.

29. The Holy Office confiscated the goods of those, such as Judaizers, whom it convicted of major heresies.

forty-two, the Lord Inquisitors Domingo Veles de Asas y Argos and Doctor don Francisco de Estrada y Escovedo presiding in the morning audience. Francisco Ruiz Marañón, bailiff of the secret prisons, appeared before them and told them that doña Blanca de Rivera had requested an audience. She was brought in. Once present, she was told that the bailiff had said she had requested an audience. She is now in one, and she should say why she requested it and tell the truth by the oath she swore.

She said, "I asked for and wanted it so that I could continue my confession and tell the whole truth." In keeping with this, she said, "When my parents died I was about nine or ten years old.[30] I was left in the charge of a cousin of mine on my mother's side, who was doña Ana Enríquez, who lived in Seville. She took care of me and after about a year, as I said, I entered the Convent of the Conception of San Miguel, where I stayed until they took me out to marry me to Diego López Ribero, my husband. Until that time, and for about a year after, more or less, I was a Catholic Christian. I had never heard of or had any knowledge of the Law of Moses. It happened that my cousin, doña Ana Enríquez, was friendly and had dealings with a Marcos Rodríguez Tristán, who is Portuguese and the uncle to doña Isabel Tristán, who lives in Mexico City,[31] and with whom he had a daughter, who is doña Isabel Duarte, wife of Diego Antúnez, now dead, whom I know to be herself an observer of the Law of Moses because she told me she was and I told her I was, and she celebrated the fasts of the Law in my house. My daughters know this, too. . . .

"One day, while we were in the house alone, my cousin doña Ana Enríquez, . . . who raised me, told me.[32] She asked if I had ever heard of the Law of Moses. I told her I hadn't, and didn't know anything other than what I'd been taught by my parents and the nuns and the convent headmistress, and that I was a Catholic Christian. Then my cousin told me that I was in error and deceived if I followed the Law of the Christians, because it wasn't right or true.

---

30. This contradicts Blanca's previous testimony that her parents died when she was five or six years old.

31. Blanca is implicating Mexico City secret Jews. Doña Isabel Tristán, a delicate, aristocratic woman known as "la Tristana," was later arrested and tortured by the Mexico City tribunal of the Holy Office. She withstood the torture and revealed nothing in her interrogations. She was burned at the stake as an unrepentant heretic on 11 April 1649. See Alberro, *Inquisition et société,* 270, 582.

32. Here Blanca narrates a typical "indoctrination scene," common to most Inquisition trials of secret Jews, in which a female relative reveals the family's secret Jewish practices to the adolescent defendant. There is no way to tell whether these scenes were as common as they appear to have been from the trial records, or whether defendants realized that inquisitors expected such a scene and would interrogate them until they got one.

The Law of Moses, which she followed and kept, was the right and true Law, and necessary for salvation.[33] She said I should leave off following the Law of the Christians. I began to reconsider whether what my cousin had said was true. I told her I would wait and see, and think it over. What she'd said to me that day still hadn't settled in my heart. I took my leave of my cousin and went back to my house. Afterward my cousin tried many times, both in her house and in mine, to pervert me and take me away from the faith and belief in the Law of Our Lord Jesus Christ, telling me that I needed to stray from it for the sake of my salvation and profess faith in the Law of Moses, as she did and as her relatives had taught her. Since my cousin had tried to persuade me so many times while I was still a young, inexperienced girl, I let myself be persuaded and fooled by her. I believed her and took what she had said to be the truth, so from that time on, when I was about sixteen years old, more or less, and was pregnant with my daughter doña María, with all my heart I passed over into faith and belief in the Law of Moses, understanding it to be right, true, and necessary for my salvation, and straying from the Law of Our Lord Jesus Christ, not taking that Law as good for my salvation, but rather the Law of Moses, which I understood at the time was contrary to the Law of Our Lord Jesus Christ.

"It weighs on me a great deal that I haven't said anything about this in my earlier audiences, but then I wasn't prepared or repentant, so instead I said I'd learned [the Law of Moses] in Mexico City, in the house of Justa Méndez, who is now dead, and not in my cousin doña Ana Enríquez's house in Seville. My cousin doña Ana Enríquez taught me and told me how to keep Saturdays as a holy day,[34] without working, putting clean clothes on and clean linens on the bed and the table, and how I should slaughter chickens and hens with a knife, instead of twisting their necks, so that they bleed out, and how I should de-vein and soak them before I roast or eat them.[35] She told me to perform certain solemn fasts in observance of the Law; especially on the tenth day of September, I should perform the fast of the High Holy Day,[36] bathing the day before at

33. The focus on salvation that Blanca reports in her indoctrination, not a part of Jewish doctrine, is indicative of the syncretism (mixing of religious doctrines) between Christianity, the religious culture that surrounded secret Jews in Castile and the Indies, and Judaism.

34. The Jewish Sabbath begins Friday night at sundown and ends Saturday night at sundown.

35. Here Blanca accurately describes the process for koshering meat (preparing it according to Jewish dietary laws).

36. Yom Kippur, which the Mexico City crypto-Jews called the "Día Grande" (Great Day, or, in its modern English parallel usage, High Holy Day) but which translates literally as the Day of Atone-

vespers[37] and putting on clean clothes and clean linens on the beds and tables. That evening I should eat fish and vegetables, but not meat,[38] and I should go the whole next day without eating or drinking until night falls and the star appears. On the High Holy Day, she said, I was to put on the best dress and jewels I had, sweep, clean, and put the house in order, and that I should get together [with her?] the next night for a supper of fish and vegetables, but not meat, and that at sundown on the first night I should light wax candles or oil lamps and put them on a table,[39] on clean linen, reciting on that night psalms and prayers of the Law, and that those who are angry with each other should reconcile and be friends, and pardon each other and embrace,[40] and that after supper on the second night the fast of the High Holy Day was over.

"She also taught me that during the week I should perform certain fasts. I should fast for the dead observers of the Law of Moses on Mondays and Wednesdays, and for the living on Thursdays.[41] The fasts could be done by whoever wanted to do them.[42] She said I should fast by eating fish and vegetables, but not meat, for supper the night before, and then go the whole next day without eating until the star comes out in the night sky, when I could once again eat the same things, but not meat. There was no ceremony other than to recite the prayers that I chose from the Law.

"She also taught me to fast the Fast of Queen Esther, going three whole days without eating.[43] Before beginning the fast, we had to eat wild amaranth with

---

ment, is one of the fasting holidays on the Jewish calendar. It falls on 10 Tishri in the Jewish calendar (September/October in the Christian calendar).

37. Vespers occur at dusk in the Christian liturgical day. Jewish holidays begin at sundown.

38. The restrictions Blanca describes are not part of Jewish dietary laws. Rather, they are similar to Christian dietary laws, which demarcate fish as food appropriate to fasts and solemn days and meat as food appropriate to feast days and joyous occasions. However, by requiring that Blanca eat only fish and vegetables the night before a fast, her cousin (inadvertently?) ensured that she would adhere to Jewish dietary laws, which prohibit the mixing of milk or milk products and meat in the same meal.

39. Candle lighting at sundown is a component of the Yom Kippur and Sabbath observances.

40. Reconciling with those who have become estranged, that is, receiving or asking for pardon for those who have wronged and from those who have been wronged, is traditional in the celebration of Yom Kippur.

41. When Jews do fast for the dead, they usually observe the fasts on the anniversary of the death. Associating fasts with particular days of the week is not part of this tradition. It resembles, instead, Catholic penitential fasting practices.

42. The excessive number of fasts per week (three, at least, as Blanca describes them) may have made them difficult for Mexico City's secret Jews to carry out. Fortunately for that community, the fasts could be carried out by a paid proxy. Fulfillment of religious obligations by paid proxy is an acceptable practice in Judaism. The obligation most often fulfilled this way is the recitation of the kaddish, the prayer for the dead. The designated proxy did not have to be a rabbi. Blanca and her daughters all earned extra money working as religious obligation-by-proxy professionals.

43. The biblical Fast of Esther did last three days and three nights, but there were no particular

water and salt for supper, and on the last night of the three, we had to begin the supper with wild amaranth and then afterward eat fish and vegetables and other things one eats during a fast. She also told me and taught me that there were many other festivals of the Law whose names she couldn't remember. She said that I wasn't to throw away my nail clippings, but rather that I should put them in the fire,[44] and other little things and ceremonies of the Law which I don't remember right now."

She was commanded to search her memory and tell the truth. . . .

[In a shortened version of the traditional warning, the inquisitors commanded Blanca to return to her prison cell, search her memory, and return prepared to tell the truth at her next audience. In subsequent audiences, Blanca continued to list names of others in Mexico City's secret Jewish community and confessed to having been paid by members of the secret Jewish community to fast for them and to having performed rituals with them that she describes as fasts. Below she denounces penanced members of the community, in other words, those who had already been arrested once by the Inquisition. If rearrested, they would automatically be burned at the stake as relapsed heretics. These were the members of Mexico City's secret Jewish community whom Blanca and her daughters had agreed to protect at all costs. At the time of this audience, Blanca had been in prison, in the torture chamber, for a year and a half.]

Twenty-third Audience

In Mexico City, Thursday, the fifth of November, in the year sixteen hundred and forty-three, the Lord Inquisitors [*sic*] Doctor don Francisco de Estrada y Escovedo presiding. He commanded that doña Blanca de Rivera be brought in. When she was present, he told her that the bailiff had told him that she had requested an audience. She was now in an audience, and she should state why she requested it and tell the whole truth, by the oath she has sworn.

She said, "I requested this audience to unburden my conscience completely

---

foods associated with the pre- and postfast meals. Queen Esther, a biblical Jewish woman married to King Ahasuerus, and her uncle Mordecai, saved their people from an extermination plot hatched by the king's evil adviser Haman. The victory is celebrated on the Jewish holiday of Purim (14 Adar in the Jewish calendar, February/March in the Christian calendar). The Fast of Esther commemorates the fast she and her uncle held when they discovered that the lives of all Jews in the kingdom were imperiled. The biblical fast lasted three days and three nights (Esther 4:16), the 14–16 of Nison (March/April in the Christian calendar), which is how Mexico City's secret Jewish community observed the holiday as well. Modern Jews hold a daylong fast, on the day before the Purim holiday.

44. Jewish law considers nail-clippings part of the body. As such, they cannot be thrown away. They must be buried in the earth or, as Blanca says, burned.

because I want to save my soul. There is nothing left for me to say. The reason I've kept secret the things I'm about to say here was so that the Holy Office wouldn't burn the people I will mention in this deposition, because they are people who have already been penanced by this tribunal.[45] It seems to me that my daughters, also doña Juana Enríquez and all of her sisters and relatives, especially doña Catalina Enríquez, got together to agree that they wouldn't denounce those who had once been prisoners here. But the salvation of my soul matters more to me, and I've realized that I cannot fully unburden my conscience without saying all that needs to be said. . . ."

[Doña Blanca proceeded to denounce secret Jews in Mexico City whom she knew to be relapsed heretics. Several were later burned at the stake. In the twenty-fourth audience, Blanca confessed that she and two of her daughters had repeatedly desecrated a Christ statute they kept in a trunk in their house.]

Twenty-fourth Audience

In Mexico City, Saturday, the seventh of November in the year sixteen hundred and forty-three, morning audience, Lord Inquisitor Doctor don Francisco Estrada y Escovedo presiding. He commanded that doña Blanca Rivera be brought in. When she was present, she was told that the bailiff had said she had requested an audience. She was now in one and should explain why she wanted one and tell the whole truth by the oath she has sworn.

She said, "I asked for it so I could confess a serious crime I committed, which, because it was so grave and atrocious, I have been afraid and ashamed to confess. Now I fear the great punishment I deserve for having committed it, but I trust in the mercy of the Holy Office and confess my crime with great pain and repentance and many tears. On my knees I beg you to be merciful with me because at that time I was in a miserable state, being a Jewess, an observer of the Law of Moses, and praying in that Law. To unburden my conscience on every point, I must say that about six or eight months before I was arrested, my daughter Margarita told me that we should flog an image of the crucified Christ.[46] We were tempted into this sacrilege because of a little

45. Doña Blanca is trying to keep the *relapsos* (people rearrested by the Inquisition after having been sentenced a first time) out of her testimony because, as she knew, it was the Inquisition's policy to burn *relapsos* at the stake as unrepentant heretics whether they confessed during their second trials or not.

46. Ritual flogging of any kind is not a part of Judaism, though ritual penitential flogging of oneself was, at the time, an accepted Catholic practice. The ritual flogging of a Christ statue suggests that some secret Jews, raised in a Christian culture, had internalized and reproduced of their own ac-

Christ we had put away in a trunk, rolled up in a caftan, because he'd come un-nailed from the Cross where he was and one of his arms had fallen off. We were taking the clothes out of that trunk when the crucifix came out and reminded us of this impulse. We did it three or four times, this way:

"We put a sleeping mat on the floor of the room where we [stored silks?] and put the crucified Christ face down on the mat. I sat down and held him by one foot. My daughter Margarita de Rivera took a whip with five tails that Diego Correa, my son-in-law, had made to whip his son Luis. With it, Margarita flogged the image of Jesus Christ, giving him five or six strokes, each time showing the implacable hatred and loathing all three of us had for Him[47] as Jewesses who did not believe in Him and wanted to avenge ourselves against His image with this horrendous act. After doing this, we put the Christ back in the trunk where we'd had it before. We would wait until the rest of the house-hold had gone to bed. Then around ten at night, three or four times the three of us committed this evil act by ourselves. It seemed to me that my other three daughters, Maria, Catalina and Clara, knew about it, too, because one of the other two, Margarita or Isabel, might have told them. I am certain that I did not tell them, because the act seemed so horrible to me that it seemed to me I should have been punished by stoning. My heart was so afflicted and inconsol-able, I don't know how it was that I didn't fall down dead. Even though it seemed to me that I deserved a thousand deaths, I didn't dare to talk about this until last night, when I resolved to tell it, even though it may cost me my life, so that I can unburden my conscience and leave behind this confusion that my guilt has caused me, trusting in the pity and mercy that this Holy Office has toward those who confess these sorts of crimes voluntarily.

"When I committed them I don't remember whether or not I maltreated the crucifix with opprobrious words or blasphemies as well. If I did do any of that, I don't remember because I have a poor memory, but my daughters Margarita and Isabel will tell you what else happened. All I remember was the act.

"The holy Christ was old, made of wood, and about one span long.[48] We brought it back with us from San Luis. He was up on a cross and while He was

---

cord contemporary Christian ideas about who Jews were (anti-Christians) and what they had done (at the time, the papacy and Christian popular culture held Jews collectively responsible for having killed Christ).

47. Blanca has not mentioned which of her other daughters was also involved in the flogging of the Christ statue. It was, according to her subsequent testimony, the youngest, Isabel.

48. "Una quarta de largo." A *cuarta* is equivalent to a span, approximately the length of a hand.

in our house we prayed to Him. But over time He came un-nailed and one of His arms fell off, which my daughter Margarita burned in the fire so that it wouldn't roll around on the floor, which is what she said.

"How should I know what her intentions were?

"I remember that we called Our Lord Jesus Christ don Manuel, and His Mother, the Holy Virgin Our Lady, doña María, names we called them to show our disdain and to mock and jeer at them to show the loathing we had for both. As a perfidious Jewess[49] I called Jesus Christ "The Un-nailed" *(el desclavado)*, which is what some of my daughters called Him, too, though I don't remember which ones."

The aforesaid Lord Inquisitor showed the aforesaid doña Blanca a holy crucifix that had been very badly treated, which was made of wood, was missing an arm, and was one span long, so she could see it and recognize it. She took it in her hands and kissed it many times, bathed it in the tears she spilled, and said that the holy crucifix he had shown her was the same as the one she and her daughters Margarita and Isabel had sacrilegiously flogged. Putting Him on the table, she demonstrated the way in which she and her daughter Isabel held Him while her daughter Margarita whipped Him. The aforesaid doña Blanca, kneeling and beating her chest, said, speaking to the holy crucifix, "Little Lord, have mercy on me. I have been bad and have left your most holy Hand and laid hands on You, for which I am very repentant and pained. Would to God that before I had done so I had died a thousand deaths, as I deserve to have done for having committed such a great offense against You."[50]

The aforesaid Lord Inquisitor showed her a whip of five tails . . . and asked the aforesaid doña Blanca if this was the one her daughter Margarita had used to flog the holy crucifix, she said, "No, it wasn't that whip with which she carried out the crime. It was another, smaller one with five tails, the same kind as Diego Correa my son-in-law had made to whip his son Luis, but I don't

---

49. The phrase "perfidious Jews" was common to anti-Jewish literature of the period. It was included in the Solemn Prayers of Good Friday, Roman Missal, until 1959 when the pope ordered it dropped. From the Solemn Prayers of Good Friday, Roman Missal, 1958: "Let us pray also for the perfidious Jews: that our God and Lord may remove the veil from their hearts; that they also may acknowledge Our Lord Jesus Christ. Almighty and Eternal God, Who dost not exclude from Thy mercy even the perfidious Jews: hear our prayers, which we offer for the blindness of that people; that acknowledging the light of Thy Truth, which is Christ, they may be delivered from their darkness. Through the same Lord Jesus Christ, Who livest and reignest with God the Father in the unity of the Holy Ghost, through all endless ages. Amen." Blanca has, in her efforts to show true repentance, adopted seventeenth-century anti-Jewish language to describe herself.

50. This short quote was recorded in the first person in the original transcript.

know where that one is. This whip you've shown me here is the one Diego Correa made to whip the black [slave] Periquillo."

She said that this was the truth, by the oath she had sworn. Warned that she should continue to think well on these things, she was commanded to return to her cell. She signed

> [signed] Blanca de Rivera[51]
> Before me
> [signed] Doctor of Jurisprudence Melchior de A[?]

[In the remainder of her audiences, Blanca continued to denounce her own heresies and those of other secret Jews.]

Final Accusation of doña Blanca Méndez de Rivera

We, the Inquisitors against depravity and apostasy, in Mexico City, in the states and provinces of New Spain, along with the Ordinary,[52] have seen a criminal case which is pending before us, and which is pending between the party of the first part, the Lord Prosecutor of this Holy Office . . . and the party of the second part, the defendant doña Blanca Méndez de Rivera, who is present, and is a native of the city of Seville in the kingdoms of Spain, and resides in Mexico City. She is the widow of Diego López Ribero, native of Castelobranco, Portugal, who died in Mexico City and who was a merchant; the daughter of Enrique Rodríguez Obregón, native of the city of Llerena in Extremadura, a slave trader who brought Blacks from Angola to New Spain, and the daughter of Margarita López, native of the city of Seville, both of whom are now dead. Because said doña Blanca Mendez de Rivera is a baptized and confirmed Christian, who enjoys all the privileges and exemptions that faithful and Catholic Christians enjoy, and should enjoy, and because, in contravention of the profession [of faith] she made in holy baptism, she has done, said, and committed, and seen done, said, and committed, many and serious crimes against that which our Holy Mother Roman Catholic Church and evangelical Law believes, holds, and preaches, passing into the observance of and belief in the dead Law of Moses, keeping it with its rites and ceremonies, and believing with all her heart that it was good and true, and that in it she

---

51. Blanca has stopped signing her name with the honorific *doña*.

52. "Junto con el ordinario." The term *the ordinary* refers to ecclesiastical justices who were part of the traditional (ordinary) Church court system, as opposed to the Inquisition.

could be saved, while pretending to be a faithful and Catholic Christian and [believing] that the Law of Our Lord Jesus Christ was not good or true, we find doña Blanca and all of her daughters, among all the many Jews and Jewesses who live in these kingdoms, to be proselytizing Jewesses, consummate rabbis, and dogmatizers. . . .

Doña Blanca Méndez de Rivera has kept this Law since the age of fifteen and was taught it in Seville by a cousin of hers who was reconciled by the Inquisition of that city, while both women lived in Duque neighborhood. The aforementioned cousin would go out to a patio in the evenings and sing aloud, "O high God of Abraham" and would slit the throats of chickens. When one of doña Blanca's daughters saw her do this, the cousin said to her, very worried, "Quiet! Quiet! You are lost!" After the aforementioned cousin and one of the cousin's sisters were reconciled, doña Blanca would go to visit them in the Penitential Prison.[53] In her presence, as obstinate Jewesses, her cousins persuaded another relative of theirs to keep the Law of Moses, as they had taught her. Doña Blanca had contact, as a Jewess, with another woman who died a prisoner of that Inquisition, and with another five who lived on Cerrasería Street, all of whom were observers of the Law of Moses, and penanced as such by the Inquisition in a celebrated *auto de fe*. . . .

She came to these kingdoms fleeing the Inquisition of Seville, changing her name from Blanca Méndez to doña Blanca de Rivera so that she would not be taken prisoner like those from Seville with whom she had declared herself to be a Jewess. The first house she lived in in Mexico City was the home of a certain Jewess, a relative of hers, who, along with her husband, had been reconciled by this Inquisition, so that [doña Blanca] might learn [from her] how best to avoid detection.

When a certain person very close to doña Blanca died in this city,[54] she and her five daughters, wearing white skirts, at three o'clock in the morning roamed the streets wailing, in a ceremony of the Law of Moses. Afterward, said doña Blanca herself became gravely ill, and her physician Doctor Rumbo ordered that she receive last rites. So as to avoid receiving the holy communion, she left the city, along with her daughters, in a carriage. When a certain

53. Blanca went to visit her cousins in prison after they had been "reconciled" with the Church at the *auto de fe* and sentenced to serve time in prison, a punishment the Inquisition understood as "penance," or penitence, whence the term *Penitential Prison*. Imprisonment as a punishment (as opposed to imprisonment while awaiting trial) was rare in early modern Europe, although it was a common inquisitorial punishment for Judaizers, especially female Judaizers, who, unlike the men, could not serve as galley slaves.

54. The prosecutor may be referring to Blanca's husband.

Catholic man approached the carriage and asked where they were going with doña Blanca so ill and when the doctor had ordered that she receive last rites, she replied sadly that Rumbo's sacrament was not enough to kill her.[55]

On the night of the burial of a particular Jewess, doña Blanca and many other Jews and Jewesses, kin and friends of the deceased, stayed all night in the dead woman's house. It is the custom of observers of the Law of Moses not to leave the house of those who have died in observance of the Law until seven days have passed.[56] It so happened that as they were cooking their supper of fish and vegetables cooked in oil, according to the Jewish rite, they heard a rumor that the Inquisition was about to descend on them. Tossing the supper over the rooftops and into the alleyways, they began to flee, the husbands taking their wives away. Doña Blanca took two of her daughters and did the same. . . .

When a certain relative of the aforesaid doña Blanca died, she and her daughters fasted for his soul, according to the Law of Moses, because it is the Jews' opinion that only those who are of their blood can be saved and receive God's mercy, even though they may be Christians. When another Jewess died, one who had been penanced by the Inquisition of Granada and rearrested by the Inquisition of Seville,[57] said doña Blanca (who was obligated to be the mourner at the burial of all the Jews who ended their miserable days in this City, as she was a great Jewish ceremony-maker, as zealous regarding the Law as she is regarding her appearance and station in life) attended her and ate the meal of fish served to the relatives. One Jewess who was eating fish with rice, which seemed to her to have been cooked in lard, stopped eating it so she would not be "treif,"[58] or stained. Another Jewess said to her that she hadn't seen any lard in the pot, and said, "My daughter, may God grant you good fortune, for He cooked this, and He has shed many tears for the death of the deceased, whom He loved very much."[59]

. . . When a certain Jewess who had been reconciled by this Holy Office was

---

55. Blanca may have been making a play on words. The doctor's last name, Rumbo, also meant lavishness, pomp, or show ("a lavish sacrament was not enough to kill her").

56. It is customary for relatives and friends of the deceased to "sit shiva" (gather in the mourners' home to offer company and comfort to the bereaved) for seven days following a death. While it is not customary for mourners to leave the "shiva house," guests may come and go as they like.

57. This may have been the mother of Blanca's patroness, Blanca Enríquez.

58. *Treif* is that which is unclean (therefore forbidden) according to Jewish dietary laws.

59. This quote is in Portuguese in the original, suggesting that Mexico City's crypto-Jews, many of whom were Portuguese immigrants, sometimes communicated among themselves in Portuguese. "Miña filla, asi Deu le dei boa ventura lo guiso, y a chorado muyto por la muerte da difunta, que la queria muyto."

in her death throes, a Catholic man approached her with a holy Christ in his hand. When she heard what he was saying to her, that she should commend herself to that Lord, who was her Redeemer, Master, and God, she opened her eyes wildly and stuck out her tongue, which, by luck, she bit off and, gushing blood, died in this horrible state. Doña Blanca Méndez de Rivera, frightened, fled and sat down on a certain pile that had fallen in front of the house until one of the other Jews, and Jewesses, present called her to tell her that the woman had died. . . .

To let everyone who observed the Law of Moses know that she was Jewish, and so that she would be known in these kingdoms and outside of them as an archive of all the Jews who are or were in Mexico City, since she arrived from Spain doña Blanca has used the following codes: "Fulano, or Fulana,[60] is like us," or "are good," "fear the Lord," "see," "are one of ours,"[61] "are friends of God."

She got together with a certain circumcised Jew who had come from Livorno to Mexico City[62] and who taught doña Blanca the precepts of the Law so that she could better her knowledge of them, as if that were necessary.[63] The precepts are not to eat meat, blood-sausage, pig blood, or fish without scales, to keep the Sabbath on Saturdays, without working from four o'clock Fridays on, and on the Sabbath put on clean shirts. . . . Women should sleep in separate beds, and not sleep with their husbands, when they have their period. Children of Jews must perform the fasts of the Law for their parents' souls, without paying another person to do it for them. In the mouth of a dead person, they must put some item of gold because Jews cannot get into heaven if they do not carry gold in their mouths.[64] When Jewesses pray the prayers of the Law, they

---

60. *Fulano* means "Mr. so-and-so," and *fulana* means "Ms. so-and-so." Both are generic terms used to refer to persons whose names are unknown or forgotten.

61. "Son de los nosos" (a phrase that mixes Spanish and Portuguese).

62. The circumcised Jew from Livorno (an Italian city with a Jewish ghetto) is Juan de León, whose jailhouse conversations were recorded by Inquisition spies and are transcribed in Lewin, *Confidencias*. Juan de León was arrested by the Inquisition in 1642.

63. The prosecutor's record of the precepts Blanca learned from Juan de León is hit-or-miss in terms of its consistency with Jewish law and tradition. The traditions and laws that accurately survived transmission from Juan de León's rabbi to Juan, to Blanca, and then to the Inquisition's prosecutor were keeping the Sabbath from sundown Fridays through sundown Saturdays, covering the head when at prayer, separation of spouses for purposes of ritual cleanliness when the wife is menstruating, abstaining from food and drink on Yom Kippur, reconciliation and forgiveness on Yom Kippur, and dietary laws prohibiting consumption of blood, pork, and fish without scales. The other traditions recorded here were either mangled beyond recognition or invented by Juan, Blanca, and/or the prosecutor.

64. This practice, erroneously identified as Jewish, may reflect an internalized acceptance of the traditional anti-Jewish association of Jews with avarice. Early modern Europeans' association of Jews

must put on head scarves and the men, hats or caps. When they are about to fast, they must wash their hands, eyes, and mouths, saying, "I wash my hands and praise You, o Lord."[65] On the fast of the High Holy Day, which falls on the September moon, they go to bathe at vespers, putting on clean clothes and eating a supper of fish without scales,[66] eggs, vegetables, chocolate,[67] but not meat, and they light wax candles, which they place on clean linen. Around the candles, they pass the night praying all the prayers of the Law without going to sleep until after midnight. They have to go all the next day without eating or drinking until night falls and the star appears. Then they once again eat fish, eggs, vegetables, chocolate, but not meat, and they beg pardon of each other, reconciling with those from whom they had been estranged, embracing, with the younger ones kissing the hands of the elders, who give them Jewish blessings, putting their right hands on the younger ones' heads and saying, "May God make you good."

On the March moon they must fast the fast of Queen Esther, during which they cannot eat or drink for three straight days as a sign of the benefice God gave his kingdom through Esther and Mordecai.[68] When they cut their nails, they throw the clippings into the fire, and when they fast for a dead Jew on the first night's supper, they eat a soup of salt and water, and other infinite, ridiculous, puerile, and superstitious ceremonies, all of which doña Blanca has observed in every detail . . . and which she has performed with many other Judaizers, with whom she has communicated and declared herself to be a Jewess. . . .

---

with greed would have been reinforced by the legal association of Jews with usury (money lending for profit), a "dishonorable" trade that the Catholic Church prohibited for its faithful but which was open to Jews.

65. "Miñas maus labare, y ati Señor alabare." This prayer, not a traditional Jewish oration, rhymes as the Inquisition's prosecutor recorded it. It is in a mixture of Spanish and Portuguese.

66. The prosecutor's account of the High Holy Day supper of "fish without scales" contradicts his previous (correct) assertion that Jewish dietary laws forbid the consumption of fish without scales. Whether the prosecutor's accusation of consumption of a pre–Yom Kippur supper of fish without scales by Mexico City's secret Jews accurately reflects their practices is unclear.

67. Chocolate, like tobacco, was new to seventeenth-century Europe, imported from the Americas. Like tobacco, when first introduced, it was considered one of the delicacies of the Indies, easy to digest and possessing curative powers. Prisoners of the Mexico City Inquisition who fell ill often claimed that they could eat only chocolate, with which they were usually provided, under doctor's orders. Doña Blanca's daughter Margarita, for example, complained of uterine pain and asked for chocolate and tobacco to ease her suffering. See Alberro, *Inquisition et société*, 254. For a study on the reception of chocolate and tobacco in early modern Spain, see Marcy S. Norton, "New World of Goods: A History of Tobacco and Chocolate in the Spanish Empire, 1492–1700" (Ph.D. diss., University of California, Berkeley, 2000).

68. On the Fast of Esther, see note 43.

When they were in Zacatecas, a Jew invited one of doña Blanca's closest relations[69] to eat. Serving the food, he put a little bit of ham on his plate. The relation of the aforementioned doña Blanca asked him if he was trying to find out whether or not he was a Jew. The other Jew replied that he wasn't ignorant. He knew this relation was a Jew, because doña Blanca and her daughters were, and because he had inherited it from his parents, who were tavern keepers in Castelobranco, and because they were Jews, everyone called their tavern the Jews' Tavern. To this, doña Blanca's relation replied that the best thing his parents ever had was that name.

Before the Inquisition arrested doña Blanca and her daughters, they agreed among themselves not to tell the truth and to say they had learned the Law of Moses from Judaizers who were now dead, since the dead could not defend themselves. . . .

Doña Blanca mocked the holy processions that take place during Holy Week and with a common cackle referred to what one black woman[70] had said, which was that with her firm faith she suffered to see the way of the passion of Our Lord and Redeemer Jesus Christ. "Every year they whip You. Every year they arrest You because they can't stand You." To which doña Blanca added, "Poor thing,"[71] which she said as a perfidious Jewess who has, as have all the Jews, a hatred of the Lord Our God rooted in her heart.

Later, when she was a prisoner in the secret prisons, she made urgent inquiries at all hours of the day and night to find out where her daughters were, yelling, sighing, and calling to them, saying "Perico, Periquillo," a sign they had agreed on at home so they could recognize each other. She was able to communicate with two of her daughters, with whom she discussed whether or not the other three had been arrested. She was afraid that they might talk and have their heads cut off, and told them not to make any mistakes in the audiences. She said they should say that everything came from *fulana*,[72] naming the dead woman, whom they had agreed to say had taught them, and that it had only been eleven years that they had used the Law of Moses, and that they should not get anyone into trouble, or get them condemned . . . or talk about other people's business. She said they should watch what they say so that they

---

69. The relation in question is doña Blanca's husband, born in Castelobranco, Portugal. Zacatecas was an important mining town in northern New Spain.

70. "Una negra." This may refer to Juliana, María de Rivera's black slave.

71. "Malaventurado" (literally, "unfortunate one"). Underlined in the original.

72. *Fulana* here is Justa Méndez, the Blancas' first landlady in Mexico City.

do not pay the price themselves, or make others pay it, and she lamented that she did not have the chance to give these instructions to her other daughters. She told her daughters to talk only about the fasts and to say they had fasted no more than four times.

. . . One of doña Blanca's daughters said that the Lord Inquisitors had told her to unburden her conscience and she had replied, "Do Your Lordships want me to condemn myself with lies?" And doña Blanca, very furious, said, "O traitors, who make us lie! They are demons, who go around spying and intimidating! May their souls be condemned to hell! . . ." Extinguishing her candle, with the same fury she said, "May their souls be extinguished in hell!"

Continuing in her communications with her daughters, she came back from an audience one day and called them by the sign "Perico, Periquillo,"[73] and told them, "We are lost and great harm is to come, great harm, ladies.[74] What are we to do? They told me that they already warned me the other day, and today once more, and that now there is no longer any help for us and that they're going to burn us. They know everything." One of her daughters responded, "Refuse them. Devil be damned." Doña Blanca said, "I don't know what I should say. If I said what I should, they'd have to burn all of Mexico City. What will my daughters have said? Is there such terrible confusion? So much company [in the prisons]? What will come to pass if not that?" With hatred, malice, and rage they all turned against the ministers of this Holy Office. They cursed them and spit.

After her cell had been changed to another, she pretended to be crazy and mute. In the audiences she asked for, she made it seem as if she wanted to despair and hang herself. She would kneel in the door of her cell to pray the way blind people do. When the door was opened, she would continue to pray, hands clasped and her eyes turned up to heaven. She would not be quiet, even when they told her to. All this was discovered to be a lie when one of the judges talked to her while she was pretending to be mute. She refused to respond to him until he threatened to take away some of her comforts. All of a sudden she spoke, saying, "No, for the love of God!" and clasped her hands. Before that she had been talking in sign.

When [housed in a cell] with one of her grandsons, she appeared to regain her senses. They agreed between them to call her doña Paula and to give him

73. Periquillo was the name of one of the family's slaves.
74. The prosecutor quotes in the first person from the records made by Inquisition spies who overheard this jailhouse conversation.

the name don Jacinto so that prisoners in the neighboring cells would not know who they were. This way, with oaths and curses (believing that no one knew who they were), they treated the Holy Office indecently. They mocked its ministers and the judges who examined and questioned them, and concluded by calling them perverse, and [clowns?]. To wear down and tire out the bailiffs, with great derision she asked them for many things. One night she maliciously extinguished her candle over and over again, calling the bailiff each time to come and light it. The last time this happened, the bailiff, who was tired, told them he did not want go, to which doña Blanca, finding herself in the dark, replied that she saw him wallowing in his own blood in Berbería.[75]

Talking with her grandson, who did not eat much at all, she said that she ate very well, as if the food were the body of a certain minister [of the Holy Office]. Then she cursed all the ministers repeatedly and said she saw herself surrounded by traitors like a captain surrounded by his enemies. "All they want to hear when they ask a question is 'Yes, my Lord, it was that way. I know. I did it.'" . . . She said she should only tell them what they already knew. . . . Her grandson counseled her to unburden her conscience completely, since they had charged him with the things they had talked about [in the cell] and he had confessed to them. She became furious with him and fought with him perpetually at all hours, lamenting that even her grandson was conspiring against her, cursing him and saying, "What a wonderful cellmate they gave me who turns around and accuses me." There must be some demon or Satan in this prison who makes it so that no one cares about Grandmother, Mother, aunts, or other relatives. . . ."

One day around six in the morning when her grandson got out of bed, he said to her, "Don't get up in that condition; it's bad for you." Doña Blanca responded, "What you've said has been much worse for me than getting out of bed naked." Cursing her grandson, whom she had requested as a cellmate, and been granted, she said, "Quiet, scoundrel! Who asked for you? How dare you curse me? You've cut off my head. I would have been better off alone than with you." When her grandson warned her once again that she should request an audience and unburden her conscience, she said, "Leave me alone, scoundrel! Dog! I don't want to ask for an audience or unburden my conscience. I don't want to do anything. I know them by now and I know what they're going to do,

75. Muslim-controlled North Africa. Blanca is apparently hexing the bailiff with the vision (or wish) that he will wind up rolling in his own blood after (presumably) being taken captive and killed in Muslim lands.

and I don't want you to say another word to me. I don't want to give them the satisfaction. What did you say, scoundrel? You're the cause of all my suffering. . . . Come, demons! What are you waiting for?" Suspecting that the prisoners on either side of her cell could hear what she said, she told her grandson to smash the plates and other things they'd been given to eat with and to scrape the lime off the walls. When they had done that, they spent the whole night grinding it all up, mixing it with water in a large earthenware jug to make a sort of mud. Then they searched out all the peepholes and cracks and plugged them up, causing a great tumult. And she, furious, burst out saying even worse things than those referred to above.

It is to be assumed, and believed, that doña Blanca de Rivera has said, done, and committed many other and serious crimes against our holy Catholic faith. . . . She is accused of being a heretical Judaizer and apostate from our holy Catholic faith. . . .

[The prosecutor requested that Blanca be "relaxed" to the secular arm of justice and that all her goods be confiscated. The following is the inquisitors' summary of the events in Blanca's trial.]

Having arrested doña Blanca de Rivera with sufficient cause, and placed her in the secret prisons of this Holy Office, on the second day she requested a voluntary audience, in which she lied and said she had been taught the Law of Moses by the aforementioned dead Jewess who had been reconciled by this Holy Office, a story she and her daughters had agreed upon before they were put in prison.[76] She confessed that her name was doña Blanca de Rivera, which she used instead of her real name, Blanca Méndez, which she had used in Spain. She confessed that she was a native of the city of Seville, born on Dados Street, and that she was more than fifty years old, and that she was the widow of Diego López Ribero, native of Castelobranco, who died in Mexico City and with whom she had lived as man and wife for more than twenty years. She confessed that she had been arrested on the seventeenth of May, sixteen hundred and forty-two, at night. When she gave her genealogy, she said she was certain that her parents and grandparents were Portuguese by caste and lineage but were very pure Old Christians, as they should have been. But it has been proven that they were all Hebrew Judaizers, New Christians, many of them penanced [by this Holy Office]. . . .

When We [the Lord Inquisitors] received the Lord Prosecutor's case against

76. The "aforementioned dead Jewess" was Justa Méndez.

her, We made a copy of the summary of the witness testimony[77] and asked her to ratify it. . . . She read the first, second, third witnesses, and seeing how many there were, she got to number sixty-nine and said, "Devil bless you! What a dust-cloud you've raised!" and with great impatience swore to tell the truth, which she did not do. [Rather,] she denied the most serious parts of the witness depositions. After consulting with her lawyer[78] . . . she gave notice to the Lord Prosecutor, and in this state she requested several voluntary audiences, and with tears and signs of repentance that appeared genuine, she confessed the whole truth, including the most atrocious deeds and crimes, asking that the Holy Office show her pity and mercy according to the repentance she showed. She said that what had kept her from telling the truth was the fear that if she told the truth she would be burned and, if not, at least be sentenced to the harshest punishments. Some of the reconciled Jews[79] had made it known to the Jews in this city and these kingdoms that they should not confess everything, because to the confession of minor crimes the Inquisition gave minor punishments, and to major crimes, major punishments. It was enough to confess one's own crimes [and not denounce others]. She protested that she would live and die as a faithful, Catholic Christian and would never again return to Judaize, and that she would bear with patience the harshest and gravest punishments given her. . . .

[The inquisitors voted to sentence Blanca to "perpetual imprisonment," which, in the language of inquisitorial custom, meant a sentence of no more than five years. They also sentenced her to wear her sanbenito in perpetuity, to hear masses and recite certain prayers, and to be publicly shamed, flogged, and exiled from the Indies. Of doña Blanca's five daughters, three, María (the eldest), Catalina (the middle child), and Clara (the "feeble-minded") died in prison. According to the autopsy the Inquisition requested for María, who died suddenly and unexpectedly, she died of a coronary embolism but had also been suffering from self-starvation and uterine difficulties.[80]

The last page in Blanca's case file is a letter of permission, dated 1 October 1647, from the Mexico City Inquisition. It allowed Blanca, her daughter Margarita (the second-oldest), and Blanca's grandsons (María and Catalina's sons)

77. The copy of the witness testimony Blanca received had the witnesses' names omitted.

78. Doña Blanca's lawyer most probably encouraged her to confess in full and reminded her that if she did not, she would be burned at the stake.

79. Secret Jews who had been punished by the Inquisition and who had repented and been "reconciled" with the Church, rather than burned at the stake.

80. Alberro, *Inquisition et société*, 256–57.

to return to Seville, in compliance with Blanca's exile from the Indies. We do not know what became of Blanca's youngest daughter, Isabel, who was twenty-one at the time of her arrest in 1642.]

The life of Blanca Mendez and her daughters is part of the larger—and still largely unexplored—history of crypto-Jews in the New World. Although there were probably conversos in the Americas since the early days of the conquest, their numbers increased following Spain's conquest and annexation of Portugal (1580–82). At the time Portugal was home to a large and relatively prosperous community of conversos, many of whom traced their roots to families who had fled Spain at the time of the Expulsion Order in 1492. During the early part of the sixteenth century, Portugal's conversos were left relatively undisturbed, but their situation began to change when King John III, starting in 1532, decided to create a Spanish-like Inquisition designed to root out heresy among this group. In 1540 the Portuguese Inquisition, based in Lisbon, organized its first *auto de fe*. Others soon followed, and from the 1580s on, following the union of the Spanish and Portuguese Crowns, conversos there faced mounting persecution. Some escaped by returning to Spain, and others moved abroad. Some of those went to the Low Countries, Amsterdam above all; still more emigrated to port cities in Spanish America, such as Cartagena de Indias, in what is Colombia today, and Veracruz. A growing number also found their way to Mexico City, capital of New Spain, Blanca and her daughters among them.

   Once in Mexico City, the Portuguese converso community enjoyed renewed prosperity. While most of the Portuguese New Christians in Mexico City were common tradesmen and shop owners, like Blanca's daughter Catalina and her husband, or seamstresses like Blanca herself, others, such as Simón Váez Sevilla, a merchant with ties to members of Blanca's family, figured among the city's wealthiest inhabitants.[81] In New Spain, the Portuguese conversos found economic opportunity, cultural familiarity, and an Inquisition with a record of inaction and indifference toward Judaizing that bordered on tolerance.

   In part, this inactivity can be attributed to the count-duke of Olivares, who, as seen in chapter 4, initiated a pro-converso policy soon after he came to power in 1621. Yet it should also be attributed to the influence that wealthy conversos of Portuguese origin acquired, not only in Madrid, where they emerged as some of the

---

81. Jonathan I. Israel, *Race, Class, and Politics in Colonial Mexico, 1610–1670* (London: Oxford University Press, 1975), 126.

Crown's principal financial backers, but also in Mexico City. Starting in the early seventeenth century, when Philip III first granted them permission to settle and trade in various parts of his empire, Portuguese conversos emerged as some of the principal players in Spain's trade with the Americas. Others, especially those who were involved in the mining and shipment of silver from the rich veins in northern New Spain to Europe, helped to advise the viceroys on financial matters. In return, these conversos enjoyed the viceroys' protection and support. It follows that the inquisitors there did little to interfere with Judaizing heresy. When the Holy Office in Mexico City received a report in 1622 that passersby could hear five hundred conversos chanting every Saturday morning in a clandestine synagogue, it filed the report and made no arrests.[82]

In the 1630s, the de facto tolerance of Judaizing heresy and the protection awarded conversos began to erode. The changeover occurred in 1641, following the revolt of the Portuguese against the monarchy of Philip IV. The king responded quickly, ordering his viceroy in New Spain, the count of Escalona, to close the colony's ports to Portuguese ships, to prohibit further Portuguese immigration, and to intercept correspondence of Portuguese merchants.[83] By the summer of 1641, a wave of anti-Portuguese sentiment swept over New Spain,[84] as rumors of a massacre of Spaniards living in Brazil, a Portuguese colony, reached Mexico City.

At the same time, Archbishop Juan de Palafox y Mendoza, a zealously religious protégé of the count-duke of Olivares, moved to instigate the removal of the count of Escalona, on the grounds that as a relative of the duke of Braganza, leader of the Portuguese revolt, he was not doing enough to implement the anti-Portuguese measures ordered by the Crown. Soon, Escalona was out; Palafox, Philip IV's choice for interim viceroy, was in; and a new and unfortunate era for Mexico City's Portuguese conversos began.

Archbishop Palafox began his term with a crackdown on vice and sin in the city, which included rounding up prostitutes and other usual suspects. While the interim viceroy had no direct power over the Holy Office, Palafox also endorsed the tribunal's prosecution of Judaizers. The tribunal itself must have been eagerly awaiting a change in viceregal regime. In financial trouble since the 1630s, the Mexico Tribunal went bankrupt on 25 November 1640. Convictions of prominent Portuguese crypto-Jews, including the merchant Simón Váez Sevilla, and the confiscation of all their

82. Alberro, *Inquisition et société,* 536.
83. Israel, *Race, Class, and Politics,* 210.
84 Ibid., 124, 199–215. The information below regarding the political precursors to the *complicidad grande,* is drawn from the same work, 199–215.

goods, would help refill its coffers. In May 1642, two months into Palafox's term as interim viceroy, the Mexico Tribunal revealed the so-called *complicidad grande* (great conspiracy) of the Portuguese conversos, a conspiracy to commit Judaizing heresy. The Holy Office began a dragnet that ended in the arrests of 150 Portuguese conversos in the space of four years (1642–46). Blanca and her daughters were among the first it detained.

Together with other tribunals of the Spanish Inquisition, the one in Mexico City operated under the authority and direct supervision of the Suprema, based in Madrid. But the Mexico Tribunal's faraway location gave its judges unofficial leeway to bend the Suprema's rules, as they did when they recruited Gaspar de Robles, a confessed Judaizer, to serve as an Inquisition spy. They also violated inquisitorial procedures when they confined Blanca to the torture chamber and secretly positioned spies to record the prisoners' jailhouse conversations, among them the revealing and incriminating words between Blanca and her daughters.[85]

In the years before her arrest, however, Blanca found new opportunities for religious expression in Mexico City, where she became a "consummate rabbi," in the words of the Inquisition prosecutor, and a "semi-rabbi," as Y. Yovel, a scholar of converso women, put it.[86] In established Jewish communities, it was traditionally the males who, as teachers (rabbis), circumcisers (mohels), and butchers (shohetim), performed the most important rituals. Women's religious roles, restricted mainly to food preparation and housekeeping, were decidedly secondary. Yet recent studies of converso communities have demonstrated that women's rites and rituals became central to the underground version of the Jewish religion.[87] Renée Levine-Melamed,

85. On the Suprema's disapproval of the Mexico Tribunal's use of Judaizer Gaspar de Robles as a spy, see Alberro, *Inquisition et société*, 544 and 544 n. 33. Alberro also notes that the tribunal took care not to tell the Suprema about its nocturnal jailhouse spies. While Nicolau Eymeric and Francisco Peña's inquisitors' manual permitted the use of "witnesses, including the Inquisition notary, well placed, under cover of darkness, to listen," Iberian tribunals did not always use them. See Alberro, *Inquisition et société*, 234–35. Housing of prisoners in the torture chamber was also highly irregular. Torture was to have been carefully regulated and should have lasted only one hour at a time. In all likelihood Blanca's imprisonment in the torture chamber, too, went unreported for fear of the Suprema's disapproval. On the Mexico Tribunal's rules for and use of torture, see Richard E. Greenleaf, *Zumárraga and the Mexican Inquisition* (Washington, DC: Academy of American Franciscan History, 1961), 23.

86. Yirmiyahu Yovel, "The New Otherness: Marrano Dualities in the First Generation," 1999 Swig Lecture, Swig Judaic Studies Program, University of San Francisco, San Francisco. Available on-line at http://www.usfca.edu/judaicstudies/lectures.html (last accessed 8 September 2003).

87. For a full-length treatment of secret Jewish women in early modern Iberia, including an assessment of the religious authority of such women relative to their families and religious communities, see Renée Levine Melammed, *Heretics or Daughters of Israel? The Crypto-Jewish Women of Castile* (New York: Oxford University Press, 1999). See also Alberro, *Inquisition et société*, 427.

for example, found that rites carried out in the privacy of the home, such as those involving food and food preparation, became central to crypto-Judaism in Castile after the expulsion.[88] Scholars have also discovered that women in secret Jewish communities assumed many of the responsibilities previously assigned to males. Like Blanca's cousin Ana Enríquez, they acted as semi-rabbis when they indoctrinated their younger relatives and when they performed traditional Jewish ritual (kosher) slaughter of poultry and other animals. Blanca herself took over the traditional function of the male synagogue caretaker when she fasted on behalf of other community members. But, as Yovel has found, these female semi-rabbis also performed rites born not of Jewish tradition but of newfound religious necessity, such as the "unbaptising" of secret Jewish children or, in Blanca's case, the flogging of crucifixes.

The rituals Blanca reports in her Inquisition trial are valuable for what they tell us about the practices of Mexico City's secret Jews more generally. While many of the heresies Blanca confessed to were indeed Jewish rituals, others were not. Among these, some were syncretic practices that conversos adopted from seventeenth-century Catholic Spain, such as associating fish with penitential fasting. Others were inversions of Jewish or Catholic rituals, such as Blanca's extinguishing of the candle and turning her back on an Easter procession. Still others represented the internalization of age-old Christian stereotypes of Jews as usurers and the killers of Christ. One of these was Blanca's reference to the practice of putting a gold coin in the mouths of the deceased—possibly a reference to the notion of Jews as money-grubbers; another, Blanca's flagellation of a crucifix, evoked the old idea of the Jewish rejection of the idea of Christ as Messiah, although this practice, evidently carried out among crypto-Jews in Spain as well, has also been interpreted as evidence that Jews considered the figure of Christ on the cross to be little more than a wooden object devoid of spiritual import.[89] Syncretic, inverted, and "stereotypical" acts were just as much a

---

88. *Heretics,* 73–93; and David Gitlitz, *Secrecy and Deceit: The Religion of the Crypto-Jews* (Philadelphia: Jewish Publication Society, 1991).

89. See Michael Alpert, "Did Spanish Crypto-Jews Desecrate Christian Sacred Images?" in *Faith and Fanaticism: Religious Fervour in Early Modern Spain,* ed. Lesley K. Twomey (Brookfield, VT: Ashgate, 1997), 85–94. On the abuse of Christ images in sixteenth- and seventeenth-century Spain, see William A. Christian Jr., *Local Religion in Sixteenth-Century Spain* (Princeton, NJ: Princeton University Press, 1981), 192–93. Christian suggests that accusations concerning the sacrilege of crucifixes were generally inflated and were essentially topoi derived from deeply ingrained obsessions about the alleged Jewish mistreatment of Christian symbols. For further examples of the desecration and flogging of crucifixes and other religious images in colonial New Spain, see Serge Gruzinski, *Images at War: Mexico from Columbus to Blade Runner (1492–2019),* trans. Heather Maclean (Durham: Duke University Press, 2001), chap. 5.

part of Blanca's Judaizing as were recognizably Jewish practices, a point that has led some scholars to question whether or not Iberia's secret Jews were really Jews.[90] In seventeenth-century Amsterdam, for example, the newly arrived "Jews of the Portuguese nation" were so far removed from traditional Jewish practices that the autochthonous Jewish community frequently required them to undergo reconversion to Judaism and to prove their Jewish ancestry by means of "purity of blood" tests similar to those utilized in Catholic Spain.[91] Even then, these Portuguese "Jews" remained a group apart.

Blanca's trial suggests that similar conditions existed in Mexico City. Juan de León, the Jew from Livorno who later moved to Mexico City, distinguished between Jews and secret Jews when he told the tribunal that "where he's from the [Jews] only worry about teaching the Old Law and keeping its precepts . . . but they don't mess with Jesus Christ Our Lord. Jews who flog crucifixes [cristos] and commit other such crimes are raised here and live as Catholics. . . . The other Jews don't think much of them."[92] Juan de León found the Mexico City Jews' rituals to be peculiar diasporic practices. In contrast, Blanca and her coreligionists could not make such a distinction. Neither could the inquisitors.

Even before Blanca's trial began, the inquisitors knew that they had arrested a "consummate rabbi" whose religious observances fueled the Judaizing heresies of the Portuguese converso community. The inquisitors consequently sought to achieve two things: obtain a full and complete confession from Blanca and also, perhaps more importantly, get her to give them the names of her accomplices. The first was contingent on the second. Blanca's aims were quite different, as she sought both to avoid serious punishment and to protect the identities of her friends. Essentially, this was an impossible task, but Blanca attempted it anyway, mainly by employing a strategy that might be called "confession-as-evasion." This strategy, couched in the kind of penitential language the inquisitors wanted to hear, entailed confession to lesser sins while professing ignorance of anything that might be construed as major heresy. In this way, Blanca hoped also to avoid torture and thus

---

90. This mix of Jewish, Christian, and anti-Christian practices was common among Mexico City's secret Jews. See, for example, Martin A. Cohen, *The Martyr: The Story of a Secret Jew and the Mexican Inquisition in the Sixteenth Century* (Philadelphia: Jewish Publication Society of America, 1973); and Alberro, *Inquisition et société,* 417–54.

91. On the practice of blood purity among Jews in seventeenth-century Amsterdam, see Miriam Bodian, *Hebrews of the Portuguese Nation: Conversos and Community in Early Modern Amsterdam* (Bloomington: Indiana University Press, 1997).

92. Alberro, *Inquisition et société,* 438, from "Proceso contra Juan Pacheco de León, alias Salomon Machorro (1642)," AGN: Inq., vol. 40, exp. 2, fols. 700, 705, 105v.

the risk of being forced to rat on her friends and accomplices. Thus, when Blanca was asked "if she knew, presumed, or suspected the reasons she was arrested and had been brought to the prisons of this Holy Office," she freely admitted to the fact of her conversion to secret Judaism but changed the details to implicate only one other secret Jew, a woman who was already dead. Blanca followed the story of her conversion with professions of penitence spun out in the hyperbolic and convoluted language of Baroque Catholicism ("My errors tear at my heart and cause streams of tears").

Unfortunately for Blanca, Inquisition spies had exposed her crocodile tears for what they were. They informed the inquisitors that Blanca, during her nocturnal conversations with her daughters, had referred to the inquisitors as "traitors, who make us lie" as well as "demons, who go around spying and intimidating." The spies had also discovered that Blanca, in a ritual that was apparently an inversion of the Jewish tradition of lighting candles to preserve the life and memory of the dead, had extinguished the flame on a candle and cursed her captors by muttering, "may their souls be extinguished in hell." Such behavior, following on the heels of her insincere, incomplete confession, aroused the inquisitors' wrath. They ordered her immediate transfer from her prison cell into the torture chamber, a tactic probably designed to frighten her and make her crack. It did.

A month in the torture chamber broke Blanca's resolve to protect her family, friends, and faith. Bit by bit she exposed those she had worked to protect, first the living members of the secret Jewish community, then the relapsed heretics who would burn at the stake if convicted a second time, and then, most importantly, herself and her daughters. But even as she revealed these details, Blanca did everything in her power to resist the Inquisition's grasp. Outside of her audiences her resistance was aggressive. She caulked the walls of the torture chamber in an attempt to stop the spying. She cursed the inquisitors, exasperated her guards, and berated her grandson for his collaboration with their interrogators (which, in truth, was no worse than her own). In contrast, in the course of her interrogations she played the part of the humble defendant, prepared to make a full confession of her heresies. In this way, even her confession of desecrating the Christ figure was a form of resistance, a way of escaping the ultimate punishment.

This latter ritual Blanca had previously been loath to confess. She and her daughters had flogged a Christ figurine that they had un-nailed from its crucifix and hidden in a trunk in their home. Blanca delayed telling the inquisitors about this most unchristian act, fearing the worst. She perhaps understood that repentant first offenders generally escaped capital punishment. But she may have wondered what her judges would do when faced with such a horrible crime. She was right to worry. Upon hearing her story, the inquisitors from the Mexico Tribunal wrote to the Suprema in a letter dated 27 November 1643. They asked whether, given the heinous nature of the heresy, they should go against Inquisition policy and condemn to death all those who had flogged, or had been accomplices in the flogging of, the Rivera family crucifix, "even if they confess to it."[93] No answer to this letter has been found, but, given the outcome of Blanca's case, it can only be assumed that the Suprema replied, "No."

Although the Inquisition did not sentence Blanca or her daughters to burn at the stake, three of her daughters, María, Catalina, and Clara, did die in prison. Blanca and her surviving daughter Margarita (the outcome of Isabel's trial and her whereabouts are unknown) underwent whipping, public shaming, and the ordeal of an *auto de fe* before being banished from the Indies. Blanca chose to serve out her exile in her native Seville, where she disappeared from the historical record. Did she, broken by the deaths of three of her daughters and so many of her friends, return to the Convent of the Conception to live as a penitent? Did she die in the Great Plague of 1649, which killed one-third of Seville's population? Or did she walk straight from the ship into her aunt's house, dismember a crucifix, and start all over again? One day a document might turn up that reveals what happened to Blanca, but at present the end of her life story eludes us.

Blanca's trial contributed directly to the decimation of Mexico City's secret Jewish community. In 1647, the year Blanca's trial ended, the Mexico Tribunal reconciled twenty-three of the city's secret Jews at an *auto de fe*. It reconciled another twenty-two at the *auto* in 1648.[94] Another thirteen were burned at a grand *auto de fe* in 1649. Among these was Isabel Tristán, a friend of the Blanca family whom Blanca had denounced in her confessions. The grand *auto* of 1649 ended the mass persecutions of Mexico City's secret Jews. The Inquisition had exhausted its prey.

FURTHER READING

The role of Jews and crypto-Jews in the Americas was the subject of a series of valuable essays assembled in Paolo Bernardini and N. Fiering, eds., *Jews and the Expansion of Europe to the West* (New York: Berghahn Books, 2001); as well as Jonathan I. Israel, *Diasporas within a*

93. Alberro, *Inquisition et société*, 574.
94. Ibid., 580–82.

Diaspora: Jews, Crypto-Jews, and World Maritime Empires (1540–1740) (Leiden: Brill, 2002). Studies relating specifically to the conversos in New Spain include Jonathan I. Israel, "Portuguese Crypto-Judaism in New Spain (1569–1642)," in his *Diasporas within a Diaspora*, 97–123; as well as his earlier study, *Race, Class, and Politics in Colonial Mexico, 1610–1670* (London: Oxford University Press, 1975). See also his insightful essay "The Portuguese in Seventeenth-Century Mexico," in his *Empires and Entrepots* (London: Hambledon Press, 1990), 311–31.

Glossary

Abjuración de levi (lit., forswearing of minor [heresies]): Inquisition punishment for those accused of relatively minor heresies. Usually included public penance in an *auto de fe*.

Abjuración de vehementi (lit., forswearing of major [heresies]): Inquisition punishment for those accused of major heresies. Usually included public renunciation of specific heresies in an *auto de fe*.

Abjure de levi. See abjuración de levi.

Alcalde: Head of municipal governments, similar to a mayor.

Alcalde mayor: A municipal judge.

Algarvesía: Valencian (southeastern Spanish) Muslim dialect. The Spanish Inquisition considered speaking Algarvesía a heretical act, one that tacitly expressed the speakers' preference for Islam over Christianity.

Apostate: A person who publicly renounces or abandons the religion she or he professes.

Audiencia: Hearing, or audience, e.g. of a prisoner with inquisitors.

Auto de fe (lit., act of faith): Public ceremony at which the Spanish Inquisition "penanced," that is, punished, convicted heretics.

Bachiller: Title used by individuals who had earned a simple university degree (roughly equivalent to a bachelor's degree in the United States).

Berbería: North Africa. (Berber, North African.)

Calificador: A canon lawyer or theologian responsible for determining the merits of an Inquisition case. Cases passed before the *calificador* after inquisitors had collected evidence but before they arrested a defendant. The *calificador*'s function was similar to that of a grand jury in Anglo-American law.

Castilian: Persons or things pertaining to Castile, the central portion of the Iberian Peninsula. Aragon and Castile were the two kingdoms at the heart of early modern Spain. *Castilian* also refers to the Spanish language.

Converso: A Christian of Jewish ancestry. *Conversos* refers both to those who personally converted from Judaism to Christianity and to their descendants. See also *New Christian, marrano.*

Corregidor: The monarch's appointed representative in municipal government in both Castile and the Americas. *Corregidores* had administrative as well as judicial duties and acted as judges in civil and criminal cases. They also served as the titular heads of local town councils.

Council of Trent: Meeting of representatives of the Catholic Church in Trent, Italy (1547–63), which established and articulated much of the Church's Counter Reformation policy and reiterated some of the Church's major tenets.

Cristiano nuevo: see *New Christian.*

Cristiano viejo: see *Old Christian.*

Crypto-Jew: Term used by historians, in place of pejoratives *(marrano, Judaizer),* to describe those baptized Christians who secretly practiced Judaism.

Diaspora (lit., scattering): The scattering of a people. As a proper noun, refers to the scattering of the Jews from Palestine after their Babylonian exile. Can also refer specifically to the dispersing of Sephardic Jews throughout North Africa, Europe, and the Middle East after their expulsion from Spain in 1492.

Don/Doña: Honorific titles connoting members of the nobility or, more informally, those of high social standing though not necessarily nobles.

Escudo: A silver coin in wide usage.

Granadinos (lit., from Granada): Granada, the last surviving Muslim kingdom on the Iberian Peninsula, was conquered by Christian Castile in 1492. The term *granadino* refers to those Muslims, and Muslim converts to Christianity, who were from this region.

Habsburgs: Members of the royal family of Spain in the sixteenth and seventeenth centuries. Their Austrian cousins, the Hapsburgs, traditionally held the office of Holy Roman Emperor.

Heresy: From the Greek *haresis,* meaning "choice," heresy is anything that contradicts Church doctrine. The Spanish Inquisition, like the Roman (papal) inquisitions before it, criminalized and punished heresy in various forms. Heresy differs from sin in that heresy contradicts Church doctrine, whereas sin acknowledges the correctness of that doctrine, even as the sin deviates from its dictates on correct behavior. (Hereticate, to make into a heretic.)

Heretic: A person who contradicts the doctrines of the Roman Catholic Church. The Spanish Inquisition, like the papal inquisitions that preceded it, criminalized heresy and prosecuted heretics with the stated intent of reforming them.

Holy Office: The first part of the Inquisition's full title, The Holy Office of the Spanish Inquisition. The Holy Office of the Spanish Inquisition had as its institutional goal the eradication of *heresy* from the provinces of the Spanish Monarchy. The Spanish Inquisition was a hybrid institution, governed at the top by the Spanish monarchs but staffed by clerics and based on a Roman (papal) model of an inquisition that had its origins in the thirteenth century.

In face ecclesia: In a church.

Infamia: A form of public disgrace, used as punishment in medieval and early modern Spanish justice systems. The Inquisition typically assigned *infamia* as a punishment to heretics convicted of serious crimes and their descendants for three generations. Those subjected to *infamia,* known as *infames,* could not hold public office, ride horses, carry arms, or wear luxury goods.

Judaizante, Judaizer: See *Judaize.*

Judaize: In inquisitorial parlance, this verb refers to practicing Judaism after one has been baptized Christian. Judaizing, one of the most serious inquisitorial crimes, was considered a heresy because it implicitly promoted the superiority of Judaism over Christianity.

Lateran Council: Refers to the Fifth Lateran Council, a church council held in Rome between 1512 and 1517 in which bishops met to discuss, create, and confirm Church policy.

Law of Moses: Judaism. Early modern Spaniards use the term as a contrast with the Law of Jesus Christ, or Christianity.

Licentiate, after Licenciado: Title used by individuals who earned an advanced university degree (roughly equivalent to a modern master's degree) in law, medicine, or theology.

Limpieza de sangre: A term of late medieval origin that referred to persons who were of exclusively Christian ancestry, or at least those who could prove this of themselves. It was used to distinguish these individuals from those whose ancestors were, or who themselves had formerly been, Jewish or Muslim. Blood purity statutes were first implemented by the municipal government of Toledo in 1449.

Marrano (lit., pig): Pejorative term of Portuguese origin used to describe converts from Judaism to Christianity and their descendants. It sometimes is used specifically to denote converts who secretly practice Judaism after their conversion.

Megorashim: The term used by "native" Jews for Jewish immigrants from Spain following the Expulsion Order of 1492.

Meshumud: Hebrew term referring to Jews who had converted to Christianity.

Morisco: A Muslim who had been baptized and converted, at least nominally, to Christianity. The term can also refer to the descendants of converts.

Moor: A Muslim, specifically one from North Africa. See *moro.*

Mohammedize: The inquisitorial crime of secretly practicing Islam after having been baptized a Christian. Mohammedizing, along with *Judaizing,* was one of the most serious inquisitorial crimes. It was considered a heresy because it implicitly promoted the superiority of Islam over Christianity.

Moro (lit., a Moor): Specifically refers to Berbers, Muslim peoples residing in North Africa, but more generally to all Muslims. A derogatory term.

Mulatto/a: An individual of mixed racial ancestry. The term, in Spain, usually referred to those born of a white Spanish father and a North African or sub-Saharan African slave mother.

Nation (Hebrew or Muslim): Term used in the early modern period with no exact contemporary equivalent. Denotes membership in an ethnic group (nation) that does not necessarily correspond with a political unit (state). Thus, before the forced conversion order of 1502, a person could be of the Muslim nation but reside in the *Castilian* (Christian) state.

New Christian: An Iberian Christian of Jewish or Muslim descent, discriminated against by *blood purity* statutes. The term *New Christian* referred to recent converts and descendants of converts, and blood purity statutes applied to both groups.

Old Christian: An Iberian Christian whose ancestors were Christian, rather than Jewish or Muslim.

Patriarch of the Indies: Honorary title generally held by the royal chaplain in Madrid. Refers to Spanish ecclesiastical jurisdiction in the New World.

Purity of blood. See limpieza de sangre.

Real (pl. reales): A small silver coin used widely in Castile.

Regidor: Title given to members of the municipal councils that ruled many cities, especially in Castile. The office was often hereditary and held by members of the local nobility.

Relapsos: Recidivists. Refers to individuals who had been tried and punished by the Inquisition and who committed the same heresy again thereafter. On the basis that their original confession and repentance had been insincere, the Inquisition had a policy of sentencing *relapsos* to burn at the stake, even if they confessed after their second arrest.

Renegade:. Refers in the sixteenth century to a person who abandons his or her faith for another. Used especially to refer to Christian and Jewish converts to Islam.

Sect of Muhammed/Law of Muhammed. Islam.

Secular Justice: Also called royal justice. Law courts, including local courts of the *corregidor,* governor, and *alcaldes,* whose ultimate authority rests with the monarchy.

Sepharad: The Hebrew name for what is now Spain and Portugal.

Sephardic/Sephardim: Terms referring to Jews of Spanish origin and their descendants.

Suprema: The Supreme Council of the *Holy Office* of the Spanish Inquisition. Created by Ferdinand and Isabella at the end of the fifteenth century, this council coordinated the activities of all the inquisitorial tribunals in Spain and its overseas territories.

Toshavim: The term that distinguished autochthonous (or native) Jews from *megorashim.*

Index